Carol Hawes

AS/400: A Practical Guide to Programming and Operations

AS/400: A Practical Guide to Programming and Operations

Donald G. Zeilenga
Donna M. Lenczycki

QED Publishing Group
Boston • London • Toronto

This book is available at a special discount when you order multiple copies. For information, contact QED Publishing Group, POB 812070, Wellesley, MA 02181-0013 or phone 617-237-5656.

P.O. Box 812070
Wellesley, MA 02181-0013

QED Publishing Group is a division of QED Information Sciences, Inc.

Library of Congress Catalog Number: 92-26867
International Standard Book Number: 0-89435-433-7

Printed in the United States of America
93 94 95 10 9 8 7 6 5 4 3 2

Library of Congress Cataloging-In-Publication Data

Zeilenga, Donald G.
AS/400 : a practical guide to programming and operations / Donald G. Zeilenga, Donna M. Lenczycki.
p. cm.
Includes index.
ISBN 0-89435-433-7
1. IBM AS/400 (Computer) I. Lenczycki, Donna M. II. Title.
QA76.8.I1237Z45 1992
005.2'45—dc20 92-26867
CIP

Contents

Introduction

The objective of this book is to introduce various aspects of the AS/400 computer system, both to systems operations and as background to the programmer who will be working on the system. It will be broken down into the following chapters:

Operations Procedures
Programming Procedures
Query Procedures
COBOL Programming Procedures
RPG Programming Procedures
Miscellaneous Information

Each chapter will explain the material covered and indicate where additional reference material can be found. Also, if applicable, each chapter will contain actual systems examples of the material.

The information in the following paragraph applies at all times on the AS/400 and will be useful.

All entry of commands will be done on screens with command lines. The command line is the line near the bottom of *any* menu screen headed 'Selection or command'. The primary screen on the

AS/400 is the one headed 'AS/400 Main Menu', also labeled 'MAIN' in the upper left-hand corner.

Major function keys (PF keys) are consistent throughout AS/400 structure. They are as follows:

1. F1—System Help, which sends context-sensitive explanatory screens depending on the cursor location on the screen.
2. F3—Exit, which stops the current activity and sends the user back one level. Usually, in an edit activity an interim screen will be displayed that will allow the user to either save or cancel the changed data.
3. F4—Prompt, which provides fill-in-the-blanks screens for command parameters and/or programming.
4. F5—Refresh, which refreshes the current screen based on activity that has occurred since the screen was initially displayed.
5. F9—Repeat, which causes the previously issued command to be displayed on the command line.
6. F10—Additional Parameters, which provides a method for viewing/entering parameters related to specific commands. It is listed on the bottom of the screen if it is active for a given command.
7. F12—Cancel, which cancels without saving and sends the user back one level.

Additional function keys and options are available on individual screens and will be addressed as needed.

Very often, displays consist of multiple screens of information. This will be noted by the appearance of 'More...' in the lower right corner of the display screen. Paging is then accomplished with the Page Up (backward) and Page Down (forward) keys. When the user has reached the end of the display, 'Bottom' will appear in the lower right corner of the display screen. In some of the manuals the term 'Roll Up' is used in place of 'Page Down' and 'Roll Down' in place of 'Page Up'.

AS/400 Control Language is considered the 'JCL' of the system. All commands entered on the command line are Control Language commands, and they can be entered individually or strung together to create a job that can be run either interactively with the terminal or in a batch environment.

Additional introductory information on AS/400 can be found in IBM Manual GC21-8211, *AS/400 System Operations: New User's Guide*, which can serve as a starting point for further study.

1

Operations Procedures

The objective of this chapter is to introduce various operational procedures of the AS/400 computer system, both to systems operations and as background to the programmer who will be working on the system. It will be broken down into the following sections:

1.1 System Startup and Stop
1.2 PC Support and Logon/Logoff
1.3 Jobs and Subsystems
1.4 Backups and Restores
1.5 Adding Terminals and Users to the System
1.6 Security

1.1 SYSTEM STARTUP AND STOP

The following sections detail AS/400 system startup and stop.

Unattended IPL

Unattended IPL is the most common IPL to start up the AS/400 and its subsystems. Procedurally, the following should occur:

1. Since the system is down, the Unit Emergency switch (red) on the system unit control panel will be in the OFF position.
2. Turn the power ON for any display stations (main console), printers, tape units, and controllers.
3. Flip the Unit Emergency switch ON.
4. Be sure the keylock switch is turned to the Normal position.
5. Flip the Power switch to turn on the system.

The IPL is complete when the Sign-On screen is displayed on the main console. If there are problems with it, the System Attention light will be illuminated and codes will appear in the Function and Data displays on the control panel. The first place to look in the event of problems is in the *AS/400 System Operations: Operator's Guide* (IBM Manual SC21-8082). Refer to Chapter 8, 'Starting Point for System Problem Handling.'

Attended IPL

Attended IPL is a less common IPL, utilized by technical support personnel when installing a new release of the operating system or changing IPL options. The attended IPL will not be detailed here. The *Operator's Guide*, part of the additional references, fully explains it in its treatment of the IPL strategies of the AS/400.

Figures 1.1 to 1.3 show and explain the major control panel components for the various AS/400 system configurations.

The AS/400 units come in three different machine types: 9402, 9404, and 9406. Units 9402 and 9404 are like personal computer towers and can fit under or alongside a desk. Unit 9406 is a much larger system that can be housed in one or more racks and can accommodate many users.

Listed below is information regarding the various features of the control panels on each AS/400:

- Power On. This light always blinks when the AS/400 is being turned off and also blinks when the 9404 and 9402 units are turned on.
- Power switch. This manual switch on the 9404 and 9406 units can be moved to the On (top) position to start the system or to

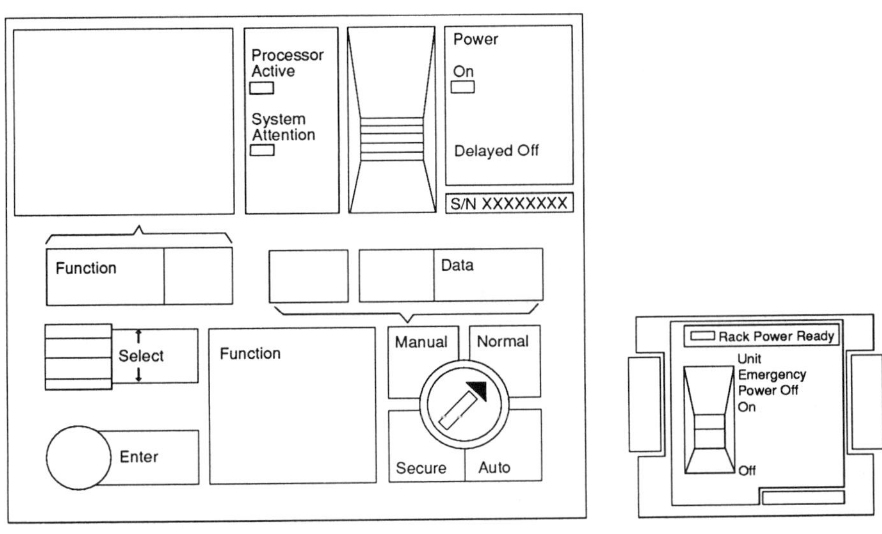

Figure 1.1. 9406 system unit control panel and Power switch.

the Delayed Off (bottom) position to stop it. On the 9402 unit there are two separate switches. Note that the optimal way to power down the system is to use the PWRDWNSYS command; otherwise, data files may have errors. The Power switch also controls an IPL when the keylock is in the manual or Normal position.

- Processor Active. This light blinks when there are programs running.
- System Attention. This light comes on and stays on when the system needs operator intervention, such as when there is a system failure.
- Function display. This display on the 9404 and 9406 units displays entered function information.
- Data display. This display on the 9404 and 9406 units displays system reference codes.*
- Select switch. This switch can be used to increase or decrease the numbers displayed on the Function display, as well as

*On the 9402 unit there is a combination display, the Function/Data display.

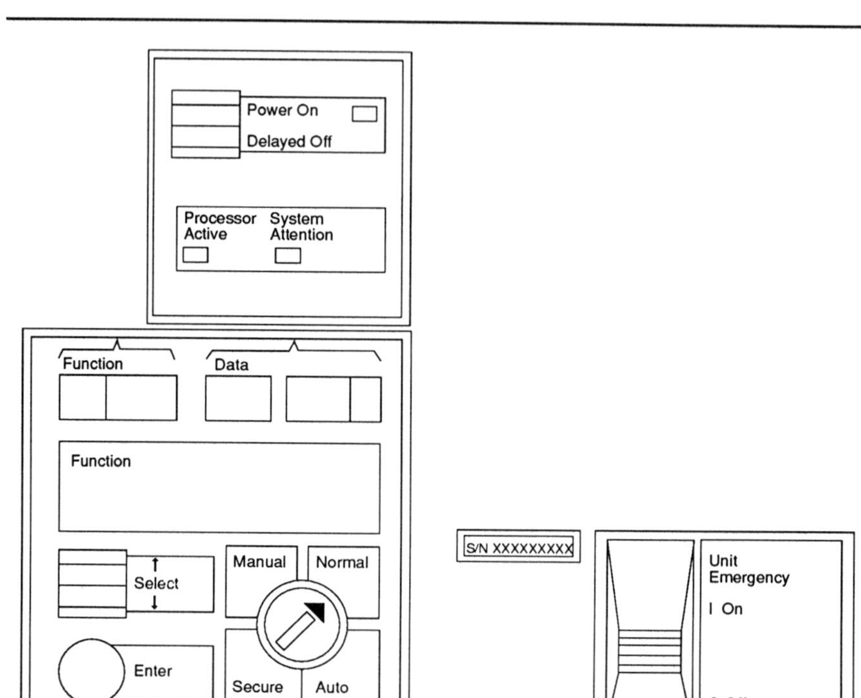

Figure 1.2. 9404 system unit control panel and Power switch.

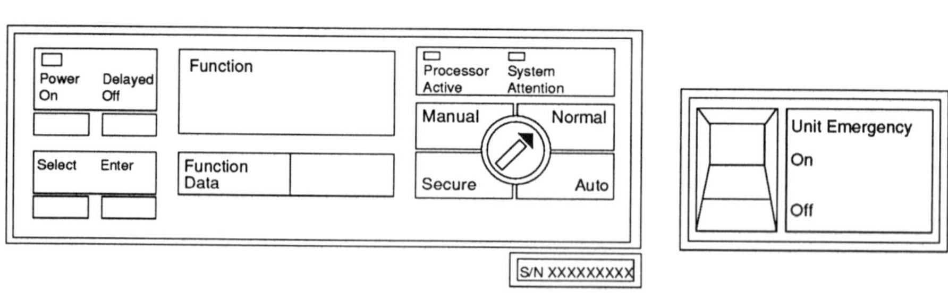

Figure 1.3. 9402 system unit control panel and Power switch.

change data in the Data display during an IPL. This also changes the Function/Data display on the 9402 unit. Only those functions allowed by the position of the keylock will be displayed, and the function itself is not sent to the processor until the Enter button is depressed.

- Enter button. This button is used to send information on the Function display to the processor or to save selected IPL information.
- Keylock switch. This switch controls IPL and power down activities on the system. There are four positions it can be in:

1. Auto—allows automatic IPLs, such as remote, by date/time, and after a power failure. It also allows power down via the Delayed Off switch/position.
2. Manual—does *not* allow the same automatic operations as Auto, but does allow manual IPLs from disk or tape.
3. Normal—allows both automatic and manual IPL operations and only allows a power down via the PWRDWNSYS command.
4. Secure—locks the control panel. With the system in Secure, only PWRDWNSYS can be used to bring it down.

Additional information on IPL options and the keylock positions is available in the *Operator's Guide*.

System Shutdown

Appearing below is the most common shutdown procedure for the AS/400. Only operations and users with proper security should be allowed this access.

1. Enter WRKACTJOB on the command line and press ENTER. Look for jobs with a job type of INT, which is basically the same as displaying all active users on the system. If there are no active jobs on the system, skip the next step and proceed to step 3. In either case, hit F3 to return to the previous screen.
2. Send a break message telling any system users to log off. Do this by entering the command SNDBRKMSG on the command line and pressing F4 (prompt) for additional param-

eters. The message(s) can be sent to those users logged on or simply to all display stations by use of the *ALLWS parameter in 'To workstation message queue'. Press ENTER to send the message.

3. Ensure that there are no tapes running in the tape drives.
4. Enter PWRDWNSYS on the command line and press F4. If there were no active users previously, the How to End parameter should be set to *IMMED (immediate power down). If there were users logged on, the operator may want to give them a few minutes to log off by specifying a controlled power down. The delay time must also be used for this, by the specification of the number of seconds to wait before the controlled power down begins.
5. The Restart After Power Down parameter specifies whether the system should remain down or immediately IPL. There are situations where system modifications take effect only after an IPL, so often the latter will be done. Press ENTER to bring down the system.

Figure 1.4 depicts the WRKACTJOB, SNDBRKMSG, and PWRDWNSYS commands.

Additional information on system startup and shutdown can be found in the *Operator's Guide.*

1.2 PC SUPPORT AND SYSTEM LOGON/LOGOFF

The following sections detail AS/400 logon, which begins on a PC with the startup of PC Support. If logging on to a dumb terminal, start with AS/400 logon, discussed subsequently.

PC Support

PC Support is accomplished on the DOS PC with the following commands:

1. At C:, key in 'CD\PCS', then press ENTER.
2. Once in the PCS directory, key in 'STARTPCS', then press ENTER.

(a)

```
                    Work with Active Jobs (WRKACTJOB)
                                                            11/29/91 09:05:05
CPU %:     .0     Elapsed time:   00:00:00     Active jobs:    135

Type options, press Enter.
  2=Change    3=Hold   4=End      5=Work with    6=Release    8=Spooled files
  9=Exclude   10=Program stack    11=Locks       13=Disconnect

Opt  Subsystem/Job  User       Type  CPU %  Function        Status
     QBATCH         QSYS       SBS      .0                   DEQW
     QCMN           QSYS       SBS      .0                   DEQW
       DPXXX        DPXXX      EVK      .0  *  -PASSTHRU     EVTW
       DPYYY        DPYYY      EVK      .0  *  -PASSTHRU     EVTW
       DPAAA        DPBBB      EVK      .0  *  -PASSTHRU     EVTW
       DPDDD        DPBBB      EVK      .0  *  -PASSTHRU     EVTW
       DPEEE        DPBBB      EVK      .0  *  -PASSTHRU     EVTW
       DPFFF        DPBBB      EVK      .0  *  -PASSTHRU     EVTW
       DPGGG        DPBBB      EVK      .0  *  -PASSTHRU     EVTW
                                                                  More. . .
Parameters or command
===>
F3=Exit      F5=Refresh   F10=Restart statistics   F11=Display elapsed data
F12=Cancel   F24=More keys
Already at top of area.
      10-02     SA        MW        KS        IM        II S2      KB
```

Figure 1.4. Shutdown command screen displays.

(b)

```
                      Send Break Message (SNDBRKMSG)

Type choices, press Enter.

Message text . . . . . . . . . .   please log off now system coming down




To work station message queue  .   *allws         Name, *ALLWS
  Library  . . . . . . . . . . .     *LIBL        Name, *LIBL
               + for more values
                                     *LIBL
Message type . . . . . . . . . .   *INFO          *INFO, *INQ
Message queue to get reply . . .   QSYSOPR        Name
  Library  . . . . . . . . . . .     *LIBL        Name, *LIBL




                                                                     Bottom
F3=Exit    F4=Prompt    F5=Refresh    F12=Cancel    F13=How to use this display
F24=More keys
    12-43     SA         MW         KS         IM         II S2          KB
```

Figure 1.4. *(cont.)*

(c)

```
                      Power Down System (PWRDWNSYS)




 Type choices, press Enter.


 How to end . . . . . . . . . . .   *CNTRLD       *CNTRLD, *IMMED
 Delay time, if *CNTRLD . . . . .   3600          Seconds, *NOLIMIT
 Restart after power down . . . .   *NO           *NO, *YES
 IPL source . . . . . . . . . . .   *PANEL        *PANEL, A, B










                                                                 Bottom
 F3=Exit   F4=Prompt   F5=Refresh   F12=Cancel   F13=How to use this display
 F24=More keys
     05-37     SA         MW         KS         IM         II S2        KB
```

Figure 1.4. *(cont.)*

3. After numerous DOS messages, you will receive the following prompts:
   - Enter common "userid"—key in your AS/400 userid, then press ENTER.
   - Enter password for common "userid"—key in your password, then press ENTER.
4. Again, after numerous DOS messages, you will see a screen headed 'AS/400 PS Support Work Station Function'. After you are connected to the AS/400, the system will send you the message 'PRESS A KEY TO CONTINUE'. Press any key.
5. After yet another set of DOS messages, you will receive the AS/400 Sign-On screen.

AS/400 Logon

AS/400 logon is accomplished by entry of a userid and password on the AS/400 Sign-On screen. Initial setup of userids and passwords generally mirrors that of mainframe systems.

When entering your userid and password on this screen, do not press ENTER until both fields have been filled. Other fields on this screen (Program/Procedure, Menu, and Current Library) need not be filled in. Note also that display of password is suppressed.

The way your userid was defined (see Section 1.6) will determine your capabilities on the AS/400.

Figure 1.5 depicts the Sign-On screen. The three fields in the upper right corner are significant:

1. 'System' is the ID of the AS/400 the user is logging on to.
2. 'Subsystem' is the subsystem controlling the sign-on. 'QINTER' is the interactive subsystem that controls user access.
3. "Display" is the ID of the physical workstation to the AS/400. This is a constant and does not change, no matter which user is logged onto that workstation.

AS/400 Logoff

To log off the AS/400, do the following:

1. Return to the AS/400 Main Menu, key in Option 90, then press ENTER. If you are on a dumb terminal, this will return

```
                                      Sign-On.

                          System . . . . . . :    S
                          Subsystem . . . . :    QINTER
                          Display . . . . . :    DPXXXS1

   User . . . . . . . . . . . . .
   Password . . . . . . . . . . .
   Program/procedure. . . . . . .
   Menu . . . . . . . . . . . . .
   Current library  . . . . . . .








                                   (C) COPYRIGHT IBM CORP. 1980, 1990.
 06-53    SA        MW        KS        IM        II S1        KB
```

Figure 1.5. Sign-On screen.

you to the Sign-On screen and you are now logged off. If you are on a PC, continue.

2. An alternate way to log off the AS/400 is to key in 'SIGNOFF' on any command line and press ENTER.
3. Both Option 90 or SIGNOFF will return you to the 'C:\PCS>'prompt.
4. At this prompt, key in 'RMVPCS ALL' and press ENTER. This command will allow you to use other PC functions without rebooting your PC.
5. Several messages will appear on your screen, all of which will request ENTER or ESCAPE. In all cases press ENTER. This will return you to 'C:\PCS>'. You can then use your PC normally.

1.3 JOBS AND SUBSYSTEMS

Jobs

There are four types of jobs on the AS/400. They may be defined as follows:

1. Interactive—starts at a terminal session. A user's sign-on, subsequent work, and sign-off constitute a single job.
2. Batch—same as a batch job on the mainframe, to execute a long-running function or print a report. A batch job is submitted to a specific job queue and is then selected to run from within that queue. The job is ended when all tasks are completed.
3. Autostart—an automatically started job to be set up at a specific time, such as at system startup. The job is ended when all tasks are completed.
4. Spooling—printing reports from an output queue by starting the writer. The job is ended when the writer is ended.

A job cannot start unless it has a job description. As illustrated in Figure 1.6, the AS/400 job description contains a collection of job attributes, such as output queue, message logging, and associated libraries.

(a)

```
                          Display Job Description
                                                                System: S
 Job description:   DPXXXJOBD     Library:   DPXXXLIB

 User profile . . . . . . . . . . . . . . . . . . :   *RQD
 CL syntax check  . . . . . . . . . . . . . . . . :   *NOCHK
 Hold on job queue  . . . . . . . . . . . . . . . :   *NO
 End severity . . . . . . . . . . . . . . . . . . :   30
 Job date . . . . . . . . . . . . . . . . . . . . :   *SYSVAL
 Job switches . . . . . . . . . . . . . . . . . . :   00000000
 Inquiry message reply  . . . . . . . . . . . . . :   *RQD
 Job priority (on job queue)  . . . . . . . . . . :   5
 Job queue  . . . . . . . . . . . . . . . . . . . :   QBATCH
   Library  . . . . . . . . . . . . . . . . . . . :     QGPL
 Output priority (on cutput queue)  . . . . . . . :   5
 Printer device . . . . . . . . . . . . . . . . . :   *USRPRF
 Output queue . . . . . . . . . . . . . . . . . . :   *USRPRF
   Library  . . . . . . . . . . . . . . . . . . . :


 Press Enter to continue.
                                                                  More...
 F3=Exit    F12=Cancel

     01-01     SA        MW        KS        IM        II S2      KB
```

Figure 1.6. Display Job Description screens.

(b)

```
                         Display Job Description
                                                            System:   S
Job description:    DPXXXJOBD     Library:    DPXXXLIB

Message logging:
  Level  . . . . . . . . . . . . . . . . . . . . . :   4
  Severity . . . . . . . . . . . . . . . . . . . . :   0
  Text . . . . . . . . . . . . . . . . . . . . . . :   *NOLIST
Log CL program commands  . . . . . . . . . . . . . :   *YES
Accounting code  . . . . . . . . . . . . . . . . . :   *USRPRF
Print text . . . . . . . . . . . . . . . . . . . . :   *SYSVAL

Routing data . . . . . . . . . . . . . . . . . . . :   QCMDI

Request data . . . . . . . . . . . . . . . . . . . :   *NONE



Device recovery action . . . . . . . . . . . . . . :   *SYSVAL

Press Enter to continue.
                                                               More...
F3=Exit    F12=Cancel

    01-01     SA        MW        KS        IM        II S2       KB
```

Figure 1.6. *(cont.)*

(c)

```
                         Display Job Description
                                                              System:   S
Job description:    DPXXXJOBD     Library:    DPXXXLIB

Time slice end pool  . . . . . . . . . . . . . . :   *SYSVAL
Text . . . . . . . . . . . . . . . . . . . . . . :   Job Description for DPXXX

Initial library list:
  DPXXXLIB
  QTEMP
  QGPL
  TSTLIB
  PRDLIB






Press Enter to continue.
                                                                 Bottom
F3=Exit    F12=Cancel

    01-01     SA        MW        KS        IM        II S2       KB
```

Figure 1.6. *(cont.)*

Subsystems

All jobs on the AS/400 execute from within subsystems. A subsystem is an environment that controls the initiation and execution of jobs. It is defined by a subsystem description that contains tables listing how jobs will start and execute from within the subsystem.

Subsystems are started and ended by individual commands as well as the system IPL and system power down. SRTSBS starts a subsystem; ENDSBS ends it. All subsystems must be ended in order to save the entire system. (See Section 1.4 for more information.)

The controlling subsystem is QCTL. It stays active on the system console even when all other subsystems are shut down for backups. The only time QCTL is shut down is when a PWRDWNSYS command has been successfully completed. The other active subsystems, controlled by QCTL, are these:

- QBATCH—all batch jobs.
- QINTER—all interactive jobs. These are terminals (PCs) signed onto the system.
- QCMN—all communication jobs. These are PCs on the network that have started their AS/400 PC Support session, whether or not they have logged on to the AS/400.
- QSPL—print writers.
- QXFPCS—PC Support.
- QSNADS—data transmission between AS/400s and other systems.

Other subsystems may exist on the AS/400, but might be inactive. You can display these, as well as the active subsystems, by entering a WRKSBSD command, pressing F4, and entering *ALL in the subsystem description parameter. Additional subsystems may be added to the system on a user-defined basis. For example, a subsystem might be created for users of a specific application, such as payroll.

Figure 1.7 depicts a subsystem description.

Additional information on jobs and subsystems can be found in the *Operator's Guide.*

(a)

```
                    Display Subsystem Description
                                                             System:   S
Subsystem description:   QSPL            Library:   QSYS
Status:   ACTIVE

Select one of the following:

     1. Operational attributes
     2. Pool definitions
     3. Autostart job entries
     4. Work station name entries
     5. Work station type entries
     6. Job queue entries
     7. Routing entries
     8. Communications entries
     9. Remote location name entries
    10. Prestart job entries

                                                                More...
Selection or command
===>
F3=Exit   F4=Prompt   F9=Retrieve   F12=Cancel
    21-07     SA          MW         KS          IM         II S1        KB
```

Figure 1.7. Subsystem description screen displays.

(b)

```
                         Display Operational Attributes
                                                                  System:   S
Subsystem description:   QSPL         Status:   ACTIVE

Subsystem description  . . . . . . . . :   QSPL
  Library  . . . . . . . . . . . . . . :     QSYS
Maximum jobs in subsystem  . . . . . . :   *NOMAX
Sign-on display file . . . . . . . . . :   QDSIGNON
  Library  . . . . . . . . . . . . . . :     QSYS
System library list entry  . . . . . . :   *NONE









Press Enter to continue.
F3=Exit   F12=Cancel
    01-01      SA         MW         KS         IM         II S1        KB
```

Figure 1.7. *(cont.)*

(c)

```
                          Display Pool Definitions
                                                                   System:   S
Subsystem description:   QSPL          Status:   ACTIVE

Pool         Storage     Activity
 ID          Size (K)     Level
  1            *BASE
  2           *SPOOL










                                                                        Bottom
Press Enter to continue.
F3=Exit   F12=Cancel
    01-01      SA         MW         KS         IM         II S1        KB
```

Figure 1.7. (*cont.*)

(d)

```
                         Display Autostart Job Entries
                                                            System:   S
Subsystem description:   QSPL          Status:   ACTIVE

Job           Job Description      Library
  (No autostart job entries)











                                                                 Bottom
Press Enter to continue.
F3=Exit   F12=Cancel
    01-01      SA         MW         KS         IM         II S1        KB
```

Figure 1.7. *(cont.)*

(e)

```
                    Display Work Station Name Entries
                                                              System:   S
Subsystem description:   QSPL          Status:   ACTIVE

Type options, press Enter.
  5=Display work station name details
Opt Name            Opt Name            Opt Name            Opt Name

  (No work station name entries)











                                                                 Bottom
F3=Exit   F9=Display all detailed descriptions  F12=Cancel
    01-01      SA         MW         KS         IM         II S1        KB
```

Figure 1.7. *(cont.)*

(f)

```
                    Display Work Station Type Entries
                                                               System:   S
Subsystem description:   QSPL          Status:   ACTIVE

Type options, press Enter.
  5=Display work station type details
Opt Type            Opt Type            Opt Type            Opt Type
  (No work station type entries)










                                                                  Bottom
F3=Exit   F9=Display all detailed descriptions  F12=Cancel
    01-01      SA         MW         KS         IM         II S1        KB
```

Figure 1.7. *(cont.)*

(g)

```
                         Display Job Queue Entries
                                                                System:   S
Subsystem description:   QSPL           Status:   ACTIVE

 Seq  Job                         Max    ---------Max by Priority--------
 Nbr  Queue        Library      Active   1   2   3   4   5   6   7   8   9
  10  QSPL         QGPL         *NOMAX   *   *   *   *   *   *   *   *   *

                                                                   Bottom
Press Enter to continue.
F3=Exit   F12=Cancel
    01-01     SA        MW        KS        IM        II S1      KB
```

Figure 1.7. *(cont.)*

(h)

```
                        Display Routing Entries
                                                              System:   S
Subsystem description:   QSPL          Status:   ACTIVE
Type options, press Enter.
  5=Display details

                                                             Start
Opt    Seq Nbr    Program      Library      Compare Value    Pos
          10      QCMD         QSYS         'QWTRPT'          1
          50      QCMD         QSYS         'QAFPWT'          1
        9999      QCMD         QSYS         *ANY

                                                                 Bottom
F3=Exit   F9=Display all detailed descriptions   F12=Cancel
    10-01      SA         MW         KS         IM         II S1        KB
```

Figure 1.7. *(cont.)*

(i)

```
                    Display Communications Entries
                                                            System:   S
Subsystem description:   QSPL          Status:   ACTIVE

                                 Job                        Default       Max
Device           Mode        Description    Library         User          Active
  (No communications entries)

















                                                                          Bottom
Press Enter to continue.
F3=Exit   F12=Cancel
    01-01      SA         MW         KS         IM         II S1        KB
```

Figure 1.7. *(cont.)*

(j)

```
                     Display Remote Location Name Entries
                                                              System:   S
Subsystem description:   QSPL          Status:   ACTIVE

Remote                          Job                       Default       Max
Location      Mode          Description    Library        User         Active
  (No remote location name entries)

                                                                       Bottom
Press Enter to continue.
F3=Exit   F12=Cancel
    01-01     SA         MW         KS         IM         II S1        KB
```

Figure 1.7. *(cont.)*

(k)

```
                         Display Prestart Job Entries
                                                                System:   S
Subsystem description:   QSPL          Status:   ACTIVE

Type options, press Enter.
  5=Display details

Opt        Program        Library        User Profile
  (No prestart job entries)










                                                                    Bottom
Press Enter to continue.
F3=Exit   F9=Display all detailed descriptions   F12=Cancel
    01-01     SA        MW        KS        IM        II S1        KB
```

Figure 1.7. *(cont.)*

1.4 BACKUPS AND RESTORES

This section deals with general backup and restore processes for the AS/400. For backups and restores for specific applications, please read the documentation for those applications.

Tape Initialization

Tape initialization must be done before any backups can be put to tape. Since each AS/400 has a different tape drive, the initialization procedure is slightly different for each one. Sample procedures for initialization of reel-to-reel and cartridge drives are as follows:

- Initialize reel-to-reel tapes (Model 9347):
  1. Enter INZTAP on the command line and press F4 (prompt).
  2. Key in 'Tape Device'—TAP01.
  3. Key in 'New Volume Identifier'—tape number.
  4. Key in 'New Owner Identifier'—AS400.
  5. Key in 'Check for Active Files'—*NO.
  6. Key in 'Tape Density'—*1600.
  7. Key in 'End of Tape Option'—*UNLOAD.
- Initialize cartridge tapes (Model 3490):
  1. Enter INZTAP on command line and press F4 (prompt).
  2. Key in 'Tape Device'—TAP01.
  3. Key in 'New Volume Identifier'—cartridge number.
  4. Key in 'New Owner Identifier'—AS400.
  5. Key in 'Check for Active Files'—*NO.
  6. Key in 'End of Tape Option'—*UNLOAD.

The system will display either a completion message after the tape has successfully been initialized or error messages if a problem has occurred during initialization.

Backups

Backups are primarily referred to as SAVEs on the AS/400. The list below is a brief explanation of the most common SAVEs. Most SAVEs are done to tape (parameter *TAP01), but they can also be done to save-file format (parameter *SAVF), which saves the file to disk to be written to tape at a later time or to be used as a disk backup. Save files are of particular value in backing up old versions of programs as emergency backup.

- SAVSYS. This command saves the main system library (QSYS) as well as user profiles and device descriptions.
- SAVDLO. This command saves the system document library (QDOC) or selected folders within that library.
- SAVLIB. This command saves one or numerous libraries.
- SAVOBJ. This command saves one or numerous objects. It *cannot* be used to restore libraries, only objects, so it is not a recommended function.
- SAVSECDTA. This command saves security data such as user profiles and authorization lists.
- SAVSTG. This command saves all system storage sector by sector. It can be compared to backing up entire disk packs on the mainframe. Individual files cannot be identified; this backup is done primarily to facilitate disaster recovery.
- SAVCHGOBJ. This command saves changed objects. It is somewhat cumbersome to use since the operator must explicitly specify libraries to be saved.
- SAVALLCHG. This is a user-generated command from QUSRTOOL that only saves changed objects. It is a much cleaner command than SAVCHGOBJ because the operator need not specify any libraries. Libraries to be backed up are identified by the command itself.

The following pages detail the steps in a site's current daily and weekly backup procedures for two AS/400s. Note that the same weekly backup procedures are used for monthly backups. The following should also be noted:

- The user-generated program CHGJOBLOGO ensures that joblogs are cleaned up on a timely basis. They are saved for one week.
- Regarding the weekly backups, step 8 represents Option 21 from the SAVE Menu. This steps the operator through the *complete* system backup.

- The SAVSTG command (step 9) is run weekly to facilitate disaster recovery.
- The user-generated command PRTSAVSTS is run weekly to list all libraries saved via the SAVSYS. This listing, in conjunction with the listing from the SAVALLCHG command, allows restoration of any damaged library to its last backup.

AS400 Daily Backup for Machine 1 and Machine 2

1. Sign on as QSECOFR; commands must be done from side 1 (DSP01).
2. Send a message that the system will be going down to do backups.
   a. Enter SNDBRKMSG and press F4.
      1) Key in message text, state time system will be down.
      2) Key in 'to work station message queue'—*ALLWS.
3. Verify that no users are on the system by entering WRKACTJOB.
   a. DSP01 with status of RUN is okay; no other job can be running.
   b. Note active subsystems (SBS under type). These same subsystems will be started again once the backups are finished.
4. Put a message break in the system by entering CHGMSGQ QSYSOPR *BREAK.

Note: If there is a message to respond to and the system didn't break, you can receive the message by pressing both the Alt key and SYSREQ and then pressing enter after the line on the very bottom of the screen appears. Enter Option 6 to display system operator messages and respond to messages. After you respond to the messages, pressing enter from the System Request Menu will return you to the Main Menu.

5. Delete old history logs by entering WRKOBJ QSYS/QHST* *FILE (Delete All But Most Current Log).
6. Save joblogs for seven days by entering CALL CHGJOBLOGO.
7. Back up changed objects, ensure that tape device is clean, load the first tape, and make the tape device ready.
   a. Enter SAVALLCHG and press F4.

1) Key in 'device names'—TAP01.
2) Key in 'expiration date'—*DAY10 (10-day save).
3) Key in 'reference date'—*SAVLIB.
4) Key in 'end of tape file option'—*UNLOAD.
5) Key in 'use chksavrst command'—*NO.
6) Key in 'chksavrst errorsonly option'—*NO.

b. When backup is finished, press F3 to erase the command line.

Note: When the backup is running you will receive messages on the bottom of the screen that zero objects were changed, one object was saved, two were excluded, etc. These messages are okay and indicate the backup is executing properly. When the backup is complete you will receive the message 'BEGIN SAVALLCHG COMMAND'. A listing will be created and should be filed in the manager's office. This listing will show the number of files saved, excluded, etc. Both printouts are printed on each machine's printer.

c. When backup is complete run JOBT to pull in tapes or JOBC to pull in cartridges. This job should be run on the mainframe to update Tape Management.

AS400 Weekly Backup for Machine 1 and Machine 2

1. Sign on as QSECOFR; commands must be done from side 1 (DSP01).

2. Send a message that the system will be going down to do backups.

a. Enter SNDBRKMSG and press F4.

1) Key in message text; state the time the system will be down.
2) Key in 'to work station message queue'—*ALLWS.

3. Verify that no users are on the system by entering WRKACTJOB.

a. DSP01 with status of 'RUN' is okay; no other job can be running.

b. Note active subsystems (SBS under type). These same subsystems will be started again once the backups are finished.

4. Put a message break in the system by entering CHGMSGQ QSYSOPR *BREAK.

Note: If there is a message to respond to and the system didn't break, you can receive the message by pressing both the Alt key and SYSREQ and then pressing enter after the line on the very bottom of the screen appears. Enter Option 6 to display system operator messages and respond to them. After you respond to the messages, press enter from the System Request Menu to return to the Main Menu.

5. Delete old history logs by entering WRKOBJ QSYS/QHST* *FILE (Delete All But Most Current Log).
6. Save joblogs for seven days by entering CALL CHGJOBLOGO.
7. Back up changed objects, ensure that the tape device is clean, load the first tape, and make the tape device ready.
   a. Enter SAVALLCHG and press F4.
      1) Key in 'device names'—TAP01.
      2) Key in 'expiration date'—*DAY10 (10-day save).
      3) Key in 'reference date'—*SAVLIB.
      4) Key in 'end of tape file option'—*UNLOAD.
      5) Key in 'use chksavrst command'—*NO.
      6) Key in 'chksavrst errorsonly option'—*NO.
   b. When the backup is finished, press F3 to erase the command line.

Note: When the backup is running you will receive messages on the bottom of the screen that zero objects were changed, one object was saved, two were excluded, etc. These messages are okay and indicate the backup is executing properly. When the backup is complete you will receive the message 'BEGIN SAVALLCHG COMMAND'. A listing will be created and should be filed in the manager's office. Both printouts are printed on each machine's printer.

8. Go to the SAVE Menu. Key in 'GO SAVE' and from the SAVE Menu, key in Option 21 to do the SAVE system backup, load the first tape, and make the tape device ready. Option 21 will come up with prompts to end the subsystem, SAVSYS, SAVLIB, SAVDLO, and start the subsystems.

a. ENDSBS.
   1) Key in 'how to end'—*IMMED.

Note: When the subsystems have ended you will receive the message 'system ended to restricted state'.

b. SAVSYS.
   1) Key in 'tape device'—TAP01.
   2) Key in 'file expiration date'—MM/DD/YY (60-day save).
   3) Key in 'end of tape option'—*LEAVE.

c. SAVLIB.
   1) Key in 'file expiration date'—MM/DD/YY (60-day save).
   2) Key in 'end of tape option'—*LEAVE.

d. SAVDLO.
   1) Key in 'file expiration date'—MM/DD/YY (60-day save).
   2) Key in 'end of tape option'—*UNLOAD.
   3) Key in 'print option'—*PRINT.

e. STRSBS—press F3 to cancel; subsystems need to be down to do SAVSTG.

9. Enter the save storage command, SAVSTG DEV(TAP01) and press F4.
   1) Key in 'file expiration date'—MM/DD/YY (60-day save).
   2) The system will power down and will restart with an IPL.
   3) Key in 'DSPMSG *SYSOPR' to display the system operator message queue. Look at save storage completion messages for CPC3724 to see if any sectors were found damaged and unreadable. If damage is detected, call IBM.

10. Print a listing of files saved (printouts of each machine will print on that machine's printer); file it in the manager's office.
Enter the Command PRTSAVSTS *ALL.

11. When the backup is complete run JOBT to pull in tapes or JOBC to pull in cartridges. This job should be run on the mainframe to update Tape Management.

12. SAVSTG tapes/cartridges should be sent offsite.

Restores

The most common restore commands on the AS/400 are:

1. RSTLIB—restore of a library or libraries from a SAVLIB. This is probably the most common restore of all. For example, if a user has detrimentally changed a number of objects within her library, we would probably restore the entire library to another (temp) name and allow her to select those objects to copy into the permanent library and delete the temp library. This is similar to what is done on the mainframe.
2. RSTOBJ—restore of an object or objects from a SAVOBJ. Since SAVOBJ is not recommended, the likelihood of using this command is slim.
3. RSTUSRPRF—restore of user profiles, from a SAVSYS or SAVSECDTA. This would occur if user profiles were damaged.
4. RSTAUT—restore of object use authority to user profiles, from a SAVSYS. When the system is completely restored, this is the last command to run.
5. RSTCFG—restore of device configurations from a SAVSYS.
6. RSTDLO—restore of documents and folders from a SAVDLO.
7. RSTLICPGM—restore of licensed programs for initial or new release installation.

Note that a *full* system restore would only be done in the case of a disaster and would be done by technical support personnel. Also, with the exception of RSTLIB and RSTOBJ, the use of most restore commands should be restricted to technical support and operations.

Additional information on backup and restore processes can be found in the *Operator's Guide* and IBM Manual SC21-8079, *AS/400 Programming: Backup and Recovery Guide.*

1.5 ADDING TERMINALS AND USERS TO THE SYSTEM

This section details the addition of terminals and users to the AS/400. It emphasizes personal computers since users typically have PCs attached to the AS/400 via the network, as opposed to dumb terminals. The following pages list and explain the commands necessary to add a user, personal computer support, and a library to the AS/400. It is worthwhile to note the importance of the F1 and F4 keys throughout this entry. F1 displays Help on the entire entry screen, or, if the user tabs to a specific field on the screen, Help will be displayed for that field alone. F4 is the prompting key.

A user need not know every required field for every command on the AS/400. Via prompting on the command, the AS/400 provides a fill-in-the-blanks format for entry of data. In addition, there are often more fields on the prompt screens than need to be filled in. Instructions will only be given below for the necessary fields. The F10 key functions as the Additional Parameters key and must be hit in order for some of the parameters for the commands listed below to be found.

CRTUSRPRF

CRTUSRPRF adds a user profile. When it is entered, hit F4 to prompt on it, entering the following and leaving the other fields as they are:

- User Profile—AS/400 userid; typically, the same as on a mainframe.
- User Class—type of user. Typically PGMR = programmer, SYSOPR = system operator, SECADM = security administrator, and so on. This field and all fields on the screen can be prompted (hit F4) to show valid values and additional information.
- Description—the user's name.
- Special Authority—if a user needs any special access, such as authority to save the system, it would be specified here by entry of a '+' on this line and the correct options. Availability of these options would be determined by the security administrator.

After ENTER has been pressed, a message confirming the addition of the user profile will appear on the bottom of the screen. The screen displays for the CRTUSRPRF command appear in Figure 1.8.

(a)

```
                     Create User Profile (CRTUSRPRF)

Type choices, press Enter.

User profile . . . . . . . . . . > DPXXX         Name
User password  . . . . . . . . .   *USRPRF       Name, *USRPRF, *NONE
Set password to expired  . . . .   *NO           *NO, *YES
User class . . . . . . . . . . . > *PGMR         *USER, *SYSOPR, *PGMR...
Current library  . . . . . . . .   *CRTDFT       Name, *CRTDFT
Initial program to call  . . . .   *NONE         Name, *NONE
  Library  . . . . . . . . . . .                 Name, *LIBL, *CURLIB
Initial menu . . . . . . . . . .   MAIN          Name, *SIGNOFF
  Library  . . . . . . . . . . .     *LIBL       Name, *LIBL, *CURLIB
Limit capabilities . . . . . . .   *NO           *NO, *PARTIAL, *YES
Text 'description' . . . . . . .   'TYPICAL PROGRAMMER'


                          Additional Parameters

Special authority  . . . . . . .   *USRCLS       *USRCLS, *NONE, *SAVSYS...

                                                                 More...
F3=Exit   F4=Prompt   F5=Refresh   F12=Cancel   F13=How to use this display
F24=More keys
     05-37     SA         MW         KS         IM         II S2        KB
```

Figure 1.8. CRTUSRPRF screen displays.

(b)

```
                    Create User Profile (CRTUSRPRF)

Type choices, press Enter.

               + for more values                   *USRCLS, *NONE, *SAVSYS...
Special environment . . . . . . .    *SYSVAL       *SYSVAL, *NONE, *S36
Display sign-on information  . .    *SYSVAL       *SYSVAL, *NO, *YES
Password expiration interval . .    *SYSVAL       1-366, *SYSVAL, *NOMAX
Limit device sessions  . . . . .    *SYSVAL       *SYSVAL, *YES, *NO
Maximum allowed storage  . . . .    *NOMAX        Kilobytes, *NOMAX
Highest schedule priority  . . .    3             0-9
Job description  . . . . . . . .    QDFTJOBD      Name
  Library  . . . . . . . . . . .      *LIBL       Name, *LIBL, *CURLIB
Group profile  . . . . . . . . .    *NONE         Name, *NONE
Owner  . . . . . . . . . . . . .    *USRPRF       *USRPRF, *GRPPRF
Group authority  . . . . . . . .    *NONE         *NONE, *ALL, *CHANGE, *USE...
Accounting code  . . . . . . . .    *BLANK
Document passwood  . . . . . . .    *NONE         Name, *NONE
Message queue  . . . . . . . . .    *USRPRF       Name, *USRPRF
  Library  . . . . . . . . . . .                  Name, *LIBL, *CURLIB

                                                                      More...
F3=Exit   F4=Prompt   F5=Refresh   F12=Cancel   F13=How to use this display
F24=More keys
     05-37     SA        MW         KS         IM         II S2         KB
```

Figure 1.8. *(cont.)*

(c)

```
                     Create User Profile (CRTUSRPRF)

 Type choices, press Enter.

 Delivery . . . . . . . . . . . .   *NOTIFY         *NOTIFY, *BREAK, *HOLD, *DFT
 Severity code filter . . . . . .   0               0-99
 Print device . . . . . . . . . .   *SYSVAL         Name. *SYSVAL
 Output queue . . . . . . . . . .   *DEV            Name, *DEV
   Library  . . . . . . . . . . .                   Name, *LIBL, *CURLIB
 Attention program  . . . . . . .   *NONE           Name, *NONE
   Library  . . . . . . . . . . .                   Name, *LIBL, *CURLIB
 User options . . . . . . . . . .   *NONE           *NONE, *CLKWD, *EXPERT...
               + for more values
 Authority  . . . . . . . . . . .   *EXCLUDE        *ALL, *CHANGE, *USE, *EXCLUDE









                                                                          Bottom
 F3=Exit   F4=Prompt   F5=Refresh   F12=Cancel   F13=How to use this display
 F24=More keys
      05-37     SA         MW         KS         IM         II S2        KB
```

Figure 1.8. *(cont.)*

ADDDIRE

ADDDIRE adds a directory entry. In effect, it attaches the AS/400 to a userid. When the command is entered, hit F4 and enter the following required fields. Other fields, such as full name and address information, are optional at this point.

- Userid—same as the userid of the profile just added.
- Address—typically the system identifier of the AS/400.
- Description—the user's name.
- User Profile—same as the userid of the profile just added.

After ENTER has been pressed, a message confirming the addition of the directory will appear on the bottom of the screen. Figure 1.9 shows the screen displays for the ADDDIRE command.

WRKCFGSTS

WRKCFGSTS starts the add of a controller, which begins the attachment of the PC to the AS/400 via the Token Ring. It will be used to copy an existing controller into a new one that corresponds with the new user profile. This process is as follows:

1. After typing the command, hit F4. For field Type enter *CTL, and for field Configuration Description enter a name or generic ID. Press ENTER; the next screen displayed is Work with Configuration Description.
2. Key in Option 8 in front of the description to be copied (in this case DPYYY). Press ENTER. The next screen displayed will have the DPYYY description on one line.
3. Key in Option 3 in front of DPYYY. Press ENTER. A prompt screen will be displayed in which the following information is to be entered, leaving the other fields as they are:
   - Controller description—identifier for the controller, usually some meaningful description for location or owner of the PC.
   - Remote control point—same as controller description.
   - Initial connection—usually *ANS, except when communication is with other systems (i.e., IBM Link), in which case the parameter is *DIAL.

(a)

```
                          Add Directory Entry (ADDDIRE)
Type choices, press Enter.

User identifier:
  User ID . . . . . . . . . . . . . > DPXXX         Character value
  Address . . . . . . . . . . . . . > S             Character value
User description . . . . . . . . . > 'TYPICAL PROGRAMMER'

User profile . . . . . . . . . . . > DPXXX         Name, *NONE
System name:
  System name . . . . . . . . . .     *LCL          Character value, *LCL, *PC
  System group . . . . . . . . . .                 Character value
Last name . . . . . . . . . . . .     *NONE

First name . . . . . . . . . . . .    *NONE
Middle name . . . . . . . . . . .     *NONE
Preferred name . . . . . . . . . .    *NONE
Full name . . . . . . . . . . . .     *DFT



                                                                      More...
F3=Exit   F4=Prompt   F5=Refresh   F12=Cancel   F13=How to use this display
F24=More keys
    06-37    SA         MW         KS         IM         II S2        KB
```

Figure 1.9. ADDDIRE screen displays.

(b)

```
                        Add Directory Entry (ADDDIRE)

 Type choices, press Enter.

 Department . . . . . . . . . . .   *NONE          Character value, *NONE
 Job title  . . . . . . . . . . .   *NONE

 Company  . . . . . . . . . . . .   *NONE

 Telephone number 1 . . . . . . .   *NONE
 Telephone number 2 . . . . . . .   *NONE
 Location . . . . . . . . . . . .   *NONE

 Building . . . . . . . . . . . .   *NONE
 Office . . . . . . . . . . . . .   *NONE
 Address line 1 . . . . . . . . .   *NONE

 Address line 2 . . . . . . . . .   *NONE



                                                                     More...
 F3=Exit   F4=Prompt   F5=Refresh   F12=Cancel   F13=How to use this display
 F24=More keys
     05-37     SA        MW        KS        IM        II S2       KB
```

Figure 1.9. *(cont.)*

(c)

```
                          Add Directory Entry (ADDDIRE)
Type choices, press Enter.

Address line 3 . . . . . . . . .   *NONE

Address line 4 . . . . . . . . .   *NONE

Text . . . . . . . . . . . . . .   *NONE

Indirect user  . . . . . . . . .   *NO          *NO, *YES










                                                                        Bottom
F3=Exit   F4=Prompt   F5=Refresh   F12=Cancel   F13=How to use this display
F24=More keys
    05-37    SA        MW        KS        IM        II S2        KB
```

Figure 1.9. *(cont.)*

- LAN remote adapter address—the Token Ring address or the burned-in address in the PC.

After ENTER has been pressed, a message confirming the addition of the controller will appear on the bottom of the screen. The screen displays related to the WRKCFGSTS command are presented in Figure 1.10.

CRTCTLAPPC

CRTCTLAPPC is an alternative for the previous command (WRKCFGSTS).* It does *not* copy an existing controller description, but does a straight add. Some additional fields must be entered. After the command has been entered, press F4, and the add controller description screen will be displayed. Enter the following fields, leaving the others as they are:

- Controller Description—identifier for the controller being added; usually some meaningful description for the location or owner of the PC.
- Link Type—*TRLAN or *LAN.
- Switched line list—Token Ring line description identifier.
- Remote network identifier—APPN.
- Remote control point—same as Controller Description.
- Initial connection—*ANS or *DIAL (see WRKCFGSTS for an explanation).
- LAN remote adapter address—the Token Ring address or the burned-in address in the PC.

After ENTER has been pressed, a message confirming the addition of the controller will appear on the bottom of the screen. Figure 1.11 is the screen display for the CRTCTLAPPC command.

---

*Either WRKCFGSTS or CRTCTLAPPC must be run to add the controller, not both.

(a)

```
                     Work with Configuration Status (WRKCFGSTS)

 Type choices, press Enter.

 Type . . . . . . . . . . . . . .   *CTL         *LIN, *CTL, *DEV
 Configuration description  . . .   *ALL         Name, generic*, *ALL, *CMN...
 Output . . . . . . . . . . . . .   *            *, *PRINT












                                                                           Bottom
 F3=Exit   F4=Prompt   F5=Refresh   F12=Cancel   F13=How to use this display
 F24=More keys
    06-37    SA        MW        KS        IM        II S2       KB
```

Figure 1.10. WRKCFGSTS screen displays.

(b)

```
                    Work with Configuration Status
                                                              System:   S
Position to  . . . . .            Starting characters

Type options, press Enter.
  1=Vary on    2=Vary off    5=Work with job    8=Work with description
  9=Display mode status ...

Opt  Lin/Ctl/Dev/Mod   Status                 -------------Job-------------
       CTLB            VARY ON PENDING
         DEVB          VARY ON PENDING
       CTL01           ACTIVE
         DSP02         SIGNON DISPLAY
         DSP01         ACTIVE                 DSP01      QSECOFR     034273
         PRT01         ACTIVE/WRITER          PRT01      QSPLJOB     034764
       DPAAA           VARY ON PENDING
         DPAAA         VARY ON PENDING
       DPYYY           ACTIVE
                                                                     More...
Parameters or command
===>
F3=Exit   F4=Prompt   F5=Refresh   F12=Cancel   F23=More Options
F24=More keys
(C) COPYRIGHT IBM CORP. 1980, 1990.
     10-02       SA        MW        KS        IM        II S2       KB
```

Figure 1.10. *(cont.)*

(c)

```
                       Work with Configuration Status
                                                              System:   S
Position to  . . . . .                  Starting characters

Type options, press Enter.
  1=Vary on    2=Vary off    5=Work with job    8=Work with description
  9=Display mode status ...

Opt  Lin/Ctl/Dev/Mod   Status                 -------------Job-------------
       CTLB            VARY ON PENDING
         DEVB          VARY ON PENDING
       CTL01           ACTIVE
         DSP02         SIGNON DISPLAY
         DSP01         ACTIVE                 DSP01       QSECOFR     034273
         PRT01         ACTIVE/WRITER          PRT01       QSPLJOB     034764
       DPAAA           VARY ON PENDING
         DPAAA         VARY ON PENDING
8      DPYYY           ACTIVE
                                                                    More...
Parameters or command
===>
F3=Exit   F4=Prompt   F5=Refresh   F12=Cancel   F23=More options
F24=More Keys
(C) COPYRIGHT IBM CORP. 1980, 1990.
    18-03    SA       MW        KS        IM        II S2       KB
```

Figure 1.10. *(cont.)*

(d)

```
                    Work with Controller Descriptions
                                                              System:   S
Position to  . . . . .              Starting characters

Type options, press Enter.
  2=Change    3=Copy    4=Delete    5=Display    6=Print    8=Work witht status
  9=Retrieve source    12=Print device addresses

Opt    Controller    Type    Text
3      DPYYY         *APPC









                                                                    Bottom
Parameters for options 2, 9 or command
===>
F3=Exit   F4=Prompt   F5=Refresh   F6=Create   F9=Retrieve   F12=Cancel
F14=Work with status
(C) COPYRIGHT IBM CORP. 1980, 1990.
    10-03    SA         MW         KS         IM         II S2       KB
```

Figure 1.10. (*cont.*).

(e)

```
                    Create Ctl Desc (APPC) (CRTCTLAPPC)

 Type choices, press Enter.

 Controller description . . . . .   DPXXX         Name
 Link type  . . . . . . . . . . . > *LAN          *LAN, *SDLC, *TDLC, *TRLAN...
 Online at IPL  . . . . . . . . . > *YES          *YES, *NO
 APPN-capable . . . . . . . . . . > *YES          *YES, *NO
 Switched line list . . . . . . . > AS400TR1      Name
                + for more values
 Maximum frame size . . . . . . . > 1994          265-8156, 265, 521, 1033...
 Remote network identifier  . . . > APPN          Name, *NETATR, *NONE
 Remote control point . . . . . . > DPXXX         Name
 Exchange identifier  . . . . . .                 00100000-FFFFFFFF
 Initial connection . . . . . . . > *ANS          *DIAL, *ANS
 Data link role . . . . . . . . . > *NEG          *NEG, *PRI, *SEC
 LAN remote adapter address . . . > 400011040088  000000000001-FFFFFFFFFFFF
 APPN CP session support  . . . . > *NO           *YES, *NO
 APPN node type . . . . . . . . . > *ENDNODE      *ENDNODE, *LENNODE...
 APPN transmission grp number . . > 1             1-20, *CALC

                                                                     More...
 F3=Exit    F4=Prompt    F5-Refresh    F10=Additional parameters    F12=Cancel
 F13=How to use this display    F24=More keys
     18-37       SA        MW        KS        IM        II S2        KB
```

Figure 1.10. *(cont.)*.

(f)

```
                    Create Ctl Desc (APPC) (CRTCTLAPPC)

 Type choices, press Enter.

 APPN minimum switched status . . > *VRYONPND    *VRYONPND, *VRYON
 Model controller description . . > *NO          *NO, *YES
 Text 'description' . . . . . . . > *BLANK


                          Additional Parameters

 Character code . . . . . . . . . > *EBCDIC       *EBCDIC, *ASCII
 Switched disconnect  . . . . . . > *YES          *YES, *NO
 Disconnect timer . . . . . . . . > 170           0-65535 seconds
 LAN DSAP . . . . . . . . . . . . > 04            04, 08, 0C, 10, 14, 18, 1C...
 LAN SSAP . . . . . . . . . . . . > 04            04, 08, 0C, 10, 14, 18, 1C...
 LAN frame retry  . . . . . . . . > 30            0-254, *CALC
 LAN connection retry . . . . . . > 30            0-254, *CALC
 LAN response timer . . . . . . . > *CALC         0-254 (0.1 seconds)
 LAN connection timer . . . . . . > 70            0-254 (0.1 seconds)
                                                                        More...
 F3=Exit   F4=Prompt   F5=Refresh   F10=Additional parameters   F12=Cancel
 F13=How to use this display    F24=More keys
     05-37        SA        MW        KS        IM        II S2        KB
```

Figure 1.10. *(cont.)*.

(g)

```
                   Create Ctl Desc (APPC) (CRTCTLAPPC)

Type choices, press Enter.

LAN acknowledgement timer  . . . > *CALC         0-254 (0.1 seconds)
LAN inactivity timer . . . . . . > 200           0-255 (0.1 seconds)
LAN acknowledgement frequency  . > 1             0-127, *CALC
LAN max outstanding frames . . . > 2             1-127, *CALC
LAN access priority  . . . . . . > 0             0-3, *CALC
LAN window step  . . . . . . . . > *NONE         1-127, *NONE
Recovery limits:
  Count limit  . . . . . . . . . > 10            0-99, *SYSVAL
  Time interval  . . . . . . . . > 5             0-120 (minutes)









                                                                      Bottom
F3=Exit   F4=Prompt   F5=Refresh   F10=Additional parameters   F12=Cancel
F13=How to use this display   F24=More keys
    05-37         SA        MW        KS        IM        II S2       KM
```

Figure 1.10. *(cont.)*.

```
                       Create Ctl Desc (APPC) (CRTCTLAPPC)

 Type choices, press Enter.

 Controller description . . . . . . > DPXXX         Name
 Link type  . . . . . . . . . . . . > *LAN          *IDLC, *LAN, *LOCAL, *SDLC...
 Online at IPL  . . . . . . . . . . > *YES          *YES, *NO
 APPN-capable . . . . . . . . . . . > *YES          *YES, *NO
 Switched line list . . . . . . . . > AS400T        Name
               + for more values
 Maximum frame size . . . . . . . .                 265-16393, 265, 521, 1033...
 Remote network identifier  . . . .   APPN          Name, *NETATR, *NONE
 Remote control point . . . . . . .   DPXXX         Name
 Exchange identifier  . . . . . . .                 00100000-FFFFFFFF
 Initial connection . . . . . . . .   *ANS          *DIAL, *ANS
 LAN remote adapter address . . . .   400012121212  000000000001-FFFFFFFFFFFF




                                                                           Bottom
 F3=Exit   F4=Prompt   F5=Refresh   F12=Cancel   F13=How to use this display
 F24=More keys
     05-37    SA          MW          KS          IM          II S1       KB
```

Figure 11.1. CRTCTLAPPC screen display.

Adding PC Support to PCs

This command adds PC Support to the DOS PC already connected to the Token Ring. After the software detailed below is installed, the PC will 'talk' to the AS/400 via the Token Ring. The following procedure should be followed:

1. At C:, change to A: and insert the AS/400 PC Support diskette into drive A.
2. At A:, enter INSTALL and press ENTER.
3. On the screen, arrow down to item 2—LAN—and press ENTER.
   - Location — AS/400 controller description ID.
   - System Name—the system ID of the AS/400.
   - System Address—the LAN adapter address of the AS/400.
   - LAN Address—Token Ring address of this PC on the network; same as that used in creating the controller on the AS/400 side.
   - Organizer—space out.
   - Work—arrow down to the field and space out.
   - Virtual Printer—arrow down to the field and space out.
4. Press ENTER to install.
5. Reboot the PC (CTL-ALT-DELETE).

At this point the user is ready to start PC Support. (Refer to Section 1.1, System Logon.)

Creating Multiple AS/400 Sessions

The creation of multiple sessions must take place at the workstation that requires multiple sessions. In most cases one AS/400 session with the alternate session capability will suffice, but some users may require two or more. This will be accomplished as follows:

1. At the PC workstation already on the AS/400, log on to the AS/400 and, once at the Main Menu, log off using Option 90.
2. At the PCS:, key in 'I:cfgwsf' and press ENTER to bring up the Workstation Function Configuration screen.
3. Press ENTER to continue.
4. Press F10, then arrow to the reverse highlighted CREATE.

5. Press ENTER to continue.
6. Press ENTER on 'Create Session Profile'.
7. When the Create Session Profile screen is displayed with SESS.DAT, key over with SESSA.DAT and press ENTER.
8. On the Session Profile screen, press ENTER on 'Standard Display'.
9. On the Standard Display Session screen, press F10 and then ENTER at the General Session Options prompt.
10. Press ENTER for 'General Session Options'.
11. On the General Session Options screen, enter the following:
    - Buffer Keystrokes—yes or no.
    - System Name—system ID of the AS/400.
    - Display Station ID—leave blank.
    - Request to Bypass AS/400 Sign-On Screen—no.
12. Press ENTER to store information.
13. Press F10 to exit.
14. Press ENTER on 'Save Session Profile and Add to Master'.
15. Press ENTER on the Verify screen.
16. On the Add Session to Master Profile screen, move the cursor to 1, press the spacebar, press ENTER, then ENTER again to verify, F10 to exit, and exit. (To add multiple sessions move the cursor to the appropriate session number; otherwise, session 1 will continually be updated.)
17. Repeat this process from step 6 to create another session profile, for SESSB.DAT, SESSC. DAT, and so on, up to a maximum of five sessions.
18. Reboot the PC (CTL-ALT-DELETE) after creating the sessions. If a LAN timeout occurs after you try the STARTPCS command, the controller and attached devices must be varied off and back on again on the AS/400 side in order to allow PCS to start.

Adding a Virtual Printer

Adding a virtual printer is done in situations where AS/400 output can be scattered among numerous printers, such as on each floor of a multifloor building. The virtual printer is assigned to the device, and any AS/400 print output is sent to that printer, no matter who is logged on at the workstation. The setup is as follows:

1. Log on to the AS/400; go to the Main Menu.
2. Select Option 11, PC Support Tasks, and press ENTER.
3. On the next screen, select Option 5, PC Support Organizer.
4. On the next screen, select Option 4, PC Support Tasks.
5. The next screen displayed is the AS/400 PC Support Menu. Space down to Option 2, Configure PC Support, and press ENTER.
6. On the next screen select Option 1, PC Support Configuration, and press ENTER.
7. Move the cursor down to Virtual Printer and press F10 to change.
8. Select Option 2, Add Printer Definition. Do the following:
   - On line 1 enter the virtual printer name (PRT1, PRT2, etc.).
   - Enter the system name—the AS/400 system ID.
   - Enter the printer device name (i.e., the system printer)—PRT01.
   - Press Enter.
9. Press F10 to exit, then select the option to save and exit. Follow the screen instructions to return to the AS/400 Main Menu.

Special Notes on Adding PC Support

For the initial PC Support for a typical user, we would use the notes from the previous sections on PC Support, multiple sessions, and the virtual printer. However, for all similar PCs, we would:

1. Copy an existing PC's PCS directory to a diskette's PCS directory by doing the following:
   - at A:, key in 'MD PCS'.
   - at C:, key in 'COPY PCS*.* A:PCS /V'.
2. Use this diskette on any PC. The PCS directory will be copied to the PC, taking with it the sample configuration, and thus eliminating the need to configure each PC individually.
3. Copy the diskette to the PC by doing the following:
   - at C:, key in 'MD PCS'.
   - at A:, key in 'COPY PCS*.* C:PCS /V'.
4. At this point, fine-tune the CONFIG.SYS and CONFIG.PCS files:

- At C:, get into the PCS directory and copy the original CONFIG.PCS to another name for backup in case of a problem. The backup name can always be deleted after the successful setup of the PC.
- Stay in the PCS directory and edit on CONFIG.PCS to modify line RTLN APPN.XXXXX, where XXXXX is the AS/400 controller description that corresponds to the PC.
- At C:, copy the original CONFIG.SYS to another name for backup in case of a problem. The backup name can always be deleted after the successful setup of the PC.
- At C:, EDLIN on CONFIG.SYS. Add the following two lines at the end:
  DEVICE = C:\PCS\EIMPCS.SYS
  DEVICE = C:\PCS\ECYDDX.SYS

5. Reboot the PC and start up PC Support. Note that you can manage multiple sessions by going into the workstation configuration function on the PC side *after* signing off the AS/400. Enter 'I:CFGWSF' and a set of screens will be presented from which master and session profiles can be altered.

Removing an Unwanted Session on the AS/400

You might remove an unwanted session in the event a printer session was set up and not needed or a user just needed to remove a session or sessions from the AS/400. The procedure as is follows:

1. At the PC workstation already on the AS/400, log off the AS/400 from the Main Menu using Option 90.
2. At the PCS:, key in 'i:cfgwsf' and press ENTER. This will put you at the Workstation Function Configuration screen.
3. Press ENTER to continue.
4. Press F10, then arrow to reverse the highlighted CHANGE.
5. Press ENTER to continue.
6. Press ENTER on 'Change Master Profile'.
7. Press F10, then select SESSIONS by pressing ENTER.
8. Select the Remove a Session from a Master option, then press ENTER.
9. Move the cursor to the session to be deleted, then hit the spacebar, then ENTER.

10. Press F10 to exit.
11. Reboot the PC after deleting the session(s).

Changing Default Color Values on the AS/400

If the user wished to change default color values for AS/400 sessions, the following procedure would be necessary:

1. The PC workstation should have a minimum of two sessions available to the AS/400. Log on to both sessions.
2. On session 1 select PC Support Tasks from the Main Menu and press ENTER.
3. On the PC Support Tasks Menu, select PC Support Organizer and press ENTER.
4. Select PC Command Prompt and press ENTER.
5. At the PCS: key in 'i:wsfcolor' and press ENTER.
6. Select session 2 and press ENTER.
7. Return to session 1.
8. Move the cursor to the color to change, then press ENTER.
9. Select the color and press ENTER.
10. View the color change(s) during the change process by returning to the alternate session.

Defining Sessions to More Than One AS/400

Defining sessions to more than one AS/400 must be done on the PC as follows:

1. Change the CONFIG.PCS, but save it first in case of a problem. Copy CONFIG.PCS to CONFIG.BKP.
2. Edit to add the following TRLI MMMMMMM1,4000ADDRESS01 before TRLI MMMMMMM2,4000ADDRESS02, where MMMMMMM1 is the system ID of machine 1, MMMMMMM2 is the system ID of machine 2, 4000ADDRESS01 is the LAN adapter address of machine 1, and 4000ADDRESS02 is the LAN adapter address of machine 2. This will attach the user to two AS/400s.
3. Change line 1 to SFLR 1, I,QIWSFLR,MMMMMMM1. This creates a shared folder for the machine-1 system.*

4. To change the session profile, get into the PCS directory and key in 'I:CFGWSF'.
5. Change C:\PCS\SESSA.DAT (if not already created, then use the Create option).
6. Enter the general session options with the following parameters:
   - Buffer Keystrokes—yes.
   - System Name—system ID of that session's AS/400.
   - Display Station ID—leave blank.
   - Request to Bypass AS/400 Sign-On Screen—no.
7. Save the session profile.
8. Exit.
9. Change SESSB.DAT (again, if not already created, then use the Create option).
10. Enter the general session options again, entering the same parameters for the *other* AS/400.
11. Save the session profile.
12. Exit. At this point one session has been created on each AS/400, and the ALT/ESC keys are used to toggle.
13. Reboot the PC (CTL-ALT-DELETE) to effect the change. The user is now ready to start PC Support.**

Enrolling Users in the AS/400

Enrolling users involves creation of the user's environment, typically a programmer's, which would most likely be done by tech support and/or a security administrator. The procedure is as follows:

1. Create a library for the user, usually named by the user (e.g., DPXXX).
2. Within the user library (DPXXX) create a job description (DPXXXJOBD). Change the attributes for the initial library

*Steps 1 through 3 add a machine-2 session to a PC already connected to machine 1. To add a machine-1 session to a PC connected to machine 2, change Steps 2 and 3 to reverse numbers (for the other system).

**Note that if the attachment to both AS/400s is successful, the backup copy of CONFIG.PCS (in this case, CONFIG.BKP) can be deleted.

list to DPXXX, QTEMP, QGPL, and any other libraries the user needs. This will set the user up so that he conducts all activity primarily in his own library without affecting any system and/or production libraries.

3. Also within the user library (DPXXX), create an output queue (DPXXXOUTQ). All batch output for the user will be stored in that queue until he prints or deletes it. The command for this is CRTOUTQ. Hit F4 to prompt and, with the exception of output queue, library name, and text (usually the user's name), take the defaults.
4. Change the previously added user profile (DPXXX) using a CHGUSRPRF command with the following:
   - Job Description—DPXXXJOBD, in library DPXXX.
   - Message Queue—DPXXX, in library QUSRSYS.
   - Output Queue—DPXXXOUTQ, in library DPXXX.
   - Current Library—DPXXX.
5. Create source files within library DPXXX by entering command CRTSRCPF. Files can be created for COBOL programs (QCBLSRC), CL programs (QCLSRC), DDS (QDDSSRC), and so on, all in library DPXXX.

More detail on source files and libraries will be provided in Chapter 2.

Additional information on adding terminals and users to the AS/400 can be found in:

- IBM Manuals SC21-9775, SC21-9776, SC21-9777, SC21-9778, and SC21-9779: *AS/400 Programming: Control Language Reference,* Volumes 1–5. Commands are referenced alphabetically throughout the five volumes, and the book steps the user through the needed parameters for any command.
- IBM Manual SC21-8197, *AS/400 PC Support: DOS Operations Reference.*

1.6 SECURITY

AS/400 security may be as general or as specific as needed. There are levels of system security, as well as levels of security against specific objects and/or functions on the system. This section will briefly explain security concepts and indicate the current levels of security that are common on the AS/400.

The main security officer on the system is userid QSECOFR. This userid can access all objects and functions and has the highest security rating in the system (SECOFR). The secondary security rating on the system is that of security administrator. In general, this rating (SECADM for short) has many of the same capabilities as QSECOFR but on a more localized level. An individual could have SECADM authority to set up user profiles, program and library security, etc., only for a *specific* department.

Typically, AS/400s are set up at security level 30. This means that everyone who logs on to the system must do so with a userid and password. In addition, users must be specifically given access to system resources.

There are five classes of user on the AS/400. One must be indicated at the time each user profile is created. The classes are hierarchical in that a higher class can perform all the functions of a lower class. They are as follows:

- SECOFR—security officer, as mentioned above.
- SECADM—security administrator, as mentioned above.
- PGMR—programmer, who would have some authority to program and test libraries.
- SYSOPR—system operator, who would have authority to perform operational tasks but not programming tasks.
- USER—user, whose authority would most likely entail the ability to log on to the system and perform his or her daily work.

Special authorities allow the use of certain functions that would be restricted by user class—for example, *ALLOBJ (all objects on the system) authority is automatically granted to someone whose user class is SECOFR. If, however, this authority were to be granted to another user whose class does *not* automatically grant that authority (SECADM, for example), that special authority would have to be granted by the security officer to the specific user profile whose class is SECADM.

Access to system menus, commands, library lists, objects, and physical files is controlled by the security officer. In addition, the owner of an object may grant authority to any object he or she owns.

Authorization lists are another method of controlling access to objects. The command CRTAUTL can create an authorization list that is then referenced in the creation of an object.

Group profiles can be created to ease the addition of user profiles. A group would share common access to files, objects, etc. Users can be grouped by job function, say, in order to simplify the assignment and administration of security.

Additional information on security can be found in: IBM Manual SC21-8083, *AS/400 Programming: Security Concepts and Planning.*

2

Programming Procedures

The objective of this chapter is to introduce various AS/400 programming procedures, primarily as background for the programmer who will be working on the system. It will be broken down into the following sections:

2.1 Basic Object and Library Concepts
2.2 Basic AS/400 Processing
2.3 AS/400 Naming Conventions
2.4 AS/400 Control Language
2.5 Moves from Test to Production

2.1 BASIC OBJECT AND LIBRARY CONCEPTS

The object orientation of the AS/400 seems very mysterious at first, but it really is not that difficult to comprehend. An object can best be described as an entity that exists on the AS/400, upon which operations can be *performed* by the AS/400. Objects include the following:

- All libraries on the AS/400
- Files within libraries

- Executable programs
- Database files
- User profiles
- Job descriptions
- Subsystem descriptions
- Device descriptions
- Line and controller descriptions for PC Support
- Queues
- Commands

A library is the highest-level object on the system. All objects exist within libraries, and within any given library there may be many different types of objects. In library ABC, for example, the following may reside:

- Executable programs, each of which is an object. These are object modules, or what we would call load modules in mainframe terminology.
- Source code files, which themselves contain members. A source code file is like a mainframe partitioned dataset in that its members have like characteristics. For example, source code file QDDSSRC contains members with raw data description specifications for database files; QCLSRC contains members with raw source code for Control Language programs; and QCBLSRC contains members with raw source code for COBOL programs. The files beginning with 'Q' will be discussed in Section 2.3, "Naming Conventions." Individual members of source code files are *not* considered objects, but when a member of a source code file is compiled successfully, its executable code becomes an object.
- Database files, including both physical and logical files. Logical files are alternate views of data, similar to alternate indexes to VSAM files.

There are system libraries, user libraries, and product libraries on the AS/400. System libraries include QUSRSYS, QSYS, etc. They contain modules that, in general, are system-wide and can be likened to SYSRES packs on the mainframe. Product libraries include data needed for licensed programs on the AS/400. User libraries include individual libraries for a given user or a given application. They can be classified as either production or test, so that users can be protected from accessing production libraries when access is not needed.

The manner in which user profiles are defined points to specific job descriptions for each user. Within the job description the user portion of the library list is set. The library list determines *what* an individual might be able to do during that session and *where* his programs/data reside.

The order in which the library list is searched is similar in concept to a STEPLIB or JOBLIB DD statement on the mainframe. For example, an individual's library list can be changed so that a test library, which includes test programs and test files, may be searched before a production library is searched. Library list search order is as follows:

1. Current (CUR)
2. System (SYS
3. Product (PRD)
4. User (USR)

The command to view a user's library list is DSPLIBL. Figure 2.1 shows the screen returned via this command. Note that even though the system (Type=SYS) libraries are shown first, the current library (Type=CUR) is *always* the first library searched. Other user libraries (Type=USR) are searched in the order in which they are displayed on the screen. The current and user portions of the library list can be changed either temporarily or permanently, depending on circumstances. System libraries may also be changed, but this would be done by technical support and is generally a system-wide parameter.

Additional basic information on libraries and objects can be found in IBM Manual GC21-9802, *AS/400 System Concepts.*

```
                     Display Library List
                                                        System:   S

Type options, press Enter.
  5=Display objects in library

Opt  Library     Type     Text
     QSYS        SYS      System Library
     QSYS2       SYS      System Library for CPI's
     QUSRSYS     SYS      *IN USE
     QHLPSYS     SYS
     DPXXXLIB    CUR      DPXXX Test Library
     DPXXXLIB    USR      DPXXX Test Library
     QTEMP       USR
     QGPL        USR      General Purpose Library
     TSTLIB      USR      Test System Library
     DPCLIB      USR      Prod System Library

                                                              Bottom
F3=Exit    F12=Cancel    F17=Top    F18=Bottom
(C) COPYRIGHT IBM CORP. 1980, 1990.
    09-03    SA       MW       KS       IM       II S2      KB
```

Figure 2.1. Display Library List screen.

2.2 BASIC AS/400 PROCESSING

This section briefly explains the processing, basic menu navigation, and commands that enable a programmer to work on the AS/400.

The AS/400 Main Menu is the first menu a user will encounter after logging on. It contains a number of options, each of which generally leads to submenus. These options are discussed briefly below:

- User Tasks—related to the user logged on to the AS/400, such as submitting jobs, sending messages, and changing a password.
- Office Tasks—related to IBM's OfficeVision, clerical functions, and PC Support. OfficeVision integrates functions such as word processing, calendaring, and electronic mail.
- General System Tasks—maintenance/operational activities such as saving and restoring files.
- Files, Libraries, and Folders—related to data and PC support.
- Programming—the programmer's menu, which contains options for question and answer functions, screen copy (useful in debugging programs), and numerous other programmer-related functions. This menu also contains an option for Programming Development Manager (PDM), probably the single most important function for the programmer in working with source programs and objects in system development (see Chapters 4 and 5).
- Communications—primarily an operations/technical support menu for work on network status, remote jobs, network configuration, etc.
- Define or Change the System—primarily a technical support menu for checking system configuration, applying program temporary fixes, and working with security.
- Problem Handling—assists programming, operations, and technical support in functions such as problem solving, message display, history log, and question and answer.
- Display a Menu—allows entry of 'GO' to access a menu without having to work through menus and submenus. Any menu (with its name in the upper left corner) can be accessed by

entry of 'GO menuname' either on the command line or through this option.

- User Support and Education—allows the user to learn how to use AS/400 functions by taking online education (basic system tutorial and Discover/Education classes), and explains System Help. System Help mainly consists of the user pressing F1 to display a Help screen. Help screens are context-sensitive, depending on the location of the cursor on the screen at the time F1 is pressed. For example, if it is at the top of a screen, Help will be displayed for the entire screen. If it is on an entry field halfway down a screen, Help will be limited to the specific field. In addition, Extended Help (more detailed help information) for any Help screen is available via the F2 key.
- PC Support Tasks—allows for upload/download options, as well as for technical support functions of PC Support definitions.

On some submenus, there is an Option 60, More Options. If it is selected, additional options under that topic will be displayed.

Some submenus also have an Option 70, Related Commands. It displays commands to shortcut to various options, selected either by option number or by command name on the command line. Users will discover that they more quickly reach frequently used options by knowing the correct command. Command structures are generally very logical. The first three positions represent the function: CRT for Create, DLT for Delete, WRK for Work, DSP for display, and so on. The second part is more variable in length and represents the type of object being worked on; for example, output queue is OUTQ; user profile, USRPRF; and message, MSG. Thus, DSPMSG represents Display Message; CRTUSRPRF, Create User Profile; and WRKOUTQ, Work with Output Queue. Another way to determine commands is to enter on the command line 'GO CMDxxx', where xxx is the function. 'GO CMDCRT', for example, will display Create commands.

Figure 2.2 displays the Main Menu and related submenus. Note that there is some functional overlap. PC Support, for example, can be reached from Main Menu or from submenu Files, Libraries, and Folders; Files, Libraries, and Folders can be

(a)

```
MAIN                         AS/400 Main Menu
                                                                  System:   S

Select one of the following:

     1. User tasks
     2. Office tasks
     3. General system tasks
     4. Files, libraries, and folders
     5. Programming
     6. Communications
     7. Define or change the system
     8. Problem handling
     9. Display a menu
    10. User support and education
    11. PC Support tasks

    90. Sign off

Selection or command
===>

F3=Exit   F4=Prompt   F9=Retrieve   F12=Cancel   F13=User support
F23=Set initial menu
    20-07      SA         MW         KS         IM         II S2        KB
```

Figure 2.2. The Main Menu and related submenus.

(b)

```
USER                                User Tasks
                                                                 System:   S

Select one of the following:

     1. Display or change your job
     2. Display messages
     3. Send a message
     4. Submit a job
     5. Work with your spooled output files
     6. Work with your batch jobs
     7. Display or change your library list
     8. Change your password
     9. Change your user profile

    60. More user task options

    90. Sign off

Selection or command
===>

F3=Exit   F4=Prompt   F9=Retrieve   F12=Cancel   F13=User support
F16=System main menu
(C) COPYRIGHT IBM CORP. 1980, 1990.
    20-07     SA        MW        KS        IM        II S2        KB
```

Figure 2.2. *(cont.)*

(c)

```
FCTSK                               Office Tasks
                                                                System:   S

Select one of the following:

     1. OfficeVision/400
     2. PC Support tasks
     3. Decision support
     4. Office security
     5. Work with system directory
     6. Documents
     7. Folders

    70. Related commands



Selection or command
===>

F3=Exit   F4=Prompt   F9=Retrieve   F12=Cancel   F13=User support
F16=System main menu
(C) COPYRIGHT IBM CORP. 1980, 1990.
    20-07      SA         MW         KS         IM         II S2        KB
```

Figure 2.2. *(cont.)*

(d)

```
SYSTEM                        General System Tasks
                                                               System:   S

Select one of the following:

     1. Jobs
     2. Status
     3. Display system operator messages
     4. Messages
     5. Files, libraries, and folders
     6. Save
     7. Restore
     8. Device operations
     9. Communications
    10. Security

    60. More system task options

Selection or command
===>

F3=Exit   F4=Prompt   F9=Retrieve   F12=Cancel   F13=User support
F16=System main menu
(C) COPYRIGHT IBM CORP. 1980, 1990.
    20-07     SA        MW        KS        IM        II S2       KB
```

Figure 2.2. *(cont.)*

(e)

```
DATA                      Files, Libraries, and Folders
                                                                System:   S

Select one of the following:

     1. Files
     2. Libraries
     3. Folders
     4. PC Support tasks









Selection or command
===>

F3=Exit   F4=Prompt   F9=Retrieve   F12=Cancel   F13=User support
F16=System main menu
(C) COPYRIGHT IBM CORP. 1980, 1990.
    20-07     SA         MW         KS         IM         II S2        KB
```

Figure 2.2. *(cont.)*

(f)

```
PROGRAM                              Programming
                                                          System:   S
Select one of the following:

     1. Programmer menu
     2. Programming Development Manager (PDM)
     3. Utilities
     4. Programming language debug
     5. Structured Query Language (SQL) pre-compiler
     6. Question and answer
     7. IBM product information
     8. Copy screen image
     9. Cross System Product/Application Execution (CSP/AE)

    50. System/36 programming

    70. Related commands

Selection or command
===>

F3=Exit   F4=Prompt   F9=Retrieve   F12=Cancel   F13=User support
F16=System main menu
(C) COPYRIGHT IBM CORP. 1980, 1990.
   20-07    SA       MW       KS       IM       II S2       KB
```

Figure 2.2. *(cont.)*

(g)

```
CMN                           Communications
                                                        System:   S

Select one of the following:

     1. Communication status
     2. Messages
     3. Remote jobs
     4. Configure communications
     5. Network management
     6. Network configuration
     7. Verify communications
     8. Send or receive files
     9. Jobs

    70. Related commands


Selection or command
===>

F3=Exit   F4=Prompt   F9=Retrieve   F12=Cancel   F13=User support
F16=System main menu
(C) COPYRIGHT IBM CORP. 1980, 1990.
    20-07     SA       MW       KS       IM       II S2       KB
```

Figure 2.2. *(cont.)*

(h)

```
DEFINE                       Define or Change the System
                                                                System:   S
Select one of the following:

     1. Configuration
     2. Work with licensed programs
     3. Security
     4. Work with support contact information
     5. Work with system resources
     6. Program temporary fix
     7. IBM product information
     8. Work with system values





Selection or command
===>

F3=Exit   F4=Prompt   F9=Retrieve   F12=Cancel   F13=User support
F16=System main menu
(C) COPYRIGHT IBM CORP. 1980, 1990.
    20-07     SA        MW        KS        IM        II S2        KB
```

Figure 2.2. *(cont.)*

(i)

```
PROBLEM                          Problem Handling
                                                              System:   S
Select one of the following:

     1. Question and answer
     2. Work with problems
     3. Network problem handling
     4. Display system operator messages
     5. Display the history log
     6. System service tools

    60. More problem handling options

    70. Related commands




Selection or command
===>

F3=Exit   F4=Prompt   F9=Retrieve   F12=Cancel   F13=User support
F16=System main menu
(C) COPYRIGHT IBM CORP. 1980, 1990.
    20-07     SA        MW        KS         IM        II S2       KB
```

Figure 2.2. *(cont.)*

(j)

```
                         Go to Menu (GO)

 Type choices, press Enter.

 Menu . . . . . . . . . . . . . . .                     Name, generic*, *ALL
   Library  . . . . . . . . . . . .    *LIBL            Name, *LIBL, *CURLIB...
 Return point . . . . . . . . . . .  *YES               *YES, *NO

                                                                          Bottom
 F3=Exit   F4=Prompt   F5=Refresh   F12=Cancel   F13=How to use this display
 F24=More keys
     05-37     SA         MW         KS         IM         II S2        KB
```

Figure 2.2. *(cont.)*.

(k)

```
SUPPORT                     User Support and Education
                                                                System:  S
Select one of the following:

     1. How to use help
     2. Search system help index
     3. How to use commands
     4. Question and answer
     5. AS/400 publications
     6. IBM product information
     7. How to handle system problems
     8. Problem handling
     9. Online ecucation





Selection or command
===>
F3=Exit   F4=Prompt   F9=Retrieve   F12=Cancel   F16=System main menu
(C) COPYRIGHT IBM CORP. 1980, 1990.
    21-07     SA        MW        KS        IM        II S2       KB
```

Figure 2.2. (*cont.*).

(l)

```
PCSTSK                          PC Support Tasks

Select one of the following:

User Tasks
     1. Copy PC document to database
     2. Copy database to PC document
     3. Work with documents in folders
     4. Work with folders
     5. PC Support Organizer

Administrator Tasks
    20. Initialize PC Support
    21. Enroll PC Support users
    22. Configure PC connections




Selection or command
===>
F3=Exit   F4=Prompt   F9=Retrieve   F12=Cancel   F13=User support
F16=System main menu
(C) COPYRIGHT IBM CORP. 1980, 1990.
    20-07     SA         MW         KS         IM         II S2       KB
```

Figure 2.2. *(cont.)*.

reached from the Main Menu or from the submenu General System Tasks. PC Support can also be reached by entry of 'GO PCSTSK' on the command line, and Files, Libraries, and Folders can be reached by entry of 'GO DATA'. In sum, the flexibility of the AS/400 allows numerous *correct* ways to get to the same place.

Additional information on basic processing can be found in *AS/400 System Concepts.*

2.3 AS/400 NAMING CONVENTIONS

This section explains general AS/400 naming as well as a site's naming conventions for the AS/400.

'Q' libraries, queues, userids, and files—normally any name beginning with 'Q'—indicates system-derived. This means that these so-named objects are, either by installation or IBM convention, installed with the AS/400 and are system defaults. The main system library, for example, library QSYS, contains user profiles, device descriptions, and systems programs, and library QLBL contains the COBOL/400 compiler. When users log on to the system, a library called QTEMP is automatically allocated to them as a workspace library for the duration of the interactive session. A generic user library called QGPL exists in which users can store data, programs, etc. When new releases of the operating system are installed, the 'Q' libraries are overlaid, so it is not recommended that users store data in them. Our convention is that each user will be allocated his or her own library to minimize use of 'Q' libraries.

Within individual user libraries (which can be compared to an individual's JCL, COBOL, or LOAD libraries on the mainframe) there are source files that also begin with 'Q'. This is a naming convention carried over from S/36 and S/38 computers. Source physical files beginning with 'Q' contain members with like source code. Thus, QCLSRC contains Control Language source code, QCBLSRC contains COBOL/400 source code, and QDDSSRC contains DDS source code.

The command to create a source physical file is CRTSRCPF. As each member is added to a source physical file, its type (DDS,

RPG, COBOL, etc.) is specified. It is important to ensure that the right member type is specified in its correct file for two reasons. First, when source code is entered with the source entry utility (SEU), a member type RPG may be prompted (with F4) so that source can be entered correctly; preliminary syntax checking is done at entry time. Second, the interactive compiler on the AS/400 looks for the correct source physical file from which to get the source code; thus, for example, source code for COBOL/400 program PGM001 would be a member type COBOL in source physical file QCBLSRC. QCBLSRC would reside in the user's individual library (DPXXXLIB, for example) to allow for a totally isolated testing environment.

Figure 2.3 shows the screen displays to create a source physical file in a user library, then the creation of a member in a source physical file. To create a member in a source file, select the Work with Members option from the PDM Menu, then enter the library and source files (DPXXXLIB and QCBLSRC in this case). From the Work with Members screen, press F6 to create a new member. Be sure that the source type parameter conforms to the source file (i.e., if the source file is QCBLSRC, the source type is CBL). Remember that Help keys are available for assistance.

Site Naming Conventions

In order to make internal AS/400 naming conventions as flexible as possible, the following standards, similar to those used on mainframes, should be established:

1. Job names are determined by the AS/400 system. Interactive job names consist of workstation ID, userid, and a system-assigned sequential number. An interactive job can be considered one logon session to the AS/400. The job begins at user sign-on and ends at user sign-off. Batch jobs are submitted with the SBMJOB command and user must submit a specific command from a library. Batch job names consist of command name, userid, and system-assigned sequential number.
2. Production batch command names should be in the format 'xxxnnn(ss)' where:

(a)

```
                  Create Source Physical File (CRTSRCPF)

Type choices, press Enter.

File . . . . . . . . . . . . . .   QCBLSRC       Name
  Library  . . . . . . . . . . .     DPXXXLIB    Name, *CURLIB
Record length  . . . . . . . . .   92            Number
Member, if desired . . . . . . .   *NONE         Name, *NONE, *FILE
Text 'description' . . . . . . .   'COBOL/400 SOURCE CODE'













                                                                      Bottom
F3=Exit   F4=Prompt   F5=Refresh   F10=Additional parameters   F12=Cancel
F13=How to use this display    F24=More keys
    09-60     SA        MW        KS        IM        II S1       KB
```

Figure 2.3. Screen displays for creation of a source physical file and a member.

(b)

```
                   Work with Members Using PDM

File  . . . . . .   QCBLSRC
  Library . . . .     DPXXXLIB            Position to . . . . .

Type options, press Enter.
  2=Edit         3=Copy       4=Delete       5=Display      6=Print
  7=Rename       8=Display description       9=Save         13=Change text...

Opt  Member      Type        Text
     PEDISP      CBL         personnel file online display program
     PEDSPL      CBL         personnel file online update program
     PER001      CBL         personnel file report print program
     PER002      CBL         personnel file update program




                                                                       Bottom
Parameters or command
===>
F3=Exit       F4=Prompt             F5=Refresh          F6=Create
F9=Retrieve   F10=Command entry     F23=More options    F24=More keys
    11-02     SA         MW         KS         IM       II S1        KB
```

Figure 2.3. *(cont.)*

(c)

```
                     Start Source Entry Utility (STRSEU)

 Type choices, press Enter.

 Source file . . . . . . . . . . . > QCBLSRC       Name, *PRV
   Library . . . . . . . . . . . . >   DPXXXLIB    Name, *LIBL, *CURLIB, *PRV
 Source member . . . . . . . . . .   PGM001        Name, *PRV, *SELECT
 Source type . . . . . . . . . . .   CBL           Name, *SAME, BAS, BASP, C...
 Text 'description' . . . . . . .    'TEST PROGRAM'

                                                                        Bottom
 F3=Exit   F4=Prompt   F5=Refresh   F12=Cancel   F13=How to use this display
 F24=More keys
    09-51     SA         MW         KS         IM         II S1        KB
```

Figure 2.3. *(cont.)*.

  - xxx is a three-position system identifier code (determined by site).
  - nnn is any three numeric digits.
  - ss is an optional suffix to distinguish between jobstreams that are identical except for input or run frequency. AS/400-suffixed jobs should use CL programs to submit parameters as needed.
3. Test batch jobs should adhere to the same restrictions as production jobs, although command names can be somewhat more flexible during the testing phase.
4. Program names can be broken down into batch, online, and display files (instead of maps) as follows:
   - Batch—should be in the format 'xxxnnn' where:
     - xxx is a three-position system identifier code.
     - nnn is any three numeric digits.
   - Online—should be in the format 'xxtttt' where:
     - xx is a two-position system identifier code (determined by site).
     - tttt is a meaningful alphabetic descriptor to the function of the program. This will also help to differentiate between batch and online programs on the AS/400, similar to distinctions between mainframe batch and online programs on the mainframe.
   - Display files—should be in the format 'xxttttd' where:
     - xx is a two-position system code.
     - tttt is a meaningful alphabetic descriptor, as used above in the online program. It should reference the principal program processing data using this display file.
     - d is a constant indicating that this is a display file.
5. Dataset names for AS/400 database files should be structured as 'xfffff(nn)' where:
   - x signifies:
     - R for reference file—a physical file containing no data, used as a data dictionary for an application.
     - P for physical file—an actual file containing data.
     - L for logical file—an alternate view of a physical file.
     - J for join logical file—an alternate view joining two physical files for reporting (not updating) data.

- fffff signifies a meaningful name for the database; i.e., if it is an address file, fffff is 'addrs'.
- nn is an optional suffix if there is more than one file of the same type; i.e., 'addrs01', 'addrs02', etc.

Additional information on naming conventions can be found in the following books:

- IBM Manual SC21-9775, *AS/400 Programming: Control Language Reference,* Volume 1. Chapter 1 lists the major IBM-supplied system libraries.
- IBM Manual SC09-1172, *AS/400 Application Development Tools: Source Entry Utility User's Guide and Reference.* SEU is the editor that allows updates to source file members. It has a number of similarities to ISPF.
- IBM Manual SC09-1173, *AS/400 Application Development Tools: Programming Development Manager User's Guide and Reference.* This illustrates use of PDM, the main development tool on the AS/400. PDM interfaces to SEU and a number of other tools on the AS/400.

2.4 AS/400 CONTROL LANGUAGE

Commands on the AS/400 function in much the same way JCL does on the mainframe, but with one important difference. Control Language also functions as a programming language on the AS/400, so that CL programs can execute as programs themselves while also calling programs written in high-level languages such as COBOL and RPG.

A CL command can be as simple as WRKOUTQ (Work with Output Queue), which already exists on the system. CL can also be created to execute multiple existing commands/programs, or even to create new commands (commands must be created to run batch jobs of multiple steps). Moreover, it can be sophisticated enough to prompt an operator for parameters, check for messages from programs (like checking for return codes), and in effect function somewhat like a cross between a CLIST and JCL on the mainframe.

Command names can be no more than 10 positions in length. CL programs must reside in source file QCLSRC in a library and must be compiled in order to create objects for execution. Entry of source code can be simplified through use of the prompt (F4) key on each line. This helps to eliminate syntax errors.

Figure 2.4 shows a simple CL program, CLI001, that does the following:

- Begins the program with PGM and ends it with ENDPGM. This is standard in any CL program.
- Declares some variables to maintain data. This must be done in order to maintain data from step to step.
- Executes the command RTVJOBA (Retrieve Job Attributes). This command retrieves certain attributes about the job being executed and puts them into the declared variables. In this example the jobname is put into variable &job and the userid is put into variable &use.
- Executes the SNDMSG command to display the message, in quotes, to the message queue attached to the userid.

This program must be compiled to become an object that can be executed interactively or in batch (via the SBMJOB command) on the AS/400.

CL programs can become considerably more complex, containing DO loops, GOTOs, and statement labels.

Additional information on CL can be found in the following books:

- *AS/400 System Concepts.*
- IBM Manual SC21-8077, *Control Language Programmer's Guide.*
- IBM Manuals SC21-9775 through SC21-9779, *AS/400 Programming: Control Language Reference,* Volumes 1–5. These manuals provide detailed information on each command in the AS/400.

```
 Columns . . . :    1  71          Browse                   DPXXXLIB/QCLSRC
 SEU==>                                                             CLI001
 FMT **  ...+... 1 ...+... 2 ...+... 3 ...+... 4 ...+... 5 ...+... 6 ...+...
        *************** Beginning of data *********************************
0001.00             PGM
0002.00             DCL        VAR(&JOB) TYPE(*CHAR) LEN(10)
0002.01             DCL        VAR(&USE) TYPE(*CHAR) LEN(10)
0003.00             RTVJOBA    JOB(&JOB) USER(&USE)
0004.00             SNDMSG     MSG('TEST PROGRAM HAS EXECUTED') TOMSGQ(&USE)
0005.00             ENDPGM
        ****************** End of data ************************************









 F3=Exit   F5=Refresh   F9=Retrieve   F10=Cursor   F12=Cancel
 F16=Repeat find   F24=More keys
                                         (C) COPYRIGHT IBM CORP. 1981, 1991.
     02-09     SA        MW        KS        IM        II S1        KB
```

Figure 2.4. CL001.

2.5 MOVES FROM TEST TO PRODUCTION

Each AS/400 can have a test library, named, for example, TSTLIB. It is used as a staging library for objects and source code of programs, commands, display files, and anything else, with the exception of databases. Each AS/400 also has a production library, named, for example, PRDLIB. Production libraries contain all source and object programs, commands, display files, etc., with the exception of databases.

Database libraries are segregated by application between production and test libraries. Library names are structured as 'xxxfnn' where:

- xxx is the three-position system code.
- f is either 'P' for production or 'T' for test.
- nn is a numeric descriptor for the AS/400 on which the library resides.

In this way file names can be the same in both test and production environments.

User libraries (format XXXXXLIB) should be created for programmers and can contain programs, queries, etc., including small data files. This will ensure a completely closed testing environment when needed.

As a site evolves in work on the AS/400, a more concrete move procedure should be set up to include file and program security. Only a limited number of individuals should have update authority for production libraries.

3

Query Procedures

The objective of this chapter is to introduce the programmer who will be working on the system to AS/400 Query, a mechanism for generating ad hoc reports in a short time.

Query doesn't require much programming expertise. Provided here are step-by-step instructions, along with examples, on how to create a simple database and create a report on that database using Query.

3.1 AS/400 QUERY

To print a simple report against a database file without the use of a high-level programming language, AS/400 has a query language that allows simple *inquiry* reports to be generated in a short time. Listed below are the steps to generate a database file as well as a query against it. These steps are illustrated, as necessary, by the screens depicted in Figures 3.1 through 3.6. At the end of this chapter are copies of both the actual report and the query definition.

1. A database file must be set up. If one already exists, skip to step 10. If not, continue.
2. Enter PDM via the Programming Menu. Select the Work

with Members option (3). If the library is in the user's library list, it need not be specified. However, the file must be specified—QDDSSRC—since DDS must be set up in order for a database file to be set up.

3. Select the option to create a member in file (F6). Name the member TESTFILE.
4. Enter the DDS source code (Figure 3.1); as the lines are being entered, prompt on them using F4 to get formatted lines for DDS. The database record contains four fields: ID number for a length of two alphanumerics; name for a length of 15 alphanumerics; pay rate for a length of five numerics with two decimal places; and hours for a length of four numerics with two decimal places.
5. After the entry is completed, save it. On the Work with Members screen, hit F23 to display 'more options' and enter Option 14 to compile.
6. Check messages to determine if the compilation was successful. If not, correct any errors and recompile.
7. To enter data in database file, return to the PDM Main Menu, Work with Object option (2).
8. Select object TESTFILE in your library, Hit F23 to display 'more options', and use Option 18 to CHANGE using DFU (data file utility). A temporary program is created to allow data entry into the database (Figure 3.2). Fields are all shown as defined, with DDS to identify individual fields.
9. Add, change, and delete functions are all available with DFU. Follow the function keys at the bottom of the screen. After data is successfully entered, save the changed file by using F3.
10. Begin Query by entering STRQRY on the command line.
11. Select the Work with Queries option (1) on the Query Utilities screen (Figure 3.3).
12. Select the Create option (1) on the Work with Queries screen. The query name need not be specified at this time.
13. Select parameters to create the query, going down the list on the Query screen (Figure 3.4). A '>' will indicate that a parameter has been selected as part of the query.
14. The system leads the user through the parameter selection,

```
 Columns . . . :    1  71          Edit                          DPXXXLIB/QDDSSRC
 SEU==>                                                                  TESTFILE
 FMT PF .....A..........T.Name++++++RLen++TDpB......Functions++++++++++++++++++
        *************** Beginning of data *************************************
0001.00                 R TESTREC
0002.00                   IDNO          2A
0003.00                   NAME         15A
0004.00                   RATE          5   2
0005.00                   HOURS         4   2
       ****************** End of data *****************************************



Prompt type . . .   PF       Sequence number . . . 0003.00

Name                                       Data      Decimal
Type       Name        Ref       Length    Type      Positions    Use
        NAME                        15       A
Functions



F3=Exit   F4=Prompt   F5=Refresh           F11=Previous record
F12=Cancel            F23=Select prompt    F24=More keys
    18-03      SA       MW         KS        IM         II S2        KB
```

Figure 3.1. Source code entry.

```
WORK WITH DATA IN A FILE                              Mode . . . . :    CHANGE
Format . . . . :    TESTREC                           File . . . . :    TESTFILE

*RECNBR:        5
 IDNO:    40
 NAME:    RED
 DATE:     1000
 HOURS:   4000










F3=Exit                  F5=Refresh                 F6=Select format
F9=Insert                F10=Entry                  F11=Change

    05-11     SA         MW        KS        IM        II S2      KB
```

Figure 3.2. Temporary program for data entry in database.

```
QUERY                              Query Utilities
                                                                    System:   S
Select one of the following:

  AS/400 Query
     1. Work with queries
     2. Run an existing query
     3. Delete a query

  Query management
    10. Work with query management forms
    11. Work with query management queries
    12. Start a query
    13. Analyze an AS/400 Query definition
    14. Start a cuery allowing AS/400 Query definitions

                                                                     More...
Selection or command
===> 1

F3=Exit   F4=Prompt   F9=Retrieve   F12=Cancel   F13=User support
F16=System main menu

    20-08     SA        MW        KS        IM        II S2       KB
```

Figure 3.3. Query Utilities screen.

```
                              Define the Query
Query . . . . . . :    TESTQRY          Option . . . . . :    CHANGE
  Library . . . . :     DPXXXLIB

Type options, press Enter. Press F21 to select all.
1=Select

Opt       Query Definition Option
     >    Specify file selections
     >    Define result fields
     >    Select and sequence fields
          Select records
          Select sort fields
          Select collating sequence
     >    Specify report column formatting
     >    Select report summary functions
     >    Define report breaks
     >    Select output type and output form
     >    Specify processing options


F3=Exit                F5=Report              F12=Cancel
F13=Layout             F18=Files              F21=Select all

     10-03      SA        MW        KS        IM        II S2      KB
```

Figure 3.4. Define the Query screen.

and as selections are being made the user may press F5 to view the report (in whatever state it is in) on the terminal. This allows a good deal of 'tweaking' of the report while it is being developed. Note also that parameter selection allows for a great deal of prompting (via the F4 key) for possible parameter values. In addition, F1 is always available for System Help.

Figure 3.5 displays the screens used to select the parameters for this particular query as well as the report display. As you view the screens, note in particular the Select Output Type and Output Form screen. A database file may be created (Output Type = 3) instead of a report, allowing the user to manipulate the file after its creation.

15. When F3 is pressed, several things can occur. Primarily, the query can be saved and run (Figure 3.6). If it is to be saved, it is at this point that it *must* be named. The name is TESTQRY in this example. Note that if the query is run interactively, it will lock up the user's terminal. This is not a problem with a small file, but a query against a larger file should be run in batch.

16. The report was sent to printer but spooled first so that it could be viewed on-screen. To view it, enter WRKSPLF on the command line, then select the job you wish to view by entering Option 5 (Display). The file name will be QPQUPRFIL and the user will be your logon ID.

17. To print the same report on the printer, enter Option 6 (Release). Note that since the query was saved, its report can be reproduced at any time using Option 2 (Run an Existing Query) from the Query screen.

(a)

```
                        Specify File Selections

Type choices, press Enter. Press F9 to specify an additional
  file selection.

  File . . . . . . . . .   TESTFILE     Name, F4 for list
    Library  . . . . . .     DPXXXLIB   Name, *LIBL, F4 for list
  Member . . . . . . . .   *FIRST       Name, *FIRST, F4 for list
  Format . . . . . . . .   TESTREC      Name, *FIRST, F4 for list









F3=Exit          F4=Prompt          F5=Report           F9=Add file
F12=Cancel       F13=Layout         F24=More keys

    06-29     SA        MW        KS        IM        II S2       KB
```

Figure 3.5. Parameter selection screens.

(b)

```
                         Define Result Fields

 Type definitions using field names or constants and operators, press Enter.
   Operators: +, -, *, /, SUBSTR, ||

 Field        Expressicn                          Column Heading      Len   Dec
 EARNINGS     rate * hcurs                        EARNINGS              7     2








                                                                          Bottom


 Field
 IDNO
 NAME
 DATE
 HOURS
                                                                          Bottom
 F3=Exit            F5=Report          F9=Insert          F11=Display text
 F12=Cancel         F13=Layout         F20=Reorganize     F24=More keys

     07-02     SA        MW        KS        IM        II S2      KB
```

Figure 3.5. *(cont.)*

(c)

```
                          Select and Sequence Fields

 Type sequence number (0-9999) for the names of up to 500 fields to
 appear in the report, press Enter.

 Seq    Field
   10   IDNO
   20   NAME
   30   RATE
   40   HOURS
   50   EARNINGS









                                                                      Bottom
 F3=Exit          F5=Report          F11=Display text       F12=Cancel
 F13=Layout       F20=Renumber       F21=Select all         F24=More keys

     07-02     SA       MW       KS       IM       II S2       KB
```

Figure 3.5. *(cont.)*

(d)

```
                        Specify Report Column Formatting

Type information, press Enter.
  Column headings: *NONE, aligned text lines

                 Column
Field            Spacing     Column Heading             Len    Dec    Edit
IDNO                0        ID NUMBER                    2


NAME                2        NAME                        15


RATE                2        RATE                         5      2



                                                                    More...
F3=Exit          F5=Report         F10=Process/previous        F12=Cancel
F13=Layout       F16=Edit          F18=Files                   F23=Long comment

    08-22     SA       MW       KS       IM       II S2       KB
```

Figure 3.5. *(cont.)*

(e)

```
                    Specify Report Column Formatting

Type information, press Enter.
  Column headings: *NONE, aligned text lines

                 Column
Field            Spacing     Column Heading              Len    Dec    Edit
HOURS               2        HOURS                         4      2


EARNINGS            2        EARNINGS                      7      2







                                                                      Bottom
F3=Exit          F5=Report        F10=Process/previous      F12=Cancel
F13=Layout       F16=Edit         F18=Files                 F23=Long comment

    08-22      SA        MW        KS        IM        II S2       KB
```

Figure 3.5. *(cont.)*

(f)

```
                    Select Report Summary Functions

Type options, press Enter.
  1=Total     2=Average     3=Minimum     4=Maximum     5=Count

---Options---    Field
                 IDNO
                 NAME
                 RATE
                 HOURS
                 EARNINGS

                                                                   Bottom
F3=Exit          F5=Report          F10=Process/previous    F11=Display text
F12=Cancel       F13=Layout         F18=Files               F23=Long comment

    07-02      SA        MW        KS        IM        II S2        KB
```

Figure 3.5. *(cont.)*

(g)

```
                        Define Report Breaks

Type break level (1-6) for up to 9 field names, press Enter.
  (Use as many fields as needed for each break level.)

Break     Sort
Level     Prty     Field
                   IDNO
                   NAME
                   RATE
                   HOURS
                   EARNINGS

                                                                  Bottom
F3=Exit          F5=Report          F10=Process/previous     F11=Display text
F12=Cancel       F13=Layout         F18=Files                F23=Long comment

   08-04      SA        MW        KS        IM        II S2       KB
```

Figure 3.5. *(cont.)*

(h)

```
                         Format Report Break

Break level . . . . . . . . :   0

Type choices, press Enter.
  (Type &field in text to have break values inserted.)




Suppress summaries . . . .      N            Y=Yes, N=No
Break text . . . . . . . .      GRAND TOTAL OF EARNINGS








F3=Exit          F5=Report          F10=Process/previous          F12=Cancel
F13=Layout       F18=Files          F23=Long comment

    10-33     SA       MW       KS       IM       II S2       KB
```

Figure 3.5. *(cont.)*

(i)

```
                    Select Output Type and Output Form

Type choices, press Enter.
  Output type . . . . . . . . . . .   2    1=Display
                                           2=Printer
                                           3=Database file

Form of output . . . . . . . . . . .   1    1=Detail
                                           2=Summary only

Line wrapping . . . . . . . . . . .   N    Y=Yes, N=No
    Wrapping width . . . . . . . .         Blank, 1-198
    Record on one page . . . . . .    N    Y=Yes, N=No




F3=Exit           F5=Report           F10=Process/previous
F12=Cancel        F13=Layout          F18=Files

    05-41     SA        MW        KS        IM        II S2       KB
```

Figure 3.5. *(cont.)*

(j)

```
                        Define Printer Output

Type choices, press Enter.

Printer  . . . . . . . . .   PRT01      *PRINT, name

Form size:
  Length . . . . . . . . .              Blank, 1-255
  Width  . . . . . . . . .   132        Blank, 1-198

Start line . . . . . . . .   3          Blank, 1-255

End line . . . . . . . . .   58         Blank, 1-255

Line spacing . . . . . . .   1          1, 2, 3

Print definition . . . . .   Y          Y=Yes, N=No



F3=Exit          F5=Report          F10=Process/previous
F12=Cancel       F13=Layout         F18=Files

    05-33     SA        MW        KS        IM        II S2        KB
```

Figure 3.5. *(cont.)*

(k)

```
                         Define Spooled Output

Type choices, press Enter.

Spool the output . . .   Y          Blank, Y=Yes, N=No

Form type  . . . . . .              Blank, name, *STD

Copies . . . . . . . .   1          Blank, 1-255

Hold . . . . . . . . .   Y          Blank, Y=Yes, N=No




F3=Exit          F5=Report          F10=Process/previous
F12=Cancel       F13=Layout         F18=Files

   05-29     SA       MW       KS       IM       II S2       KB
```

Figure 3.5. *(cont.)*

(l)

```
                              Specify Cover Page

Type choices, press Enter.
  Print cover page . . . . .   Y             Y=Yes, N=No

  Cover page title
TEST QUERY REPORT

F3=Exit           F5=Report          F10=Process/previous
F12=Cancel        F13=Layout         F18=Files

    05-33      SA        MW        KS        IM        II S2        KB
```

Figure 3.5. *(cont.)*

(m)

```
                   Specify Page Headings and Footings

Type choices, press Enter.
  (Type &date, &time, and &page, or choose standard page headings.)

  Print standard
    page headings . . . . .    N              Y=Yes, N=No

  Page heading
EARNINGS REPORT AS OF &date



  Page footing
PAGE &page






F3=Exit          F5=Report          F10=Process/previous
F12=Cancel       F13=Layout         F18=Files

    07-33    SA        MW        KS        IM        II S2        KB
```

Figure 3.5. *(cont.)*

(n)

```
                         Specify Processing Options

  Type choices, press Enter.

  Use rounding . . . . . . . . . . .     Y    Blank, Y=Yes, N=No

  Ignore decimal
    data errors . . . . . . . . . .      Y    Blank, Y=Yes, N=No











  F3=Exit            F5=Report           F10=Process/previous
  F12=Cancel         F13=Layout          F18=Files

      05-41     SA        MW        KS        IM        II S2        KB
```

Figure 3.5. *(cont.)*

(o)

```
                              Display Report
                                          Report width . . . . . :      59
 Position to line  . . . . .          Shift to column . . . . . . .
 Line   ....+....1....+....2....+....3....+....4....+....5....+....
        ID NUMBER    NAME                   RATE    HOURS       EARNINGS
000001     00        SMITH                 10.00    40.00         400.00
000002     10        JONES                 10.00    40.00         400.00
000003     20        BLACK                 10.00    40.00         400.00
000004     30        WHITE                 10.00    40.00         400.00
000005     40        RED                   10.00    40.00         400.00
000006     50        BLUE                  15.50    40.00         620.00
000007     60        GREEN                 15.50    40.00         620.00
000008     70        YELLOW                15.50    40.00         620.00
000009     80        ADAM                  15.50    40.00         620.00
000010     90        GOLD                  15.50    40.00         620.00
000011
000012                                          GRAND TOTAL OF EARNINGS
000013                                              TOTAL       5,100.00
***** ********    End of report    ********

                                                                      Bottom
F3=Exit     F12=Cancel     F19=Left     F20=Right     F21=Split

    03-32      SA        MW        KS        IM        II S2       KB
```

Figure 3.5. *(cont.)*

```
                         Exit this Query

Type choices, press Enter.

  Save definition . . .   Y              Y=Yes, N=No

  Run option . . . . . .  1              1=Run interactively
                                         2=Run in batch
                                         3=Do not run

For a saved definition:
  Query . . . . . . . .   TESTQRY        Name
    Library . . . . . .     DPXXXLIB     Name, F4 for list

  Text . . . . . . . . .  QUERY ON TEST FILE

  Authority . . . . . .   *CHANGE        *CHANGE, *ALL, *EXCLUDE, *USE
                                         authorization list name


F4=Prompt      F5=Report      F12=Cancel      F13=Layout
F14=Define the query

    12-29     SA        MW        KS        IM        II S2      KB
```

Figure 3.6. Saving and running the query.

Additional information on Query can be found in the following books:

- IBM Manual SC21-9614, *AS/400 Query: User's Guide.*
- IBM Manual SC09-1169, *AS/400 Application Development Tools: Data File Utility User's Guide and Reference.* DFU allows maintenance on database files.
- IBM Manual SC21-9620, *AS/400 Programming: Data Description Specifications Reference.* This book explains data description specifications for physical and logical database files, display files (screens), and printer files (reports). See also Chapter 2, which illustrates the basic setup of physical database files on the AS/400.

Query Report and Definition

```
                    TEST QUERY REPORT
   QUERY NAME . . . . . TESTQRY
   LIBRARY NAME . . . . DPDMLLIB

   FILE          LIBRARY       MEMBER        FORMAT
   TESTFILE      DPDMLLIB      TESTFILE      TESTREC

   DATE . . . . . . . . 06/14/91
   TIME . . . . . . . . 17:02:59

                   QUERY ON TEST FILE

            EARNINGS REPORT AS OF 06/14/91

ID NUMBER  NAME                RATE    HOURS          EARNINGS

   00      SMITH              10.00    40.00            400.00
   10      JONES              10.00    40.00            400.00
   20      BLACK              10.00    40.00            400.00
   30      WHITE              10.00    40.00            400.00
   40      RED                10.00    40.00            400.00
   50      BLUE               15.50    40.00            620.00
   60      GREEN              15.50    40.00            620.00
   70      YELLOW             15.50    40.00            620.00
   80      ADAM               15.50    40.00            620.00
   90      GOLD               15.50    40.00            620.00

                                    GRAND TOTAL OF EARNINGS
                                    TOTAL         5,100.00

* * *  E N D  O F  R E P O R T  * * *
```

```
5728QU1 R03 M00 900824          IBM AS/400 Query                                         Page    1

  Query . . . . . . . . . . . . . . . . . . . TESTQRY
    Library . . . . . . . . . . . . . . . . . DPDMLLIB
  Query text  . . . . . . . . . . . . . . . . QUERY ON TEST FILE
  Collating sequence  . . . . . . . . . . . . EBCDIC

  Processing options
    Use rounding  . . . . . . . . . . . . . . Yes
    Ignore decimal data errors  . . . . . . . Yes

  Special conditions

    *** All records selected by default ***


Selected files

  ID     File           Library       Member        Record Format

  T01    TESTFILE       DPDMLLIB      TESTFILE      TESTREC

Result fields

  Name        Expression                                  Column Heading          Len  Dec

  EARNINGS    rate * hours                                EARNINGS                  7    2

Ordering of selected fields

  Field           Sort      Ascending/  Break  Field
  Name            Priority  Descending  Level  Text

  IDNO
  NAME
  RATE
  HOURS
  EARNINGS

Report column formatting and summary functions
  Summary functions:  1-Total, 2-Average, 3-Minimum, 4-Maximum, 5-Count
                                                                             ____Overrides____
  Field           Summary    Column                            Dec                Dec  Numeric
  Name            Functions  Spacing  Column Headings     Len  Pos           Len  Pos  Editing

  IDNO                       0        ID NUMBER             2
  NAME                       2        NAME                 15
  RATE                       2        RATE                  5    2
  HOURS                      2        HOURS                 4    2
```

```
5728QU1 R03 M00 900824          IBM AS/400 Query                                  Page    2

Report column formatting and summary functions (continued)
  Summary functions:  1-Total, 2-Average, 3-Minimum, 4-Maximum, 5-Count
                                                                              Overrides
  Field            Summary    Column                              Dec            Dec  Numeric
  Name             Functions  Spacing  Column Headings       Len  Pos       Len  Pos  Editing

  EARNINGS         1          2        EARNINGS                7    2

Report breaks

  Break  New   Suppress   Break
  Level  Page  Summaries  Text

  0      No    No         GRAND TOTAL OF EARNINGS

Selected output attributes

  Output type . . . . . . . . . . . . . . . Printer
  Form of output  . . . . . . . . . . . . . Detail
  Line wrapping . . . . . . . . . . . . . . No


Printer Output

  Printer device  . . . . . . . . . . . . . PRT01
  Report size
    Length  . . . . . . . . . . . . . . . .  66
    Width . . . . . . . . . . . . . . . . . 132
  Report start line . . . . . . . . . . . .   3
  Report end line . . . . . . . . . . . . .  56
  Report line spacing . . . . . . . . . . . Single space
  Print definition  . . . . . . . . . . . . Yes


Printer Spooled Output

  Spool the output  . . . . . . . . . . . . Yes
  Form type . . . . . . . . . . . . . . . . (Defaults to value in print file, QPQUPRFIL)
  Copies  . . . . . . . . . . . . . . . . .   1
  Hold  . . . . . . . . . . . . . . . . . . Yes
```

```
5728QU1 R03 M00 900824          IBM AS/400 Query                                      Page    3

Cover Page

  Print cover page  . . . . . . . . . . . . Yes
    Cover page title
      TEST QUERY REPORT


Page headings and footings

  Print standard page heading . . . . . . No

    Page heading
      EARNINGS REPORT AS OF &date

    Page footing
      PAGE &page

              * * * * *   E N D   O F   Q U E R Y   P R I N T   * * * * *
```

4

COBOL Programming Procedures

The objective of this chapter is to introduce COBOL programming principles on the AS/400 to programmers who will be working on the system. This will be a 'learn by doing' approach. Following this introduction is the summary of a COBOL/400 exercise.

The chapter will be broken down into sections. If applicable, each section will contain systems examples of the material. Included are the following major topics:

- Use of data description specifications (DDS) to set up database files—reference files, physical files, and logical files.
- COBOL/400 batch programming—basic report generation and file updates.
- Use of DDS to set up screen display files.
- COBOL/400 online programming—display and update processing.

This chapter is not meant to teach COBOL from scratch; rather, it is meant as a reference tool for using COBOL on the AS/400. If the programmer has never worked with COBOL or is somewhat rusty on COBOL concepts, it is strongly recommended that there be some sort of review before this chapter is begun. There are many COBOL manuals available to acquaint the programmer with the language, as well as numerous PC-based and in-person classes on the subject.

4.1 AS/400 COBOL EXERCISE SUMMARY

The following outlines the COBOL/400 programming exercise. All source code, DDS, objects, and database files should reside in each programmer's library to minimize problems. Since the creation of files is so closely connected with the testing of programs, the programmer will begin with the creation of a database file.

1. Create an empty physical file as a reference file. The source member will be called PERSRFL and should contain the descriptions for the following fields:
   - Last Name—x(15)
   - First Name—x(10)
   - Middle Initial—x(01)
   - SS Number—9(09)
   - Fund—9(02)
   - Department—9(03)
   - Street Address Line 1—x(20)
   - Street Address Line 2—x(20)
   - City—x(20)
   - State—x(02)
   - Zip—x(05)
   - Weekly Salary—s9(5)v99
2. Once the source is entered, the member should be compiled to create its object. Remember, since this is only a reference file, no data will *ever* reside in this object.
3. Before the first COBOL/400 program is written, a physical file must be created. This member will be called PERSPFL. Use all the fields from the reference file PERSRFL, in the same order. Make the file keyed, by SS Number (unique). Compile the member to create its object. Data file utility (DFU) may be used through PDM to add/change data in the database file, but since DFU does only very rudimentary

edits, be careful. Be sure to look at the object after the entry operation to ensure that the data was entered properly. Another option for this check would be to run a Query against the file.

4. Write a COBOL/400 batch program, PER001, to print a listing of the PERSPFL database file. Merely read the file in key sequence and print a detail line for each record read. Include SS Number, Last Name, First Name, Middle Initial, Fund, Department, and Weekly Salary on each detail line. Display Edit Weekly Salary (z,zz9.99) and display SS Number with dashes. Put a heading on the report such as 'AS/400 Test Report 1' along with current date, time, and page number. Display a final total of the number of database records read.
5. Write another COBOL/400 batch program, PER002, using PER001 as a skeleton. This program will update the PERSPFL database and print a report of the updates. Again, read the file sequentially, but update the Weekly Salary field. The value of the update amount will be determined by entry of a PARM into the COBOL program via a Control Language program. The PARM should be defined as x(4), both to CL and COBOL, but should be moved to a field V9999 in the program. Print the report as in the previous step, with the following changes:
   - Change the report heading to 'AS/400 Update Report'.
   - Edit the PARM to ensure that it is numeric, displaying an error message on the report and terminating the program if it is invalid.
   - Add another field to the detail line, displaying salary both before and after the updates. This will probably necessitate adding a second detail line to the report.
   - Display the PARM amount on the report.
   - Audit-trail the number of updates.
6. Create a physical file containing Fund and Department, as previously defined in PERSRFL, and a new field, Department Description (X(50)). This file should be called PERSTFL. After compiling the DDS, use DFU in PDM to load the database.

7. Create a join logical file, PERSJFL, which joins PERSPFL and PERSTFL on Fund and Department. Retain all fields from both files. The primary file will be PERSPFL, and the key to PERSJFL will be SS Number. This join is being done to bring Department Description into the file for the next inquiry program.
8. Write a simple COBOL/400 online inquiry program, PEDISP, to run against the join file, PERSJFL. Display all fields in PERSJFL, with one database record per screen. Allow for key entry (both partial and full) and paging by SS Number. Display SS Number with dashes. Set up function key 3 as program exit. Use DDS to create the source for the screen, PEDISPD.
9. Create a logical file, PERSLFL, that will contain all fields from PERSRFL. The key to the file will be Last Name, First Name, and Middle Initial. Compile the DDS source to create the logical file. Physical file PERSPFL must exist before the logical path can be created.
10. Write a COBOL/400 online update program, PEDSPL, to run against the logical file, PERSLFL. Display all fields in PERSLFL, allowing for key entry. Allow changes to existing records as well as addition of new records. Function key 3 is program exit, and function key 12 cancels the current update, allowing a new key entry. Use DDS to create the source for the screen, PEDSPLD. The following edit rules must apply:
    - Changes may not be made to names of existing records.
    - All other fields may be updated.
    - The Zip Code, Weekly Salary, Fund, and Department fields must be numeric.
    - Fund and Department fields must be edited against PERSTFL. PERSTFL must have a corresponding entry.
    - The SS Number field must be numeric, and an error message must be displayed if a duplicate SS number is entered.
    - First position(s) of Name fields and City and State fields *may not* be numeric.

4.2 AS/400 DATA DESCRIPTION SPECIFICATIONS—FILES

This section introduces AS/400 data description specifications (DDS) for file creation.

DDS functions as the mechanism whereby files are described to the AS/400. DDS source code members reside in a source physical file called QDDSSRC inside a user's library. The members in QDDSSRC are compiled to created the object, which can then become the actual files upon which operations can be performed. Additionally, once the members are compiled to become objects, the COBOL Copy command can be used to bring the file layouts into COBOL programs. The COBOL exercise uses four different types of files:

1. Reference files—similar to a data dictionary, this file type does not store any physical data but can be used to reference the names and attributes of all the data for a given application. Selected data fields can then be used from the reference file in the creation of physical and logical files in order to maintain consistent naming conventions across files.
2. Physical files—data files that can be keyed or not keyed.
3. Logical files—files which provide alternate views of a physical file, and can be compared to VSAM alternate keys. The main difference is that logical file keys need not be contiguous.
4. Join logical files—a type of logical file in which fields from two (or more) physical files can be combined into a single record format for use in an inquiry (only) program.

DDS is columnar in format; certain data must appear in certain columns in each record. The easiest way to ensure that data is being captured correctly is to prompt on each line (F4) while doing entry. In this way fields are entered quickly and automatically placed in the correct columns. In addition, on all prompted screens F1 can be pressed for either generic Help on the screen or specific Help to a particular field.

In the COBOL exercise summary steps 1 through 3 and steps 6, 7, and 9 relate to the setup of database files. Steps 1 and 2 relate to reference files, 3 and 6 to physical files, 7 to a join logical file, and 9 to a logical file. In the subsections following are write-ups of each of the types of files being created, along with the actual DDS source code corresponding to the file.

Reference Files

Reference files are used to create a type of data dictionary. All attributes and name(s) of data fields for a particular application can be defined in one place and referenced by physical, logical, and join files throughout the application. Here are the important things to remember about reference files:

- The source member being edited in QDDSSRC is called PERSRFL, with a TYPE of PF (physical file). It is *very* important to indicate the correct TYPE for any member being created/edited, since prompting with the F4 key is dependent on the correct TYPE being specified, as well as the correct compiler at compile time. The record name referenced in the first line of DDS is PERSREC. Record names are always referenced by an 'R' in the Name Type field.
- Fields in the reference file generally have Name, Length, Attribute, Alias, and Column Heading fields entered. Note that even though the Name field allows up to ten positions, RPG programs allow a maximum of six positions for data names. For ease of future programs, it is best to allow only six positions for data names. Also, the Alias field allows an additional data name to be entered to identify a field. The alias is typically set up to look like a COBOL data name, but any dashes ('–') must be entered as underscores ('_'). When the number is copied into the COBOL program, the conversion will automatically be made. Additionally, the Column Heading field refers to the way a report generated by AS/400 Query or another utility might be headed if that field were selected to be printed.
- In our example the field LSTNAM is 15 alphanumeric positions with an alias of LAST_NAME and a column heading of 'LAST' 'NAME'. The reason for separating the Column Heading fields is to ensure that in the reports the two fields will

appear on separate lines. Fields such as COLHDG and ALIAS are entered under the Function column. There are numerous functions, both at the record and field levels, that can be coded.

- Numeric fields, such as WKYSAL, are identified as such because they indicate decimal positions (in this case, 2). If the field had no decimal positions, 0 would have to be entered in the Decimal Position field in order to be considered numeric.
- When all fields have been entered and the member has been saved, the DDS must be compiled (Option 14 from the Work with Members Using PDM screen) so its object can be created. Remember to do a WRKOUTQ to check if the compile was successful. Also remember that since this is a reference file, *no* data can reside in it. A physical file must be created before data can be loaded.

The DDS source for the reference file, PERSRFL, is in Listing 4.1.

Physical Files

Physical files are those that physically contain data. Things to remember about them are as follows:

- The source member being edited in QDDSSRC is called PERSPFL, with a TYPE of PF. (An additional physical file, PERSTFL, is also created for the COBOL exercise, and the steps to create it are the same as for PERSPFL.) The record name referenced in the DDS is PERSPREC. Record names are always referenced by an 'R' in the Name Type field.
- The REF function indicates the location of the reference file. In this case it is PERSRFL (defined in the previous step), and it should be in a library in the user's library list (as indicated by *LIBL). Normally, *LIBL will be used rather than an explicitly specified library, so that files can be more generic in nature.
- Unique refers to a unique key structure. If it were not specified, duplicate keys would be allowed.
- Text is merely a comment field for the file's title.

```
5728PW1 R03M00   900824                    SEU SOURCE LISTING

SOURCE FILE . . . . . . . .    DPDMLLIB/QDDSSRC
MEMBER  . . . . . . . . . .    PERSRFL

SEQNBR*...+... 1 ...+... 2 ...+... 3 ...+... 4 ...+... 5 ...+... 6 ...+... 7 ...+... 8 ...+... 9 ...+... 0
  100                R PERSREC
  200                  LSTNAM       15A          ALIAS(LAST_NAME)
  300                                            COLHDG('LAST' 'NAME')
  400                  FSTNAM       10A          ALIAS(FIRST_NAME)
  401                                            COLHDG('FIRST' 'NAME')
  402                  MIDINT        1A          ALIAS(MIDDLE_INIT)
  403                                            COLHDG('MIDDLE' 'INITIAL')
  404                  SSNUM         9           ALIAS(SOCSEC_NUM)
  405                                            COLHDG('SOCIAL' 'SECURITY' 'NUMBER')
  406                  FUND          2           ALIAS(FUND_CODE)
  407                                            COLHDG('FUND')
  408                  DEPT          3           ALIAS(DEPT_CODE)
  409                                            COLHDG('DEPT')
  410                  ADDR1        20A          ALIAS(ADDR_LN1)
  411                                            COLHDG('ADDRESS' 'LINE' '1')
  412                  ADDR2        20A          ALIAS(ADDR_LN2)
  413                                            COLHDG('ADDRESS' 'LINE' '2')
  414                  CITY         20A          ALIAS(ADDR_CITY)
  415                                            COLHDG('CITY')
  416                  STATE         2A          ALIAS(ADDR_ST)
  417                                            COLHDG('STATE')
  418                  ZIP           5A          ALIAS(ADDR_ZIP)
  419                                            COLHDG('ZIP')
  420                  WKYSAL        7  2        ALIAS(WLKY_SAL)
  500                                            COLHDG('WEEKLY' 'SALARY')

                        * * * *  E N D  O F  S O U R C E  * * * *
```

Listing 4.1. DDS source for PERSRFL.

- Since the data fields have been defined in the reference file, data attributes need not be defined, and 'R' must be placed in the REF field in DDS. However, if a field were to be added to the physical file that had not been defined to the reference file, it could be defined here or even referenced from another physical file.
- Key field(s) can be defined by the specification of the proper field(s) *after* all other fields in the file. Keys are noted by a 'K' in the Name Type field, respecifying a field or group of fields that were previously defined in the file.
- When all fields have been entered and the member has been saved, the DDS must be compiled (Option 14 from the Work with Members Using PDM screen) so its object can be created. Remember to do a WRKOUTQ to check if the compile was successful. Data can now be loaded into the file via Option 18 (Change Using DFU) on the Work with Objects Using PDM screen. DFU allows entry into database files and does some rudimentary edits such as ensuring that numerics are in numeric fields, but it does *not* do specific program-type edits.

The DDS source for the physical files PERSPFL and PERSTFL is shown in Listings 4.2 and 4.3, respectively.

Logical Files

Logical files provide alternate views of physical files. Things to remember about them are:

- The source member being edited in QDDSSRC is called PERSLFL, with a TYPE of LF (logical file). The record name referenced in the DDS is PERSPREC. Record names are always referenced by an 'R' in the Name Type field.
- The PFILE function indicates the location of the physical file to which the logical view is connected. In this case it is PERSPFL in the user's library list (as indicated by *LIBL). Normally, *LIBL is used rather than an explicitly named library, so that files can be more generic in nature.
- If all fields in the physical file are to be available to the logical view, the record name must be the same as that in the physical file (in this case PERSPREC) and no data fields need be

```
5728PW1 R03M00  900824                    SEU SOURCE LISTING

SOURCE FILE . . . . . . . .   DPDMLLIB/QDDSSRC
MEMBER  . . . . . . . . . .   PERSPFL

SEQNBR*...+... 1 ...+... 2 ...+... 3 ...+... 4 ...+... 5 ...+... 6 ...+... 7 ...+... 8 ...+... 9 ...+... 0
                                            REF(*LIBL/PERSRFL)
                                            UNIQUE
                R PERSPREC                  TEXT('PERSONNEL FILE')
                  LSTNAM    R
                  FSTNAM    R
                  MIDINT    R
                  SSNUM     R
                  FUND      R
                  DEPT      R
                  ADDR1     R
                  ADDR2     R
                  CITY      R
                  STATE     R
                  ZIP       R
                  WKYSAL    R
                K SSNUM

                     * * * *   E N D   O F   S O U R C E   * * * *
```

Listing 4.2. Source for PERSPFL.

```
5728PW1 R03M00  900824                    SEU SOURCE LISTING

SOURCE FILE . . . . . . .  DPDMLLIB/QDDSSRC
MEMBER  . . . . . . . . .  PERSTFL

SEQNBR*...+... 1 ...+... 2 ...+... 3 ...+... 4 ...+... 5 ...+... 6 ...+... 7 ...+... 8 ...+... 9 ...+... 0
   100                                         REF(*LIBL/PERSRFL)
   200                                         UNIQUE
   300            R PERSTREC                   TEXT('TABLE FILE')
   800              FUND      R
   900              DEPT      R
  1000              DESCR          50A         ALIAS(TAB_DESC)
  1001                                         COLHDG('DEPARTMENT')
  1600            K FUND
  1700            K DEPT

                      * * * *   E N D   O F   S O U R C E   * * * *
```

Listing 4.3. Source for PERSTFL.

specified. If, however, only some of the fields on the physical file are to be included in the logical file, the record name must be unique and fields from the physical file must be explicitly stated.

- Key field(s) can be defined by the specification of the proper field(s) *after* all other fields in the file. Keys are noted by a 'K' in the Name Type field, respecifying a field or group of fields that were previously defined in the file.
- When all fields have been entered and the member has been saved, the DDS must be compiled (Option 14 from the Work with Members Using PDM screen) so its object can be created. Remember to do a WRKOUTQ to check if the compile was successful. Once the object has been created, any data loaded to the physical file will also update the logical file. Additionally, any data loaded to the logical file will update the physical file.

The DDS source for the logical file PERSLFL is in Listing 4.4.

Join Logical Files

Join logical files are a special type of logical file in which fields from two or more physical files can be combined into a single record format for use in inquiry programs. *No* updates can be done to join logical files. Things to remember about them are:

- The source member being edited in QDDSSRC is called PERSJFL, with a TYPE of LF. It is a join logical file of physical files PERSPFL and PERSTFL. They share common fields, Fund and Department, on which the join file will be created.
- There is always a primary file in a join file, and in this case the primary file is PERSPFL, because it is specified first on the PERSJREC JFILE function statement.
- An additional statement, the join function, is entered on the following line with a TYPE of 'J' (for join), also indicating the two files being joined.
- JFLD functions indicate the fields on which the files are to be joined. In this case, it is Fund and Dept on both files; however, the fields could be named differently as long as they implied the same fields.

```
5728PW1 R03M00  900824                  SEU SOURCE LISTING

SOURCE FILE . . . . . . . .   DPDMLLIB/QDDSSRC
MEMBER  . . . . . . . . . .   PERSLFL

SEQNBR*...+... 1 ...+... 2 ...+... 3 ...+... 4 ...+... 5 ...+... 6 ...+... 7 ...+... 8 ...+... 9 ...+... 0
  300                R PERSPREC                      PFILE(*LIBL/PERSPFL)
 1501                K LSTNAM
 1502                K FSTNAM
 1503                K MIDINT

                     * * * *  E N D  O F  S O U R C E  * * * *
```

Listing 4.4. Source for PERSLFL.

- Data fields named in the join file come from the file in which they reside. However, Fund and Dept reside in both files, so the JREF function indicates that they are to be taken from the PERSPFL record.
- The file can be keyed or not. In this case, the join file is keyed by SSNUM. Keys are noted by a 'K' in the Name Type field.
- When all fields have been entered and the member has been saved, the DDS must be compiled (Option 14 from the Work with Members Using PDM screen) so its object can be created. Remember to do a WRKOUTQ to check if the compile was successful. Once the object has been created, any data loaded to the physical and logical files will be reflected in the join logical file the next time it is referenced in a program.

The DDS source for the join logical file PERSJFL is in Listing 4.5.

Additional information on DDS files in COBOL can be found in the following books:

- IBM Manual SC21-9659, *Database Guide.* Chapters 2 through 6 explain the setup of physical and logical files very thoroughly.
- IBM Manual SC09-1169, *AS/400 Application Development Tools: Data File Utility User's Guide and Reference*. DFU allows maintenance of database files.
- IBM Manual SC21-9620, *AS/400 Programming: Data Description Specifications Reference.* This manual provides detailed information on DDS, with Chapters 2 and 3 referring specifically to database files.

4.3 AS/400 COBOL BATCH PROGRAMMING

COBOL/400 in batch mode refers to report and update programs that do *not* use screen layouts for display/maintenance of data. All COBOL/400 source code resides in source physical file QCBLSRC in a user's library. The members in QCBLSRC are compiled to create the objects, which can than become the executable programs. The COBOL/400 exercise assigns two types of batch programs:

```
5728PW1 R03M00  900824                    SEU SOURCE LISTING

SOURCE FILE . . . . . . .   DPDMLLIB/QDDSSRC
MEMBER  . . . . . . . . .   PERSJFL

SEQNBR*...+... 1 ...+... 2 ...+... 3 ...+... 4 ...+... 5 ...+... 6 ...+... 7 ...+... 8 ...+... 9 ...+... 0
   300                R PERSJREC                JFILE(PERSPFL PERSTFL)
   301                                          TEXT('PERS JOIN LOGICAL FILE')
   302                J                         JOIN(PERSPFL PERSTFL)
   303                                          JFLD(FUND FUND)
   304                                          JFLD(DEPT DEPT)
   305                  LSTNAM
   306                  FSTNAM
   307                  MIDINT
   308                  SSNUM
   309                  FUND                    JREF(PERSPFL)
   310                  DEPT                    JREF(PERSPFL)
   311                  DESCR
   312                  ADDR1
   313                  ADDR2
   314                  CITY
   315                  STATE
   316                  ZIP
   317                  WKYSAL
  1501                K SSNUM

                    * * * *  E N D  O F  S O U R C E  * * * *
```

Listing 4.5. Source for PERSJFL.

1. A report print program, which merely takes a database file and moves the fields to a print line. Its specifications are detailed in step 4 of the AS/400 COBOL exercise summary. This program is set up to run interactively, which means that its execution will tie up the user's AS/400 session until it has finished running. If the program runs quickly, this is not a problem, but if it is long-running, it is better to submit the job to a batch queue in order to release the terminal.
2. An update and report program, which takes the same database file and does calculations and updates to a numeric field, printing a report with before and after fields. Its specifications are detailed in step 5 of the AS/400 COBOL exercise summary. This program also accepts a PARM from an AS/400 data area and is executed in a batch queue by a command connected to a Command Language (CL) program.

Report Print Program

Basically, the report print program sequentially processes a database file and prints the contents of each record on a detail line. COBOL/400 and COBOL on the mainframe are very similar in concept in this instance. There are, however, certain points to mention:

- The source member being edited in QCBLSRC is called PER001, with a TYPE of CBL. PER001 is also the Program-ID. Source and object computer are IBM-AS400.
- Fields in the FILE-CONTROL paragraph are similar to those on mainframe. When a database file is used, the ASSIGN is to DATABASE-XXXXXXX, where XXXXXXX is the name of the database being processed. In addition, if the database is keyed, the RECORD KEY clause must indicate that it is an EXTERNALLY-DESCRIBED-KEY. That way, the key information will be extracted from the database description. In addition, when an output report is generated, the ASSIGN is to PRINTER-YYYYYYY, where YYYYYYY is the name of an output queue on the AS/400. It is the value for where the output will go unless the user's job description dictates that output will go elsewhere—to a different queue, for example.
- The FD is typical of COBOL, except when the COPY statement is used to bring in a record description previously de-

scribed via DDS. The format for this copy is COPY DD-ZZZZZZ OF XXXXXXX, where ZZZZZZ is the record name created with DDS and XXXXXXX is the database name previously used in the ASSIGN clause. The COPY statement converts the DDS-formatted code to COBOL-formatted code.

- In the Procedure Division ACCEPT statements are used to obtain system data such as date and time. Note that the former reserved word, CURRENT-DATE, is no longer valid in AS/400 COBOL. The date is formatted YYMMDD and must be reformatted to print in normal MM/DD/YY format. The time is formatted HHMMSSFF and also must be reformatted to print in normal HH:MM format.
- File I/O for a database file is the same as that for processing a VSAM file. File Status field(s) can be set up for database I/O, but were not set up for this simple program. They should be set up for any update processes.
- Printing report lines is the same as in any other COBOL program.
- After the program is keyed in it must be compiled (Option 14 from the Work with Members Using PDM screen). After 14 is entered F4 is pressed to prompt for COBOL/400 compile options. In this way the programmer has the option of controlling the compilation. If, for example, she wishes to change the name of the object created as a result of the compilation, or the library into which it is compiled, those names can be changed here. Also, F10 for additional parameters (both source listing options and generation options) allows the programmer to determine what will appear on the output listing. F1 for Help in these instances assists in explaining the parameters. For example, the Source Listing option, *APOST, allows single quotes (') to replace double quotes ("). If this option were not specified, the compile of this program would contain errors. Another way to specify these options is to insert them in the source code themselves via the PROCESS statement at the front of the source code. It is better, however, to specify them at compile time than to taint source code with compiler options.
- Once the program has compiled, check the output listing in the output queue for errors. If there are any, correct them and recompile the program.
- To execute the program, enter 'CALL PER001' on the com-

mand line. Input will be inhibited for a short time since the program is running interactively. The report should be in the output queue for review.

- Note that the file(s) being processed by any program must be in the library list of the programmer. If, for example, a production program is being tested, and the programmer wishes to use test files located in a different library, the order of the programmer's library list can be altered either by a CHGLIBL command or by an ADDLIBLE command. For the AS/400 COBOL exercise programs to execute, however, programs and data should all reside in the same (the programmer's) library.

The COBOL/400 source for the program PER001 appears in Listing 4.6. It includes the COPY expansions. A sample of the output report appears in Listing 4.7.

Update and Report Program

Basically, the update and report program builds on the report print program, using it as a skeleton and adding additional functionality. It sequentially processes a database file, updates a single field on each record based on an external parameter, and prints the contents of each record (both before and after update) on a detail line. There are certain issues to be aware of with this program:

- The source member being edited in QCBLSRC is called PER002, with a TYPE of CBL.
- The FILE-STATUS for the database file is utilized, both in the WORKING-STORAGE SECTION and the Procedure Division.
- The LINKAGE SECTION is used to retain the parameter being passed to the program from the CL program. Note also that the USING statement is used on the Procedure Division header.
- The DECLARATIVES section at the beginning of the Procedure Division provides a standardized error-handling procedure for file-error handling that is not explicitly stated in the source code. Its use is explained well in the *COBOL/400 Reference*, part of the additional references..
- Note that the database file is opened for I/O in this program.
- The GOBACK statement is used instead of the STOP RUN statement, since the program is called by a CL program and should return to that program at the completion of its execution.

```
5728CB1 R03 M00 900824          AS/400 COBOL Source          DPDMLLIB/PER001

STMT SEQNBR -A 1 B..+....2....+....3....+....4....+....5....+....6....+....7..IDENTFCN  S  COPYNAME

   1  000100 IDENTIFICATION DIVISION.
   2  000200 PROGRAM-ID.  PER001.
   3  000300 AUTHOR. DML.
   4  000400 DATE-WRITTEN. 05/91.
   5  000500 DATE-COMPILED.

   6  000600 ENVIRONMENT DIVISION.
   7  000700 CONFIGURATION SECTION.
   8  000800 SOURCE-COMPUTER. IBM-AS400.
   9  000900 OBJECT-COMPUTER. IBM-AS400.
  10  001000 INPUT-OUTPUT SECTION.
  11  001100 FILE-CONTROL.
  12  001200     SELECT PERS-FILE ASSIGN TO DATABASE-PERSPFL
  13  001300     ORGANIZATION IS INDEXED
  14  001400     ACCESS IS SEQUENTIAL
  15  001500     RECORD KEY IS EXTERNALLY-DESCRIBED-KEY.
  16  001600     SELECT REPT-FILE ASSIGN TO PRINTER-QPRINT.
  17  001700 DATA DIVISION.
  18  001800 FILE SECTION.
  19  001900 FD  PERS-FILE.
  20  002000 01  PERS-RECORD.
  21  002100     COPY DD-PERSPREC OF PERSPFL.
     +000001*    I-O FORMAT:PERSPREC    FROM FILE PERSPFL    OF LIBRARY DPDMLLIB        PERSPREC
     +000002*                           PERSONNEL FILE                                  PERSPREC
     +000003*THE KEY DEFINITIONS FOR RECORD FORMAT  PERSPREC                            PERSPREC
     +000004*  NUMBER                 NAME                RETRIEVAL    TYPE    ALTSEQ   PERSPREC
     +000005*    0001     SOCSEC-NUM                       ASCENDING    AN      NO      PERSPREC
  22 +000006         05   PERSPREC.                                                     PERSPREC
  23 +000007              06 LAST-NAME             PIC X(15).                           PERSPREC
     +000008*                          LAST NAME                                        PERSPREC
  24 +000009              06 FIRST-NAME            PIC X(10).                           PERSPREC
     +000010*                          FIRST NAME                                       PERSPREC
  25 +000011              06 MIDDLE-INIT           PIC X(1).                            PERSPREC
     +000012*                          MIDDLE INITIAL                                   PERSPREC
  26 +000013              06 SOCSEC-NUM            PIC X(9).                            PERSPREC
     +000014*                          SOCIAL SECURITY NUMBER                           PERSPREC
  27 +000015              06 FUND-CODE             PIC X(2).                            PERSPREC
     +000016*                          FUND                                             PERSPREC
  28 +000017              06 DEPT-CODE             PIC X(3).                            PERSPREC
     +000018*                          DEPT                                             PERSPREC
  29 +000019              06 ADDR-LN1              PIC X(20).                           PERSPREC
     +000020*                          ADDRESS LINE 1                                   PERSPREC
  30 +000021              06 ADDR-LN2              PIC X(20).                           PERSPREC
     +000022*                          ADDRESS LINE 2                                   PERSPREC
  31 +000023              06 ADDR-CITY             PIC X(20).                           PERSPREC
     +000024*                          CITY                                             PERSPREC
  32 +000025              06 ADDR-ST               PIC X(2).                            PERSPREC
     +000026*                          STATE                                            PERSPREC
  33 +000027              06 ADDR-ZIP              PIC X(5).                            PERSPREC
     +000028*                          ZIP                                              PERSPREC
  34 +000029              06 WLKY-SAL              PIC S9(5)V9(2)    COMP-3.            PERSPREC
     +000030*                          WEEKLY SALARY                                    PERSPREC
  35  002200 FD  REPT-FILE.
  36  002300 01  REPT-LINE         PIC X(132).
  37  002400 WORKING-STORAGE SECTION.
```

Listing 4.6. Source for program PER001.

```
5728CB1 R03 M00 900824          AS/400 COBOL Source          DPDMLLIB/PER001

STMT SEQNBR -A 1 B..+....2....+....3....+....4....+....5....+....6....+....7..IDENTFCN  S  COPYNAME

  38  002500 01  IND-AREA.
  39  002600     05 PERS-IND        PIC X(01)        VALUE SPACE.
  40  002700        88  END-OF-PERS                  VALUE 'Y'.
  41  002800 01  COUNTERS.
  42  002900     05 REC-COUNT       PIC 9(5)         VALUE 0.
  43  003000     05 LIN-COUNT       PIC 9(5)         VALUE 51.
  44  003100     05 PAG-COUNT       PIC 9(5)         VALUE 0.
  45  003200 01  EDIT-AREA.
  46  003300     05 EDIT-SSN.
  47  003400        10 SSN-123      PIC X(03)        VALUE SPACE.
  48  003500        10 SSN-45       PIC X(02)        VALUE SPACE.
  49  003600        10 SSN-6789     PIC X(04)        VALUE SPACE.
  50  003700     05 DISP-SSN.
  51  003800        10 DISP-123     PIC X(03).
  52  003900        10 DISP-D1      PIC X(01)        VALUE '-'.
  53  004000        10 DISP-45      PIC X(02).
  54  004100        10 DISP-D2      PIC X(01)        VALUE '-'.
  55  004200        10 DISP-6789    PIC X(04).
  56  004300     05 EDIT-TIME.
  57  004400        10 TIME-HH      PIC 9(02)        VALUE ZERO.
  58  004500        10 TIME-MM      PIC 9(02)        VALUE ZERO.
  59  004600        10 TIME-SS      PIC 9(02)        VALUE ZERO.
  60  004700        10 TIME-FF      PIC 9(02)        VALUE ZERO.
  61  004800     05 DISP-TIME.
  62  004900        10 DISP-HH      PIC X(02).
  63  005000        10 DISP-C1      PIC X(01)        VALUE ':'.
  64  005100        10 DISP-MM      PIC X(02).
  65  005200        10 DISP-C2      PIC X(01)        VALUE ':'.
  66  005300        10 DISP-SS      PIC X(02).
  67  005400     05 EDIT-DATE.
  68  005500        10 DATE-YY      PIC 9(02)        VALUE ZERO.
  69  005600        10 DATE-MO      PIC 9(02)        VALUE ZERO.
  70  005700        10 DATE-DD      PIC 9(02)        VALUE ZERO.
  71  005800     05 DISP-DATE.
  72  005900        10 DISP-MO      PIC X(02).
  73  006000        10 DISP-S1      PIC X(01)        VALUE '/'.
  74  006100        10 DISP-DD      PIC X(02).
  75  006200        10 DISP-S2      PIC X(01)        VALUE '/'.
  76  006300        10 DISP-YY      PIC X(02).
  77  006400 01  WS-REPT-HDGS.
  78  006500     05 WS-REPT-HDG-1.
  79  006600        10 FILLER       PIC X(01)        VALUE SPACE.
  80  006700        10 PT-DATE      PIC X(08)        VALUE SPACE.
  81  006800        10 FILLER       PIC X(50)        VALUE SPACE.
  82  006900        10 FILLER       PIC X(20)
  83  007000           VALUE 'AS/400 TEST REPORT 1'.
  84  007100        10 FILLER       PIC X(43)        VALUE SPACE.
  85  007200        10 FILLER       PIC X(5)         VALUE 'PAGE '.
  86  007300        10 PT-PAGE      PIC ZZZZ9.
      007400
  87  007500     05 WS-REPT-HDG-2.
  88  007600        10 FILLER       PIC X(01)        VALUE SPACE.
  89  007700        10 PT-TIME      PIC X(08)        VALUE SPACE.
  90  007800        10 FILLER       PIC X(123)       VALUE SPACE.
      007900
```

Listing 4.6. *(cont.)*

```
5728CB1 R03 M00 900824          AS/400 COBOL Source          DPDMLLIB/PER001

STMT SEQNBR -A 1 B..+....2....+....3....+....4....+....5....+....6....-....7..IDENTFCN  S  COPYNAME

  91  008000     05 WS-COL-HDGS.
  92  008100        10 FILLER       PIC X(01)       VALUE SPACE.
  93  008200        10 FILLER       PIC X(09)       VALUE 'LAST NAME'.
  94  008300        10 FILLER       PIC X(07)       VALUE SPACE.
  95  008400        10 FILLER       PIC X(10)       VALUE 'FIRST NAME'.
  96  008500        10 FILLER       PIC X(01)       VALUE SPACE.
  97  008600        10 FILLER       PIC X(02)       VALUE 'MI'.
  98  008700        10 FILLER       PIC X(01)       VALUE SPACE.
  99  008800        10 FILLER       PIC X(11)       VALUE 'SOC SEC NUM'.
 100  008900        10 FILLER       PIC X(01)       VALUE SPACE.
 101  009000        10 FILLER       PIC X(03)       VALUE 'FND'.
 102  009100        10 FILLER       PIC X(01)       VALUE SPACE.
 103  009200        10 FILLER       PIC X(03)       VALUE 'DPT'.
 104  009300        10 FILLER       PIC X(01)       VALUE SPACE.
 105  009400        10 FILLER       PIC X(14)       VALUE 'ADDRESS LINE 1'.
 106  009500        10 FILLER       PIC X(07)       VALUE SPACE.
 107  009600        10 FILLER       PIC X(14)       VALUE 'ADDRESS LINE 2'.
 108  009700        10 FILLER       PIC X(07)       VALUE SPACE.
 109  009800        10 FILLER       PIC X(04)       VALUE 'CITY'.
 110  009900        10 FILLER       PIC X(17)       VALUE SPACE.
 111  010000        10 FILLER       PIC X(02)       VALUE 'ST'.
 112  010100        10 FILLER       PIC X(01)       VALUE SPACE.
 113  010200        10 FILLER       PIC X(03)       VALUE 'ZIP'.
 114  010300        10 FILLER       PIC X(03)       VALUE SPACE.
 115  010400        10 FILLER       PIC X(08)       VALUE 'WKLY SAL'.
 116  010500        10 FILLER       PIC X(02)       VALUE SPACE.
      010600
 117  010700     05 WS-DET-LINE.
 118  010800        10 FILLER       PIC X(01)       VALUE SPACE.
 119  010900        10 DET-LAST     PIC X(15).
 120  011000        10 FILLER       PIC X(01)       VALUE SPACE.
 121  011100        10 DET-FIRST    PIC X(10).
 122  011200        10 FILLER       PIC X(01)       VALUE SPACE.
 123  011300        10 DET-MI       PIC X(01).
 124  011400        10 FILLER       PIC X(02)       VALUE SPACE.
 125  011500        10 DET-SSN      PIC X(11).
 126  011600        10 FILLER       PIC X(01)       VALUE SPACE.
 127  011700        10 DET-FUND     PIC X(02).
 128  011800        10 FILLER       PIC X(02)       VALUE SPACE.
 129  011900        10 DET-DEPT     PIC X(03).
 130  012000        10 FILLER       PIC X(01)       VALUE SPACE.
 131  012100        10 DET-ADDR1    PIC X(20).
 132  012200        10 FILLER       PIC X(01)       VALUE SPACE.
 133  012300        10 DET-ADDR2    PIC X(20).
 134  012400        10 FILLER       PIC X(01)       VALUE SPACE.
 135  012500        10 DET-CITY     PIC X(20).
 136  012600        10 FILLER       PIC X(01)       VALUE SPACE.
 137  012700        10 DET-ST       PIC X(02).
 138  012800        10 FILLER       PIC X(01)       VALUE SPACE.
 139  012900        10 DET-ZIP      PIC X(05).
 140  013000        10 FILLER       PIC X(01)       VALUE SPACE.
 141  013100        10 DET-SAL      PIC ZZ,ZZ9.99.
 142  013200        10 FILLER       PIC X(01)       VALUE SPACE.
      013300
 143  013400     05 WS-EOJ-LINE.
```

Listing 4.6. *(cont.)*

```
5728CB1 R03 M00 900824            AS/400 COBOL Source              DFDMLLIB/PER001

STMT SEQNBR -A 1 B..+....2....+....3....+....4....+....5....+....6....+....7..IDENTFCN  S  COPYNAME

 144  013500         10 FILLER      PIC X(01)       VALUE SPACE.
 145  013600         10 FILLER      PIC X(45)
 146  013700            VALUE 'TOTAL NUMBER OF DATABASE RECORDS PROCESSED
 147  013800         10 EDJ-COUNT   PIC ZZZZ9.
      013900
 148  014000 PROCEDURE DIVISION.
      014100 MAIN-PROCESSING SECTION.
      014200 MAINLINE-PARA.
 149  014300     OPEN INPUT PERS-FILE.
 150  014400     OPEN OUTPUT REPT-FILE.
 151  014500     ACCEPT EDIT-DATE FROM DATE.
 152  014600     ACCEPT EDIT-TIME FROM TIME.
 153  014700     PERFORM 0600-FORMAT THRU 0600-EXIT.
 154  014800     PERFORM 0100-READ-PRINT THRU 0100-EXIT
      014900         UNTIL END-OF-PERS.
 155  015000     MOVE REC-COUNT TO EDJ-COUNT.
 156  015100     MOVE WS-EDJ-LINE TO REPT-LINE.
 157  015200     WRITE REPT-LINE AFTER ADVANCING 2 LINES.
 158  015300     CLOSE   PERS-FILE
      015400             REPT-FILE.
 159  015500     STOP RUN.
      015600
      015700 0100-READ-PRINT.
 160  015800     PERFORM 0200-READ-PERS THRU 0200-EXIT.
 161  015900     IF END-OF-PERS GO TO 0100-EXIT.
 163  016000     PERFORM 0300-MOVE-DATA THRU 0300-EXIT.
 164  016100     PERFORM 0400-PRINT-REPT THRU 0400-EXIT.
      016200 0100-EXIT.
      016300     EXIT.
      016400
 165  016500 0200-READ-PERS.
 166  016600     READ PERS-FILE AT END
 167  016700         MOVE 'Y' TO PERS-IND
 168  016800         GO TO 0200-EXIT.
 169  016900     ADD 1 TO REC-COUNT.
      017000 0200-EXIT.
      017100     EXIT.
      017200
 170  017300 0300-MOVE-DATA.
 171  017400     MOVE LAST-NAME      TO  DET-LAST.
 172  017500     MOVE FIRST-NAME     TO  DET-FIRST.
 173  017600     MOVE MIDDLE-INIT    TO  DET-MI.
 174  017700     MOVE SOCSEC-NUM     TO  EDIT-SSN.
 175  017800     MOVE SSN-123        TO  DISP-123.
 176  017900     MOVE SSN-45         TO  DISP-45.
 177  018000     MOVE SSN-6789       TO  DISP-6789.
 178  018100     MOVE DISP-SSN       TO  DET-SSN.
 179  018200     MOVE FUND-CODE      TO  DET-FUND.
 180  018300     MOVE DEPT-CODE      TO  DET-DEPT.
 181  018400     MOVE ADDR-LN1       TO  DET-ADDR1
 182  018500     MOVE ADDR-LN2       TO  DET-ADDR2.
 183  018600     MOVE ADDR-CITY      TO  DET-CITY.
 184  018700     MOVE ADDR-ST        TO  DET-ST.
 185  018800     MOVE ADDR-ZIP       TO  DET-ZIP.
 186  018900     MOVE WLKY-SAL       TO  DET-SAL.
```

Listing 4.6. *(cont.)*

```
5728CB1 R03 M00 900824          AS/400 COBOL Source          DPDMLLIB/PER001

STMT SEQNBR -A 1 B..+....2....+....3....+....4....+....5....+....6....+....7..IDENTFCN  S  COPYNAME

       019000
       019100 0300-EXIT.
       019200     EXIT.
       019300
 187   019400 0400-PRINT-REPT.
       019500
 188   019600     IF LIN-COUNT GREATER THAN 50
 189   019700         PERFORM 0500-HEAD-RTN THRU 0500-EXIT.
 190   019800     MOVE WS-DET-LINE     TO  REPT-LINE.
 191   019900     WRITE REPT-LINE AFTER ADVANCING 1 LINE.
 192   020000     ADD 1  TO  LIN-COUNT.
       020100 0400-EXIT.
       020200     EXIT.
       020300
 193   020400 0500-HEAD-RTN.
 194   020500     ADD 1 TO PAG-COUNT.
 195   020600     MOVE PAG-COUNT       TO  PT-PAGE.
 196   020700     MOVE DISP-DATE       TO  PT-DATE.
 197   020800     MOVE DISP-TIME       TO  PT-TIME.
 198   020900     MOVE WS-REPT-HDG-1   TO  REPT-LINE.
 199   021000     WRITE REPT-LINE AFTER ADVANCING PAGE.
 200   021100     MOVE WS-REPT-HDG-2   TO  REPT-LINE.
 201   021200     WRITE REPT-LINE AFTER ADVANCING 1 LINE.
 202   021300     MOVE WS-COL-HDGS     TO  REPT-LINE.
 203   021400     WRITE REPT-LINE AFTER ADVANCING 2 LINES.
 204   021500     MOVE SPACES          TO  REPT-LINE.
 205   021600     WRITE REPT-LINE AFTER ADVANCING 1 LINE.
 206   021700     MOVE ZERO            TO  LIN-COUNT.
       021800
       021900 0500-EXIT.
       022000     EXIT.
       022100
 207   022200 0600-FORMAT.
 208   022300     MOVE DATE-MO         TO  DISP-MO.
 209   022400     MOVE DATE-DD         TO  DISP-DD.
 210   022500     MOVE DATE-YY         TO  DISP-YY.
 211   022600     MOVE DISP-DATE       TO  PT-DATE.
 212   022700     MOVE TIME-HH         TO  DISP-HH.
 213   022800     MOVE TIME-MM         TO  DISP-MM.
 214   022900     MOVE TIME-SS         TO  DISP-SS.
 215   023000     MOVE DISP-TIME       TO  PT-TIME.
       023100
       023200 0600-EXIT.
       023300     EXIT.

                    * * * * *   E N D   O F   S O U R C E   * * * * *
```

Listing 4.6. *(cont.)*

```
                                        AS/400 TEST REPORT 1                                                      PAGE     1

LAST NAME          FIRST NAME MI SOC SEC NUM FND DPT ADDRESS LINE 1       ADDRESS LINE 2           CITY                 ST ZIP   WKLY SAL

Mertz              Fred       A  040-40-4040 02  003 333 Willow                                    Wheaton              IL 60187     297.30
Majkowski          Don           098-76-3456 01  001 123 Cheese Lane                               Green Bay            WI 65655   8,201.66
Ricardo            Lucy       M  111-11-1111 01  001 321 E 68th St.                                New York             NY 10000     205.04
Smith              CCC           123-32-3232 01  001 2323                                          Chicago              IL 60606     900.00
Jones              AA         L  222-22-222t 01  001 123 main st                                   Chicago              il 60606      90.00
Ricardo            Ricky      A  222-22-2222 01  002 321 E. 68th St.     Apt 1                     New York             NY 10000     281.90
Petrie             Rob           222-23-2121 01  001 147 Bonnie Meadow Rd                          New Rochelle         NY 10505   5,126.04
Smith              BBB           232-32-2223 01  001 23323                                         Wheaton              IL 60187      90.00
Mertz              Ethel         333-33-3333 02  001 333 Willow                                    Wheaton              IL 60187      46.10
Petrie             Laura         456-75-5555 03  003 147 Bonnie Meadow Rd                          New Rochelle         NY 10505     717.63
Taylor             Bee           555-55-5555 01  001 333 Main St                                   Mayberry             NC 33333     205.04
Smith              AAA           566-55-5555 01  001 1234                                          Chicago              IL 60606      90.00
Anderson           Neal          567-89-6666 01  001 Halas Hall                                    Lake Forest          IL 60000  10,252.10
Taylor             Andy          666-66-6665 01  002 333 Main St                                   Mayberry             NC 33333     433.00
Fife               Barney        666-66-6666 03  003 Boarding House      555 Spruce St             Mayberry             NC 44444     230.64
Brown              Murphy        678-91-2345 01  001 Newsroom                                      Washington           DC 30303     717.63
Campbell           Otis       A  777-77-7777 04  400 County Jail         Suite 1                   Mayberry             NC 44444      56.35
Pyle               Gomer         888-88-8888 04  400 Marine Boot Camp                              Ft Pendleton         CA 90909     307.55
Stone              Harry         899-88-8888 01  001 123 Bowery                                    New York             NY 10101     900.00
Taylor             Opie          900-00-0000 07  700 233 Elm St                                    Mayberry             NC 44444     303.42
Taylor             C             908-76-9800 01  001 dddd                                          Chicago              IL 60606      90.00
Banks              Ernie         909-09-0909 03  003 Wrigley Field                                 Chicago              IL 60606   1,449.61
Pyle               Goober        999-99-9999 05  500 Filling Station                               Mayberry             NC 44444      76.86

TOTAL NUMBER OF DATABASE RECORDS PROCESSED      23
```

Listing 4.7. PER001 output report.

- A data area is created so that the Parameter field can be passed to the program. It is created externally to the COBOL program by means of the command CRTDTAARA. Any updates to the field use the command CHGDTAARA. Data areas within libraries are often used as what could be considered control cards in the mainframe environment.
- A Command Language (CL) program must be created to extract the data area as well as to call the COBOL program to execute. The variable associated with the data area must be declared, the data area must be retrieved (with the command RTVDTAARA), and the COBOL program must be called. The CL program source must reside in file QCLSRC with a TYPE of CLP (Command Language program) and must be compiled (again, Option 14 from the Work with Members Using PDM screen).
- A command must be created so that the CL program can be executed in the QBATCH subsystem so as not to tie up the workstation while the program is executing. A member in file QCMDSRC must be created with a TYPE of CMD that contains the statement CMD. Then the member must be compiled (Option 14) and F4 must be pressed for parameters to be entered. The PROGRAM TO PROCESS COMMAND parameter must contain the name of the CL program created in the previous step. This is the only required parameter.
- The final step for executing the program is command SBMJOB. Press F4 to prompt on the command, entering the command created in the previous step on the COMMAND TO RUN parameter. Other parameters on this screen may be modified, but default values based on the user's job description will be sufficient.

The COBOL source for the program PER002, including copybooks, is in Listing 4.8. The CL source for program PER002CL and command source for PER002CMD are in Listing 4.9 and Listing 4.10. And two samples of output reports, as follows, are in Listing 4.11 and Listing 4.12:

1. A valid update run.
2. A run with an invalid parameter, abnormally terminating processing.

```
                                AS/400 COBOL Source
STMT SEQNBR -A 1 B..+....2....+....3....+....4....+....5....+....6....+....7..IDENTFCN  S  COPYNAME

   1  000100 IDENTIFICATION DIVISION.
   2  000200 PROGRAM-ID.  PER002.
   3  000300 AUTHOR. DML.
   4  000400 DATE-WRITTEN. 05/91.
   5  000500 DATE-COMPILED.

   6  000600 ENVIRONMENT DIVISION.
   7  000700 CONFIGURATION SECTION.
   8  000800 SOURCE-COMPUTER. IBM-AS400.
   9  000900 OBJECT-COMPUTER. IBM-AS400.
  10  001000 INPUT-OUTPUT SECTION.
  11  001100 FILE-CONTROL.
  12  001200     SELECT PERS-FILE ASSIGN TO DATABASE-PERSPFL
  13  001300         ORGANIZATION IS INDEXED
  14  001400         ACCESS IS DYNAMIC
  15  001500         RECORD KEY IS EXTERNALLY-DESCRIBED-KEY
  16  001600         FILE STATUS IS PERS-FILE-STATUS.
  17  001700     SELECT REPT-FILE ASSIGN TO PRINTER-QPRINT.
  18  001800 DATA DIVISION.
  19  001900 FILE SECTION.
  20  002000 FD  PERS-FILE.
  21  002100 01  PERS-RECORD.
  22  002200     COPY DD-PERSPREC OF PERSPFL.
     +000001*    I-O FORMAT:PERSPREC    FROM FILE PERSPFL    OF LIBRARY DPDMLLIB          PERSPREC
     +000002*                           PERSONNEL FILE                                     PERSPREC
     +000003*THE KEY DEFINITIONS FOR RECORD FORMAT  PERSPREC                               PERSPREC
     +000004*  NUMBER                  NAME          RETRIEVAL      TYPE    ALTSEQ         PERSPREC
     +000005*   0001    SOCSEC-NUM                    ASCENDING      AN       NO           PERSPREC
  23 +000006          05  PERSPREC.                                                        PERSPREC
  24 +000007              06 LAST-NAME               PIC X(15).                            PERSPREC
     +000008*                           LAST NAME                                          PERSPREC
  25 +000009              06 FIRST-NAME              PIC X(10).                            PERSPREC
     +000010*                           FIRST NAME                                         PERSPREC
  26 +000011              06 MIDDLE-INIT             PIC X(1).                             PERSPREC
     +000012*                           MIDDLE INITIAL                                     PERSPREC
  27 +000013              06 SOCSEC-NUM              PIC X(9).                             PERSPREC
     +000014*                           SOCIAL SECURITY NUMBER                             PERSPREC
  28 +000015              06 FUND-CODE               PIC X(2).                             PERSPREC
     +000016*                           FUND                                               PERSPREC
  29 +000017              06 DEPT-CODE               PIC X(3).                             PERSPREC
     +000018*                           DEPT                                               PERSPREC
  30 +000019              06 ADDR-LN1                PIC X(20).                            PERSPREC
     +000020*                           ADDRESS LINE 1                                     PERSPREC
  31 +000021              06 ADDR-LN2                PIC X(20).                            PERSPREC
     +000022*                           ADDRESS LINE 2                                     PERSPREC
  32 +000023              06 ADDR-CITY               PIC X(20).                            PERSPREC
     +000024*                           CITY                                               PERSPREC
  33 +000025              06 ADDR-ST                 PIC X(2).                             PERSPREC
     +000026*                           STATE                                              PERSPREC
  34 +000027              06 ADDR-ZIP                PIC X(5).                             PERSPREC
     +000028*                           ZIP                                                PERSPREC
  35 +000029              06 WLKY-SAL                PIC S9(5)V9(2)    COMP-3.             PERSPREC
     +000030*                           WEEKLY SALARY                                      PERSPREC
  36  002300 FD  REPT-FILE.
  37  002400 01  REPT-LINE          PIC X(132).
```

Listing 4.8. Source for PER002.

```
                                AS/400 COBOL Source

STMT SEQNBR -A 1 B..+....2....+....3....+....4....+....5....+....6....+....7..IDENTFCN  S  COPYNAME

  38  002500 WORKING-STORAGE SECTION.
  39  002600 01  MISC-FLDS.
  40  002700     05 PERS-IND       PIC X(01)       VALUE SPACE.
  41  002800        88 END-OF-PERS                 VALUE 'Y'.
  42  002900     05 INC-RATE       PIC V9999       VALUE ZERO.
  43  003000     05 INP-PARM-NUM   PIC 9999        VALUE ZERO.
  44  003100     05 NEW-RATE       PIC 99V9999     VALUE ZERO.
  45  003200     05 OLD-SAL        PIC S9(05)V99   VALUE ZERO.
  46  003300 01  COUNTERS.
  47  003400     05 REC-COUNT      PIC 9(5)        VALUE 0.
  48  003500     05 UPDT-COUNT     PIC 9(5)        VALUE 0.
  49  003600     05 LIN-COUNT      PIC 9(5)        VALUE 51.
  50  003700     05 PAG-COUNT      PIC 9(5)        VALUE 0.
  51  003800 01  PERS-FILE-STATUS.
  52  003900     05  PERS-FS       PIC X(02)       VALUE '00'.
  53  004000         88  PERS-OK                   VALUE '00'.
  54  004100 01  EDIT-AREA.
  55  004200     05 EDIT-SSN.
  56  004300        10 SSN-123     PIC X(03)       VALUE SPACE.
  57  004400        10 SSN-45      PIC X(02)       VALUE SPACE.
  58  004500        10 SSN-6789    PIC X(04)       VALUE SPACE.
  59  004600     05 DISP-SSN.
  60  004700        10 DISP-123    PIC X(03).
  61  004800        10 DISP-D1     PIC X(01)       VALUE '-'.
  62  004900        10 DISP-45     PIC X(02).
  63  005000        10 DISP-D2     PIC X(01)       VALUE '-'.
  64  005100        10 DISP-6789   PIC X(04).
  65  005200     05 EDIT-TIME.
  66  005300        10 TIME-HH     PIC 9(02)       VALUE ZERO.
  67  005400        10 TIME-MM     PIC 9(02)       VALUE ZERO.
  68  005500        10 TIME-SS     PIC 9(02)       VALUE ZERO.
  69  005600        10 TIME-FF     PIC 9(02)       VALUE ZERO.
  70  005700     05 DISP-TIME.
  71  005800        10 DISP-HH     PIC X(02).
  72  005900        10 DISP-C1     PIC X(01)       VALUE ':'.
  73  006000        10 DISP-MM     PIC X(02).
  74  006100        10 DISP-C2     PIC X(01)       VALUE ':'.
  75  006200        10 DISP-SS     PIC X(02).
  76  006300     05 EDIT-DATE.
  77  006400        10 DATE-YY     PIC 9(02)       VALUE ZERO.
  78  006500        10 DATE-MO     PIC 9(02)       VALUE ZERO.
  79  006600        10 DATE-DD     PIC 9(02)       VALUE ZERO.
  80  006700     05 DISP-DATE.
  81  006800        10 DISP-MO     PIC X(02).
  82  006900        10 DISP-S1     PIC X(01)       VALUE '/'.
  83  007000        10 DISP-DD     PIC X(02).
  84  007100        10 DISP-S2     PIC X(01)       VALUE '/'.
  85  007200        10 DISP-YY     PIC X(02).
  86  007300 01  WS-REPT-HDGS.
  87  007400     05 WS-REPT-HDG-1.
  88  007500        10 FILLER      PIC X(01)       VALUE SPACE.
  89  007600        10 PT-DATE     PIC X(08)       VALUE SPACE.
  90  007700        10 FILLER      PIC X(50)       VALUE SPACE.
  91  007800        10 FILLER      PIC X(20)
  92  007900           VALUE 'AS/400 UPDATE REPORT'.
```

Listing 4.8. *(cont.)*

```
                              AS/400 COBOL Source

STMT SEQNBR -A 1 B..+....2....+....3....+....4....+....5....+....6....+....7..IDENTFCN  S  COPYNAME

  93 008000         10 FILLER      PIC X(43)       VALUE SPACE.
  94 008100         10 FILLER      PIC X(5)        VALUE 'PAGE '.
  95 008200         10 PT-PAGE     PIC ZZZZ9.
     008300
  96 008400      05 WS-REPT-HDG-2.
  97 008500         10 FILLER      PIC X(01)       VALUE SPACE.
  98 008600         10 PT-TIME     PIC X(08)       VALUE SPACE.
  99 008700         10 FILLER      PIC X(123)      VALUE SPACE.
     008800
 100 008900      05 WS-COL-HDGS.
 101 009000         10 FILLER      PIC X(01)       VALUE SPACE.
 102 009100         10 FILLER      PIC X(09)       VALUE 'LAST NAME'.
 103 009200         10 FILLER      PIC X(07)       VALUE SPACE.
 104 009300         10 FILLER      PIC X(10)       VALUE 'FIRST NAME'.
 105 009400         10 FILLER      PIC X(01)       VALUE SPACE.
 106 009500         10 FILLER      PIC X(02)       VALUE 'MI'.
 107 009600         10 FILLER      PIC X(01)       VALUE SPACE.
 108 009700         10 FILLER      PIC X(11)       VALUE 'SOC SEC NUM'.
 109 009800         10 FILLER      PIC X(01)       VALUE SPACE.
 110 009900         10 FILLER      PIC X(03)       VALUE 'FND'.
 111 010000         10 FILLER      PIC X(01)       VALUE SPACE.
 112 010100         10 FILLER      PIC X(03)       VALUE 'DPT'.
 113 010200         10 FILLER      PIC X(01)       VALUE SPACE.
 114 010300         10 FILLER      PIC X(14)       VALUE 'ADDRESS LINE 1'.
 115 010400         10 FILLER      PIC X(07)       VALUE SPACE.
 116 010500         10 FILLER      PIC X(14)       VALUE 'ADDRESS LINE 2'.
 117 010600         10 FILLER      PIC X(07)       VALUE SPACE.
 118 010700         10 FILLER      PIC X(04)       VALUE 'CITY'.
 119 010800         10 FILLER      PIC X(17)       VALUE SPACE.
 120 010900         10 FILLER      PIC X(02)       VALUE 'ST'.
 121 011000         10 FILLER      PIC X(01)       VALUE SPACE.
 122 011100         10 FILLER      PIC X(03)       VALUE 'ZIP'.
 123 011200         10 FILLER      PIC X(13)       VALUE SPACE.
     011300
 124 011400      05 WS-DET-LINE.
 125 011500         10 FILLER      PIC X(01)       VALUE SPACE.
 126 011600         10 DET-LAST    PIC X(15).
 127 011700         10 FILLER      PIC X(01)       VALUE SPACE.
 128 011800         10 DET-FIRST   PIC X(10).
 129 011900         10 FILLER      PIC X(01)       VALUE SPACE.
 130 012000         10 DET-MI      PIC X(01).
 131 012100         10 FILLER      PIC X(02)       VALUE SPACE.
 132 012200         10 DET-SSN     PIC X(11).
 133 012300         10 FILLER      PIC X(01)       VALUE SPACE.
 134 012400         10 DET-FUND    PIC X(02).
 135 012500         10 FILLER      PIC X(02)       VALUE SPACE.
 136 012600         10 DET-DEPT    PIC X(03).
 137 012700         10 FILLER      PIC X(01)       VALUE SPACE.
 138 012800         10 DET-ADDR1   PIC X(20).
 139 012900         10 FILLER      PIC X(01)       VALUE SPACE.
 140 013000         10 DET-ADDR2   PIC X(20).
 141 013100         10 FILLER      PIC X(01)       VALUE SPACE.
 142 013200         10 DET-CITY    PIC X(20).
 143 013300         10 FILLER      PIC X(01)       VALUE SPACE.
 144 013400         10 DET-ST      PIC X(02).
```

Listing 4.8. *(cont.)*

```
                                  AS/400 COBOL Source

STMT SEQNBR -A 1 B..+....2....+....3....+....4....+....5....+....6....+....7..IDENTFCN  S  COPYNAME

 145  013500          10 FILLER       PIC X(01)        VALUE SPACE.
 146  013600          10 DET-ZIP      PIC X(05).
 147  013700          10 FILLER       PIC X(01)        VALUE SPACE.
 148  013800          10 DET-SAL      PIC ZZ,ZZ9.99.
 149  013900          10 FILLER       PIC X(01)        VALUE SPACE.
      014000
 150  014100       05 WS-DET-LINE2.
 151  014200          10 FILLER       PIC X(01)        VALUE SPACE.
 152  014300          10 FILLER       PIC X(15)
 153  014400             VALUE ' OLD SALARY:   '.
 154  014500          10 DET2-OLD-SAL      PIC ZZ,ZZ9.99.
 155  014600          10 FILLER       PIC X(15)
 156  014700             VALUE ' NEW SALARY:   '.
 157  014800          10 DET2-NEW-SAL      PIC ZZ,ZZ9.99.
      014900
 158  015000       05 WS-EOJ-LINE1.
 159  015100          10 FILLER       PIC X(01)        VALUE SPACE.
 160  015200          10 FILLER       PIC X(36)
 161  015300             VALUE 'NUMBER OF DATABASE RECORDS READ
 162  015400          10 EOJ-COUNT  PIC ZZZZ9.
 163  015500          10 FILLER       PIC X(41)
 164  015600             VALUE '    NUMBER OF DATABASE RECORDS UPDATED
 165  015700          10 EOJ-COUNT2 PIC ZZZZ9.
      015800
 166  015900       05 WS-EOJ-LINE2.
 167  016000          10 FILLER       PIC X(01)        VALUE SPACE.
 168  016100          10 FILLER       PIC X(30)
 169  016200             VALUE 'VALUE OF UPDATE PARAMETER
 170  016300          10 EOJ-PARM     PIC .9999.
      016400
 171  016500 01    ERRORFLAG          PIC X(01)        VALUE SPACE.
 172  016600       88 ERROR-OCCURRED                     VALUE '1'.
      016700
 173  016800 01    ERROR-DATA.
 174  016900       05 ERROR-PRINT      PIC X(35).
 175  017000       05 OP-NAME          PIC X(10).
 176  017100       05 FILLER           PIC X(17)
 177  017200          VALUE 'FILE STATUS =   '.
 178  017300       05 STATUS-VALUE     PIC X(02).
      017400
 179  017500 01    ERROR-MSGS.
 180  017600       05 ERROR-FILE       PIC X(35)
 181  017700          VALUE 'ERROR ON PERSPFL OPERATION WAS
 182  017800       05 ERROR-PARM       PIC X(35)
 183  017900          VALUE 'NONNUMERIC PARM VALUE IS
      018000
 184  018100 LINKAGE SECTION.
 185  018200 01    INP-PARM           PIC X(4).
 186  018300 PROCEDURE DIVISION USING INP-PARM.
      018400 DECLARATIVES.
      018500 I-O-ERROR SECTION.
      018600       USE AFTER STANDARD ERROR PROCEDURE ON I-O.
      018700 I-O-ERROR-ROUTINE.
 187  018800       MOVE PERS-FILE-STATUS TO STATUS-VALUE.
 188  018900       SET ERROR-OCCURRED TO TRUE.
```

Listing 4.8. *(cont.)*

```
                               AS/400 COBOL Source

STMT SEQNBR -A 1 B..+....2....+....3....+....4....+....5....+....6....+....7..IDENTFCN  S  COPYNAME

     019000 END DECLARATIVES.
     019100 MAIN-PROCESSING SECTION.
     019200 MAINLINE-PARA.
 189 019300     MOVE 'OPEN   ' TO OP-NAME.
 190 019400     OPEN I-O PERS-FILE.
 191 019500     IF ERROR-OCCURRED
 192 019600         MOVE ERROR-FILE TO ERROR-PRINT
 193 019700         GO TO 9999-ERROR-TERMINATE.
 194 019800     OPEN OUTPUT REPT-FILE.
 195 019900     ACCEPT EDIT-DATE FROM DATE.
 196 020000     ACCEPT EDIT-TIME FROM TIME.
 197 020100     PERFORM 0700-EDIT-PARM THRU 0700-EXIT.
 198 020200     IF ERROR-OCCURRED
 199 020300         GO TO 9999-ERROR-TERMINATE.
 200 020400     MOVE INP-PARM TO INP-PARM-NUM.
 201 020500     MULTIPLY INP-PARM-NUM BY .0001 GIVING INC-RATE.
 202 020600     COMPUTE NEW-RATE = 1 + INC-RATE.
 203 020700     PERFORM 0600-FORMAT THRU 0600-EXIT.
 204 020800     PERFORM 0100-READ-PRINT THRU 0100-EXIT
     020900          UNTIL END-OF-PERS.
 205 021000     MOVE REC-COUNT TO EOJ-COUNT.
 206 021100     MOVE UPDT-COUNT TO EOJ-COUNT2.
 207 021200     MOVE WS-EOJ-LINE1 TO REPT-LINE.
 208 021300     WRITE REPT-LINE AFTER ADVANCING PAGE.
 209 021400     MOVE INC-RATE TO EOJ-PARM.
 210 021500     MOVE WS-EOJ-LINE2 TO REPT-LINE.
 211 021600     WRITE REPT-LINE AFTER ADVANCING 2 LINES.
 212 021700     CLOSE  PERS-FILE
     021800            REPT-FILE.
     021900     GOBACK.
     022000
 213 022100 0100-READ-PRINT.
 214 022200     PERFORM 0200-READ-PERS THRU 0200-EXIT.
 215 022300     IF END-OF-PERS GO TO 0100-EXIT.
 217 022400     PERFORM 0250-UPDATE-PERS THRU 0250-EXIT.
 218 022500     PERFORM 0300-MOVE-DATA THRU 0300-EXIT.
 219 022600     PERFORM 0400-PRINT-REPT THRU 0400-EXIT.
     022700 0100-EXIT.
     022800     EXIT.
     022900
 220 023000 0200-READ-PERS.
 221 023100     MOVE 'READ' TO OP-NAME.
 222 023200     READ PERS-FILE NEXT AT END
 223 023300          MOVE 'Y' TO PERS-IND
 224 023400          GO TO 0200-EXIT.
 225 023500     IF ERROR-OCCURRED
 226 023600          MOVE ERROR-FILE TO ERROR-PRINT
 227 023700          GO TO 9999-ERROR-TERMINATE.
 228 023800     ADD 1 TO REC-COUNT.
     023900 0200-EXIT.
     024000     EXIT.
     024100
 229 024200 0250-UPDATE-PERS.
 230 024300     MOVE 'REWRITE' TO  OP-NAME.
 231 024400     MOVE WLKY-SAL  TO  OLD-SAL.
```

Listing 4.8. *(cont.)*

```
STMT SEQNBR -A 1 B..+....2....+....3....+....4....+....5....+....6....+....7..IDENTFCN  S  COPYNAME

 232  024500     COMPUTE WLKY-SAL =  NEW-RATE * WLKY-SAL.
 233  024600     REWRITE PERS-RECORD
      024700         INVALID KEY
 234  024800             MOVE ERROR-FILE TO ERROR-PRINT
 235  024900             MOVE PERS-FILE-STATUS TO STATUS-VALUE
 236  025000             GO TO 9999-ERROR-TERMINATE.
 237  025100     ADD 1 TO UPDT-COUNT.
      025200 0250-EXIT.
      025300     EXIT.
      025400
 238  025500 0300-MOVE-DATA.
 239  025600     MOVE LAST-NAME      TO  DET-LAST.
 240  025700     MOVE FIRST-NAME     TO  DET-FIRST.
 241  025800     MOVE MIDDLE-INIT    TO  DET-MI.
 242  025900     MOVE SOCSEC-NUM     TO  EDIT-SSN.
 243  026000     MOVE SSN-123        TO  DISP-123.
 244  026100     MOVE SSN-45         TO  DISP-45.
 245  026200     MOVE SSN-6789       TO  DISP-6789.
 246  026300     MOVE DISP-SSN       TO  DET-SSN.
 247  026400     MOVE FUND-CODE      TO  DET-FUND.
 248  026500     MOVE DEPT-CODE      TO  DET-DEPT.
 249  026600     MOVE ADDR-LN1       TO  DET-ADDR1.
 250  026700     MOVE ADDR-LN2       TO  DET-ADDR2.
 251  026800     MOVE ADDR-CITY      TO  DET-CITY.
 252  026900     MOVE ADDR-ST        TO  DET-ST.
 253  027000     MOVE ADDR-ZIP       TO  DET-ZIP.
 254  027100     MOVE OLD-SAL        TO  DET2-OLD-SAL.
 255  027200     MOVE WLKY-SAL       TO  DET2-NEW-SAL.
      027300
      027400 0300-EXIT.
      027500     EXIT.
      027600
 256  027700 0400-PRINT-REPT.
      027800
 257  027900     IF LIN-COUNT GREATER THAN 50
 258  028000         PERFORM 0500-HEAD-RTN THRU 0500-EXIT.
 259  028100     MOVE WS-DET-LINE    TO  REPT-LINE.
 260  028200     WRITE REPT-LINE AFTER ADVANCING 1 LINE.
 261  028300     MOVE WS-DET-LINE2   TO  REPT-LINE.
 262  028400     WRITE REPT-LINE AFTER ADVANCING 1 LINE.
 263  028500     ADD 2  TO  LIN-COUNT.
      028600 0400-EXIT.
      028700     EXIT.
      028800
 264  028900 0500-HEAD-RTN.
 265  029000     ADD 1 TO PAG-COUNT.
 266  029100     MOVE PAG-COUNT       TO  PT-PAGE.
 267  029200     MOVE DISP-DATE       TO  PT-DATE.
 268  029300     MOVE DISP-TIME       TO  PT-TIME.
 269  029400     MOVE WS-REPT-HDG-1   TO  REPT-LINE.
 270  029500     WRITE REPT-LINE AFTER ADVANCING PAGE.
 271  029600     MOVE WS-REPT-HDG-2   TO  REPT-LINE.
 272  029700     WRITE REPT-LINE AFTER ADVANCING 1 LINE.
 273  029800     MOVE WS-COL-HDGS     TO  REPT-LINE.
 274  029900     WRITE REPT-LINE AFTER ADVANCING 2 LINES.
```

Listing 4.8. *(cont.)*

```
                         AS/400 COBOL Source

STMT SEQNBR -A 1 B..+....2....+....3....+....4....+....5....+....6....+....7..IDENTFCN  S  COPYNAME

 275  030000      MOVE SPACES          TO  REPT-LINE.
 276  030100      WRITE REPT-LINE AFTER ADVANCING 1 LINE.
 277  030200      MOVE ZERO            TO  LIN-COUNT.
      030300
      030400 0500-EXIT.
      030500      EXIT.
      030600
 278  030700 0600-FORMAT.
 279  030800      MOVE DATE-MO         TO  DISP-MO.
 280  030900      MOVE DATE-DD         TO  DISP-DD.
 281  031000      MOVE DATE-YY         TO  DISP-YY.
 282  031100      MOVE DISP-DATE       TO  PT-DATE.
 283  031200      MOVE TIME-HH         TO  DISP-HH.
 284  031300      MOVE TIME-MM         TO  DISP-MM.
 285  031400      MOVE TIME-SS         TO  DISP-SS.
 286  031500      MOVE DISP-TIME       TO  PT-TIME.
      031600
      031700 0600-EXIT.
      031800      EXIT.
      031900
 287  032000 0700-EDIT-PARM.
 288  032100      IF INP-PARM NOT NUMERIC
 289  032200          MOVE SPACE TO ERROR-DATA
 290  032300          MOVE ERROR-PARM TO ERROR-PRINT
 291  032400          MOVE INP-PARM TO OP-NAME
 292  032500          SET ERROR-OCCURRED TO TRUE.
      032600
      032700 0700-EXIT.
      032800      EXIT.
      032900
 293  033000 9999-ERROR-TERMINATE.
 294  033100      MOVE 'PER002 TERMINATING ABNORMALLY' TO REPT-LINE.
 295  033200      WRITE REPT-LINE AFTER ADVANCING PAGE.
 296  033300      MOVE ERROR-DATA TO REPT-LINE.
 297  033400      WRITE REPT-LINE AFTER ADVANCING 1 LINE.
 298  033500      CLOSE PERS-FILE
      033600            REPT-FILE.
      033700      GOBACK.

                  * * * * *   E N D   O F   S O U R C E   * * * * *
```

Listing 4.8. *(cont.)*

```
5728PW1 R03M00  900824                    SEU SOURCE LISTING

SOURCE FILE . . . . . . .  DPDMLLIB/QCLSRC
MEMBER  . . . . . . . . .  PER002CL

SEQNBR*...+... 1 ...+... 2 ...+... 3 ...+... 4 ...+... 5 ...+... 6 ...+... 7 ...+... 8 ...+... 9 ...+... 0
  100             PGM
  301             DCL        VAR(&PER) TYPE(*CHAR) LEN(4) VALUE('    ')
  302             RTVDTAARA  DTAARA(PERVAR) RTNVAR(&PER)
  500             CALL       PGM(PER002) PARM(&PER)
  700             ENDPGM

                       * * * *  E N D  O F  S O U R C E  * * * *
```

Listing 4.9. CL source for PER002CL.

```
5728PW1 R03M00  900824                    SEU SOURCE LISTING

SOURCE FILE . . . . . . . .   DPDMLLIB/QCMDSRC
MEMBER  . . . . . . . . . .   PER002CMD

SEQNBR*...+... 1 ...+... 2 ...+... 3 ...+... 4 ...+... 5 ...+... 6 ...+... 7 ...+... 8 ...+... 9 ...+... 0
  100 CMD

                      * * * *  E N D  O F  S O U R C E  * * * *
```

Listing 4.10. Command source for PER002CMD.

```
                                              AS/400 UPDATE REPORT                                                      PAGE    1

LAST NAME       FIRST NAME MI SOC SEC NUM FND DPT ADDRESS LINE 1       ADDRESS LINE 2       CITY                 ST ZIP

Mertz           Fred       A  040-40-4040 02  003 333 Willow                                 Wheaton              IL 60187
 OLD SALARY:    1,142.54 NEW SALARY:    1,143.68
Majkowski       Don           098-76-3456 01  001 123 Cheese Lane                            Green Bay            WI 65655
 OLD SALARY:   31,519.78 NEW SALARY:   31,551.29
Ricardo         Lucy       M  111-11-1111 01  001 321 E 68th St.                             New York             NY 10000
 OLD SALARY:      787.97 NEW SALARY:      788.75
Smith           CCC           123-32-3232 01  001 2323                                       Chicago              IL 60606
 OLD SALARY:    3,458.78 NEW SALARY:    3,462.23
Jones           AA         l  222-22-222t 01  001 123 main st                                Chicago              il 60606
 OLD SALARY:      345.86 NEW SALARY:      346.20
Ricardo         Ricky      A  222-22-2222 01  002 321 E. 68th St.      Apt 1                 New York             NY 10000
 OLD SALARY:    1,083.34 NEW SALARY:    1,084.42
Petrie          Rob           222-23-2121 01  001 147 Bonnie Meadow Rd                       New Rochelle         NY 10505
 OLD SALARY:   19,699.87 NEW SALARY:   19,719.56
Smith           BBB           232-32-2223 01  001 23323                                      Wheaton              IL 60187
 OLD SALARY:      345.86 NEW SALARY:      346.20
Mertz           Ethel         333-33-3333 02  001 333 Willow                                 Wheaton              IL 60187
 OLD SALARY:      177.14 NEW SALARY:      177.31
Petrie          Laura         456-75-5555 03  003 147 Bonnie Meadow Rd                       New Rochelle         NY 10505
 OLD SALARY:    2,757.91 NEW SALARY:    2,760.66
Taylor          Bee           555-55-5555 01  001 333 Main St                                Mayberry             NC 33333
 OLD SALARY:      787.97 NEW SALARY:      788.75
Smith           AAA           566-55-5555 01  001 1234                                       Chicago              IL 60606
 OLD SALARY:      345.86 NEW SALARY:      346.20
Anderson        Neal          567-89-6666 01  001 Halas Hall                                 Lake Forest          IL 60000
 OLD SALARY:   39,399.83 NEW SALARY:   39,439.22
Taylor          Andy          666-66-6665 01  002 333 Main St                                Mayberry             NC 33333
 OLD SALARY:    1,664.05 NEW SALARY:    1,665.71
Fife            Barney        666-66-6666 03  003 Boarding House       555 Spruce St         Mayberry             NC 44444
 OLD SALARY:      886.35 NEW SALARY:      887.23
Brown           Murphy        678-91-2345 01  001 Newsroom                                   Washington           DC 30303
 OLD SALARY:    2,757.91 NEW SALARY:    2,760.66
Campbell        Otis       A  777-77-7777 04  400 County Jail          Suite 1               Mayberry             NC 44444
 OLD SALARY:      216.54 NEW SALARY:      216.75
Pyle            Gomer         888-88-8888 04  400 Marine Boot Camp                           Ft Pendleton         CA 90909
 OLD SALARY:    1,181.93 NEW SALARY:    1,183.11
Stone           Harry         899-88-3888 01  001 123 Bowery                                 New York             NY 10101
 OLD SALARY:    3,458.78 NEW SALARY:    3,462.23
Taylor          Opie          900-00-0000 07  700 233 Elm St                                 Mayberry             NC 44444
 OLD SALARY:    1,166.05 NEW SALARY:    1,167.21
Taylor          C             908-76-9800 01  001 dddd                                       Chicago              IL 60606
 OLD SALARY:      345.86 NEW SALARY:      346.20
Banks           Ernie         909-09-0909 03  003 Wrigley Field                              Chicago              IL 60606
 OLD SALARY:    5,570.98 NEW SALARY:    5,576.55
Pyle            Goober        999-99-9999 05  500 Filling Station                            Mayberry             NC 44444
 OLD SALARY:      295.35 NEW SALARY:      295.64
```

Listing 4.11. Valid update run.

```
NUMBER OF DATABASE RECORDS READ         23   NUMBER OF DATABASE RECORDS UPDATED        23

VALUE OF UPDATE PARAMETER      .0010
```

Listing 4.11. *(cont.)*

```
PER002 TERMINATING ABNORMALLY
NONNUMERIC PARM VALUE IS          NNNN
```

Listing 4.12. Output run with invalid parameter.

Additional COBOL/400 Batch Programming Features

COBOL/400 allows for a great deal of the functionality of COBOL II, including in-line performs, DO loops, and IF-ENDIF structures. These functions are not required for COBOL/400 programming, but can lend some structure to programs. They have not been utilized in the sample programs in this exercise, but they can be very valuable and should be considered for future use.

Periodically, programs do abend. If they do, a break message is generally sent to the individual submitting the job. The program will not continue/stop until a response is entered. The standard responses are:

- C—cancel processing without a dump.
- R—retry the operation.
- D—cancel processing and dump the COBOL identifiers.
- F—cancel processing and dump *all* identifiers.

Any dumps go to queue QPGMDUMP and can be viewed/printed from there.

There is a debugging tool available on the AS/400. It can be started by the command STRDBG and ended by the command ENDDBG. In between, breakpoints can be set, data fields can be interrogated, and so on. The complete list of debug commands can be viewed on the CMDDBG menu. In addition, Chapter 3 of the *COBOL/400 User's Guide* leads the programmer through the debug process.

Additional information on COBOL/400 batch programming can be found in the following books:

- IBM Manual SC09-1158, *COBOL/400 User's Guide*. This book details ways to write, compile, test, debug, and run COBOL/400 programs.
- IBM Manual SC09-1240, *COBOL/400 Reference*. This book details program structure and Procedure Division statements for successfully running AS/400 COBOL programs.
- IBM Manuals SC21-9775 through SC21-9779, *CL Reference* Volumes 1–5. These books provide detailed information about each CL command on the AS/400.

- IBM Manual SC21-8076, *Command Reference Summary*. This book summarizes the commands in the *CL Reference*.

4.4 AS/400 DATA DESCRIPTION SPECIFICATIONS—SCREENS

This section introduces AS/400 DDS for display file (screen) creation. Note that the terms 'display file,' 'transaction file,' and 'screen' are used almost interchangeably.

DDS is the mechanism that describes screens to the AS/400. DDS source code members reside in a source physical file called QDDSSRC inside a user's library. The members in QDDSSRC are compiled to create the objects that are the actual display files upon which operations can be performed. Additionally, once members are compiled to become objects, the COBOL Copy command can be used to bring the screen layouts into COBOL programs. The COBOL exercise creates two screens:

1. An inquiry-only screen, which displays data from a database file.
2. An update screen, which allows adds and updates to a database file.

DDS is columnar in format; certain data must appear in certain columns in each record. The easiest way to ensure that data is being captured correctly is to prompt on each line (F4) while doing entry. In this way fields are entered quickly and automatically placed in the correct columns. In addition, on all prompted screens, F1 can be pressed to give either generic Help on the screen or specific Help to a particular field.

The simplest approach to the coding of DDS for screens is to first review the specifications for the COBOL exercise—step 8 describes the inquiry program, and step 10 describes the update program. Then determine the format of the screen itself, as would be done for a CICS program. Next, review the books listed at the end of this section, particularly Chapter 4 in the *COBOL/400 User's Guide*. It is important to see exactly how the screen layouts interact with the COBOL statements in order to get the total picture.

Inquiry and Update DDS

Since the screen data fields have been previously defined in physical and/or logical files, it makes sense to utilize the REF function at the beginning of the screen. That way, common data names and attributes can be used in DDS and in the COBOL program. There is, however, a way to reference field(s) from databases other than via the REF statement on a field level—the REFFLD statement.

Display files can have multiple record formats, as evidenced by multiple 'R' entries in the Name Type field. It makes sense to have multiple record formats when there is a prompt on the top of the screen, with data based on that prompt displayed on the rest of a screen. This is true in the COBOL online programs.

CA and CF keys are used widely at file and record levels. They are used to activate particular function keys to a program, and they are used to turn on indicators when function keys are pressed. The main difference between the two is that CA keys are command attention keys, which transmit no input data from the device, and CF keys are command function keys, which transmit changed data. *DDS Reference* explains both types very effectively.

Screen fields are coded in a very straightforward manner. If a field has a name, data may be moved to it from a program or it may be keyed into by the operator. If it is referenced from a database file, an 'R' must be coded in the REF field; if not, its Length and Data Type fields must be entered and REF left blank. The Use field determines if the field is input only ('I'), output only (' ', the default), or input/output ('B'). The beginning LINE and POSITION must be entered in the LOCATION fields. If a field is unnamed, a literal may be entered in the FUNCTIONS area—this is used for headings and prompts.

Indicators turned on or off in a COBOL program can be linked to indicators in display files related to data fields for purposes of display, controlling functions such as error conditions and display attributes.

The FUNCTIONS area is used for a number of options, such as display edit codes, literals, error messages, and display attributes, at the file, record, and field levels. They are explained very well in *DDS Reference*. A few of the functions used here are:

- CHGINPDFT—a file-, record- or field-level keyword is used to change input defaults for input (I or B) fields. For example, the input default for alphanumeric fields is uppercase; if CHGINPDFT(LC) is specified at the file level, upper- and lowercase characters are valid entries.
- DSPATR—a field-level keyword for any field on the screen. For example, screen prompts might be highlighted by the specification of DSPART(HI).
- EDTCDE—a field-level keyword to edit numeric output fields. There is a table of edit codes in *DDS Reference*.
- ERRMSG—used in conjunction with indicators, this field-level function controls the display of error messages if the corresponding indicator is turned on. In addition, if the indicator number is specified following the last quotation mark of the error message, the indicator is automatically turned off without the program having to handle it. An example of this is ERRMSG ('INPUT ERROR' 98). If Indicator 98 were turned on, the following would occur when the screen was redisplayed: the message in quotes would appear at the bottom of the screen (the last line of all screens is reserved for error messages), the field(s) in error would be in reverse video, and Indicator 98 would be turned off.
- INDARA—this file-level function implies that the program will not use the indicators automatically provided with the screen's object and will explicitly code them in the high-level language program. In our examples this is done only in the update screen.
- OVERLAY—used on a multi-record format screen, this record-level function indicates that this record is to overlay any others on the display device, without any display already on the screen being deleted.
- PROTECT—this record-level function is used in conjunction with overlay to protect input-capable fields from a *previous* record. If a second screen overlays the first, input is prohibited in fields from the initial screen. This is used in the update screen in our example.

The inquiry source member in QDDSSRC is PEDISPD, while the update source member in QDDSSRC is PEDSPLD, both with TYPEs of DSPF.

The DDS source for the inquiry and update screens appears in Listing 4.13.

Additional information on DDS screens in COBOL can be found in the following books:

- IBM Manual SC21-9620, *Data Description Specifications Reference.* This manual provides detailed information on DDS, with Chapter 4 devoted specifically to display files.
- IBM Manual SC09-1158, *COBOL/400 User's Guide.* Chapter 4, in particular, explains the use of transaction files.
- IBM Manual SC09-1171, *Application Development Tools: Screen Design Aid User's Guide and Reference*. This guide steps the user through this AS/400 utility, which helps in the creation of screens by creating DDS source as the user 'paints' the screen. This can be used *after* the user has gained some familiarity with and understanding of basic DDS.

4.5 AS/400 COBOL ONLINE PROGRAMMING

COBOL/400 in online mode refers to inquiry and update programs that use display stations for display/maintenance of data. All COBOL/400 source code resides in source physical file QCBLSRC inside a user's library. The members in QCBLSRC are compiled to create the objects, which can then become the executable programs. The COBOL/400 exercise assigns two types of online programs:

1. Inquiry program—merely takes a database file and moves the fields to the screen, based on key fields entered by the user. The specifications for the program are detailed in step 8 of the AS/400 COBOL exercise summary. It is set up to run interactively, which means that the program's execution will tie up an AS/400 session until the user ends it.
2. Update program—based on key fields entered by the user; database records can either be added or updated. Its specifi-

```
5728PW1 R03M00   900824                    SEU SOURCE LISTING

SOURCE FILE . . . . . . .   DPDMLLIB/QDDSSRC
MEMBER  . . . . . . . . .   PEDISPD

SEQNBR*...+... 1 ...+... 2 ...+... 3 ...+... 4 ...+... 5 ...+... 6 ...+... 7 ...+... 8 ...+... 9 ...+... 0
           *PERSONNEL  DISPLAY FILE FOR PERSJFL
                                                    REF(PERSJFL)
                     R PERPRM                       TEXT('SSN PROMPT')
                                                    CA03(03 'END OF PROGRAM')
                                                    CA07(07 'PREVIOUS RECORD')
                                                    CA08(08 'NEXT RECORD')
                                                1  5'PERSONNEL INQUIRY'
         A                                      3  5'SS NUMBER'
         A             SSNUM      R          I  3 15
         A  99                                      ERRMSG('FILE AT TOP OR BOTTOM.     +
         A                                          PRESS RESET, THEN ENTER VALID NUMBE+
         A                                          R' 99)
         A  98                                      ERRMSG('FILE ERROR. PRESS RESET, TH+
         A                                          EN ENTER OR F3' 98)
         A                                      5  5'USE F3 TO END PROGRAM. USE ENTER T+
         A                                          O ENTER ANOTHER SS NUMBER'
         A           R PERFLDS                      TEXT('PERSONNEL DISPLAY')
         A                                          CA03(03 'END OF PROGRAM')
                                                    CA07(07 'PREVIOUS RECORD')
                                                    CA08(08 'NEXT RECORD')
         A                                          OVERLAY
         A                                      7  5'SS NUMBER'
         A             SSEDIT         11A       7 20
         A                                      8  5'LAST NAME'
         A             LSTNAM     R             8 20
         A                                      9  5'FIRST NAME'
         A             FSTNAM     R             9 20
         A                                      9 35'MID INIT'
         A             MIDINT     R             9 45
         A                                     10  5'ADDRESS'
         A             ADDR1      R            10 20
         A             ADDR2      R            11 20
         A                                     12  5'CITY'
         A             CITY       R            12 20
         A                                     12 45'STATE'
         A             STATE      R            12 55
         A                                     12 60'ZIP'
         A             ZIP        R            12 65
         A                                     14  5'FUND/DEPT'
         A             FUND       R            14 20
         A                                     14 23'-'
         A             DEPT       R            14 25
         A                                     15  5'DESCRIPTION'
         A             DESCR      R            15 25
         A                                     17  5'WEEKLY SALARY'
         A             WKYSAL     R            17 25EDTCDE(A)
         A                                     19  5'USE F7 TO PAGE BACKWARD, F8 TO PAG+
         A                                          E FORWARD'

                        * * * *   E N D   O F   S O U R C E   * * * *
```

Listing 4.13. Source for the inquiry and update screens.

```
5738PW1 R03M00  900824                SEU SOURCE LISTING

SOURCE FILE . . . . . . .   DPDMLLIB/QDDSSRC
MEMBER  . . . . . . . . .   PEDSPLD

SEQNBR*...+... 1 ...+... 2 ...+... 3 ...+... 4 ...+... 5 ...+... 6 ...+... 7 ...+... 8 ...+... 9 ...+... 0
   100      *PERSONNEL  DISPLAY FILE FOR PERSLFL - UPDATE
   200                                            REF(PERSLFL)
   300                                            INDARA
   500               R PERPRM                     TEXT('NAME PROMPT')
   600                                            CA03(03 'END OF PROGRAM')
   700                                            CA12(12 'CANCEL UPDATE')
   800                                            CHGINPDFT(LC)
   900                                        1  5'PERSONNEL UPDATE'
  1000                                            DSPATR(RI)
  1100      A                                 3  5'ENTER NAME'
  1200      A                                 4  5'LAST'
  1300      A          LSTNAM    R        I  4 15
  1301      A  97                                 ERRMSG('FIELD(S) IN ERROR. PRESS RE+
  1302      A                                     SET, CORRECT DATA' 97)
  1600      A                                 4 32'FIRST'
  1700      A          FSTNAM    R        I  4 38
  1701      A  96                                 ERRMSG('FIELD(S) IN ERROR. PRESS RE+
  1702      A                                     SET, CORRECT DATA' 96)
  2000      A                                 4 50'MIDDLE INITIAL'
  2100      A          MIDINT    R        I  4 65
  2101      A  95                                 ERRMSG('FIELD(S) IN ERROR. PRESS RE+
  2102      A                                     SET, CORRECT DATA' 95)
  2800      A  98                                 ERRMSG('FILE ERROR. PRESS RESET, TH+
  2900      A                                     EN ENTER, F3 OR F12' 98)
  3000      A                                 6  5'USE F3 TO END PROGRAM. USE ENTER T+
  3100      A                                     O UPDATE, F12 TO CANCEL'
  3200      A                                     DSPATR(RI)
  3201               R PERMSG                     TEXT('MESSAGES')
  3202      A                                     CA03(03 'END OF PROGRAM')
  3203                                            CA12(12 'CANCEL UPDATE')
  3204                                            OVERLAY
  3205      A          CONMSG        50A      7  5
  3400      A        R PERFLDS                    TEXT('PERSONNEL UPDATE')
  3500      A                                     CA03(03 'END OF PROGRAM')
  3600                                            CA12(12 'CANCEL UPDATE')
  3601                                            OVERLAY
  3800                                            CHGINPDFT(LC)
  3900      A  87                                 PROTECT
  4000      A                                 9  5'SS NUMBER'
  4100      A          SSNUM     R        B  9 20
  4301      A  94                                 ERRMSG('FIELD(S) IN ERROR. PRESS RE+
  4302      A                                     SET, CORRECT DATA' 94)
  4303      A  98                                 ERRMSG('DUP SS NUM. RECORD NOT ADDE+
  4304      A                                     D. PRESS RESET, CORRECT DATA' 98)
  4400      A                                10  5'ADDRESS'
  4500      A          ADDR1     R        B 10 20
  4600      A          ADDR2     R        B 11 20
  4700      A                                12  5'CITY'
  4800      A          CITY      R        B 12 20
  4801      A  93                                 ERRMSG('FIELD(S) IN ERROR. PRESS RE+
  4802      A                                     SET, CORRECT DATA' 93)
  5100      A                                12 45'STATE'
  5200      A          STATE     R        B 12 55
```

Listing 4.13. *(cont.)*

```
5728PW1 R03M00  900824                          SEU SOURCE LISTING

SOURCE FILE . . . . . . . .   DPDMLLIB/QDDSSRC
MEMBER  . . . . . . . . . .   PEDSPLD

SEQNBR*...+... 1 ...+... 2 ...+... 3 ...+... 4 ...+... 5 ...+... 6 ...+... 7 ...+... 8 ...+... 9 ...+... 0
 5201      A  92                                    ERRMSG('FIELD(S) IN ERROR. PRESS RE+
 5202      A                                        SET, CORRECT DATA' 92)
 5500      A                                  12 60'ZIP'
 5600      A            ZIP        R        B 12 65
 5601      A  91                                    ERRMSG('FIELD(S) IN ERROR. PRESS RE+
 5602      A                                        SET, CORRECT DATA' 91)
 5900      A                                  14  5'FUND/DEPT'
 6000      A            FUND       R        B 14 20
 6001      A  90                                    ERRMSG('FIELD(S) IN ERROR. PRESS RE+
 6002      A                                        SET, CORRECT DATA' 90)
 6300      A                                  14 23'-'
 6400      A            DEPT       R        B 14 25
 6401      A  89                                    ERRMSG('FIELD(S) IN ERROR. PRESS RE+
 6402      A                                        SET, CORRECT DATA' 89)
 6700      A                                  16  5'WEEKLY SALARY'
 6800      A            WKYSAL     R        B 16 25EDTCDE(A)
 7000                                               CMP(GT 0)
 7200      A            MSGLIN        50A     20  5
 7300                                               DSPATR(RI)

                          * * * *  E N D  O F  S O U R C E  * * * *
```

Listing 4.13. *(cont.)*

cations are detailed in step 10 of the AS/400 COBOL exercise summary. It, too, is set up to run interactively.

Inquiry Program

The inquiry program displays database records based on key fields entered on a prompt screen. Many of the characteristics of COBOL/400 in the batch environment are similar to those of COBOL/400 in the online environment, but because of the use of display files (created as described in Section 4.4), there are some unique programming considerations, such as the following:

- The source member being edited in QCBLSRC is called PEDISP, with a TYPE of CBL.
- Fields in the FILE-CONTROL paragraph differ when a display file is used. The ASSIGN is to WORKSTATION-DDDDDDD, where DDDDDDD is the name of the display file, and ORGANIZATION IS TRANSACTION is required. Also, CONTROL-AREA is CCCCCCC, where CCCCCCC is defined as control fields in WORKING-STORAGE that track program execution by loading the control-area fields with each read operation on the transaction file.
- In the FD the COPY statement is used to bring in the display file description previously described with DDS. The format for this copy is COPY DDS-ALL-FORMATS OF FFFFFFF, where FFFFFFF is the display file name created with DDS, that which was previously used in the ASSIGN clause. The COPY statement converts the DDS-formatted code to COBOL-formatted code.
- In the FD the COPY statement for the display file is different from that for database files. The format is COPY DDS-ALL-FORMATS OF FFFFFFF, where FFFFFFF is the display file referenced in the previous step. The COPY statement converts the DDS code to COBOL code with the following distinctions:
  - Each record layout has an input screen and an output screen. The input screen is what is read into the program, and the output screen is what is sent to the display device.
  - Each record layout redefines the other. It is very important to note this so that data is coordinated properly from record layout to record layout.

- Any indicators defined inside the record layout (such as those corresponding to function keys) always appear at the front of the record layout. Indicators are 1-position binary fields, which are turned on (value of binary 1) or off (value of binary 0) on the basis of actions that occur in the program. If indicators are duplicated on different formats on the screen, they must be explicitly referenced in the Procedure Division. For example, if function key 3 (referenced by IN03) is used to exit the program both from SCREEN1 and SCREEN2, it must be referenced as IN03 OF SCREEN1-I or IN03 OF SCREEN2-I, depending on which screen was previously read.
- Any data fields defined in the screen layout that are duplicated within record layouts must also be explicitly referenced in the Procedure Division.
- Note that screen heading literals are not part of the COBOL code. If you wish to look at the headings, reference the DDS code.

• In the Procedure Division the program is coded in a top-down manner. The operator remains in the program (unlike CICS, where the user exits and reenters the program), and program logic must account for this.
• File I/O for a transaction file is the same as that for any other file. Transaction files must be written before they can be read. If a multiple record format file is written, the FORMAT must be specified and fields must be moved to the output record. If a multiple record format file is read, the format need not be specified since it is assumed that it is the same as the one just read.
• After the program is keyed in, it must be compiled (Option 14 from the Work with Members Using PDM screen). After entering 14, press F4 to prompt for COBOL/400 compile options. They are the same as those discussed in the batch environment.
• Once the program has compiled, check the output listing in the output queue for errors. If there are any, correct them and recompile the program.
• To execute the program, enter 'CALL PEDISP' on the command line. The program will control the workstation until the user ends the execution.

- Note that if the program goes into a loop (or otherwise ties up the workstation), the user can press the ALT/SYSRQ keys to start an alternate session. When the System Request Menu is displayed, Option 2 (End Previous Request) should be selected. Perhaps at this point the programmer should utilize the debugging features available, which were detailed in Section 4.3.
- Note that the file(s) being processed by any program must be in the programmer's library list. If, for example, a production program is being tested, and the programmer wishes to use test files located in a different library, the order of the programmer's library list can be altered either by a CHGLIBL command or by an ADDLIBLE command. For the AS/400 COBOL exercise programs to execute, however, programs and data should all reside in the same (the programmer's) library.

Listing 4.14 presents the COBOL/400 source for the program PEDISP. Also presented are two sample screen layouts:

1. The prompt screen.
2. The prompt screen plus the resulting detail screen.

These appear in Figures 4.1 and 4.2, respectively.

Update Program

Basically, the update program builds on the inquiry program, using it as a skeleton and adding additional functionality. It adds or updates database records based on key fields entered on a prompt screen, incorporating edit logic and use of a second database file for edit purposes. Additional programming techniques used in this program follow:

- The source member being edited in QCBLSRC is called PEDSPL, with a TYPE of CBL.
- The FILE-STATUS for the database files is utilized, both in the WORKING-STORAGE SECTION and the Procedure Division.

```
5728CB1 R03 M00 900824          AS/400 COBOL Source          DPDMLLIB/PEDISP

STMT SEQNBR -A 1 B..+....2....+....3....+....4....+....5....+....6....+....7..IDENTFCN  S  COPYNAME

   1  000100 IDENTIFICATION DIVISION.
   2  000200 PROGRAM-ID.   PEDISP.
   3  000300 AUTHOR. DML.
   4  000400 DATE-WRITTEN. 07/91.
   5  000500 DATE-COMPILED.

   6  000600 ENVIRONMENT DIVISION.
   7  000700 CONFIGURATION SECTION.
   8  000800 SOURCE-COMPUTER. IBM-AS400.
   9  000900 OBJECT-COMPUTER. IBM-AS400.
  10  001000 INPUT-OUTPUT SECTION.
  11  001100 FILE-CONTROL.
  12  001200     SELECT PERS-DSPL ASSIGN TO WORKSTATION-PEDISPD
  13  001300         ORGANIZATION IS TRANSACTION
  14  001400         CONTROL-AREA IS WS-CONTROL.
  15  001500     SELECT PERS-FILE ASSIGN TO DATABASE-PERSJFL
  16  001600         ORGANIZATION IS INDEXED
  17  001700         ACCESS IS DYNAMIC
  18  001800         FILE STATUS IS PERS-STATUS
  19  001900         RECORD KEY IS EXTERNALLY-DESCRIBED-KEY.
  20  002000 DATA DIVISION.
  21  002100 FILE SECTION.
  22  002200 FD  PERS-DSPL.
  23  002300 01  DSPL-RECORD.
  24  002400     COPY DDS-ALL-FORMATS OF PEDISPD.
  25 +000001       05  PEDISPD-RECORD PIC X(166).                                   <-ALL-FMTS
     +000002*  INPUT FORMAT:PERPRM        FROM FILE PEDISPD    OF LIBRARY DPDMLLIB    <-ALL-FMTS
     +000003*                            SSN PROMPT                                 <-ALL-FMTS
  26 +000004       05  PERPRM-I        REDEFINES PEDISPD-RECORD.                    <-ALL-FMTS
  27 +000005           06 PERPRM-I-INDIC.                                           <-ALL-FMTS
  28 +000006               07 IN03                  PIC 1  INDIC 03.                <-ALL-FMTS
     +000007*                            END OF PROGRAM                             <-ALL-FMTS
  29 +000008               07 IN07                  PIC 1  INDIC 07.                <-ALL-FMTS
     +000009*                            PREVIOUS RECORD                            <-ALL-FMTS
  30 +000010               07 IN08                  PIC 1  INDIC 08.                <-ALL-FMTS
     +000011*                            NEXT RECORD                                <-ALL-FMTS
  31 +000012               07 IN99                  PIC 1  INDIC 99.                <-ALL-FMTS
     +000013*                            FILE AT TOP OR BOTTOM.     PRESS RESET, TH <-ALL-FMTS
  32 +000014               07 IN98                  PIC 1  INDIC 98.                <-ALL-FMTS
     +000015*                            FILE ERROR. PRESS RESET, THEN ENTER OR F3  <-ALL-FMTS
  33 +000016           06 SSNUM                 PIC X(9).                           <-ALL-FMTS
     +000017*                            SOCIAL SECURITY NUMBER                     <-ALL-FMTS
     +000018* OUTPUT FORMAT:PERPRM       FROM FILE PEDISPD    OF LIBRARY DPDMLLIB   <-ALL-FMTS
     +000019*                            SSN PROMPT                                 <-ALL-FMTS
  34 +000020       05  PERPRM-O        REDEFINES PEDISPD-RECORD.                    <-ALL-FMTS
  35 +000021           06 PERPRM-O-INDIC.                                           <-ALL-FMTS
  36 +000022               07 IN99                  PIC 1  INDIC 99.                <-ALL-FMTS
     +000023*                            FILE AT TOP OR BOTTOM.     PRESS RESET, TH <-ALL-FMTS
  37 +000024               07 IN98                  PIC 1  INDIC 98.                <-ALL-FMTS
     +000025*                            FILE ERROR. PRESS RESET, THEN ENTER OR F3  <-ALL-FMTS
     +000026*  INPUT FORMAT:PERFLDS      FROM FILE PEDISPD    OF LIBRARY DPDMLLIB   <-ALL-FMTS
     +000027*                            PERSONNEL DISPLAY                          <-ALL-FMTS
  38 +000028       05  PERFLDS-I       REDEFINES PEDISPD-RECORD.                    <-ALL-FMTS
  39 +000029           06 PERFLDS-I-INDIC.                                          <-ALL-FMTS
  40 +000030               07 IN03                  PIC 1  INDIC 03.                <-ALL-FMTS
```

Listing 4.14. Source for PEDISP.

```
5728CB1 R03 M00 900824          AS/400 COBOL Source          DPDMLLIB/PEDISP
STMT SEQNBR -A 1 B..+....2....+....3....+....4....+....5....+....6....+....7..IDENTFCN  S  COPYNAME

     +000031*                             END OF PROGRAM                                <-ALL-FMTS
  41 +000032             07 IN07                    PIC 1  INDIC 07.                  <-ALL-FMTS
     +000033*                             PREVIOUS RECORD                               <-ALL-FMTS
  42 +000034             07 IN08                    PIC 1  INDIC 08.                  <-ALL-FMTS
     +000035*                             NEXT RECORD                                   <-ALL-FMTS
     +000036* OUTPUT FORMAT:PERFLDS       FROM FILE PEDISPD    OF LIBRARY DPDMLLIB     <-ALL-FMTS
     +000037*                             PERSONNEL DISPLAY                             <-ALL-FMTS
  43 +000038       05  PERFLDS-O        REDEFINES PEDISPD-RECORD.                     <-ALL-FMTS
  44 +000039           06 SSEDIT                    PIC X(11).                        <-ALL-FMTS
  45 +000040           06 LSTNAM                    PIC X(15).                        <-ALL-FMTS
     +000041*                             LAST NAME                                     <-ALL-FMTS
  46 +000042           06 FSTNAM                    PIC X(10).                        <-ALL-FMTS
     +000043*                             FIRST NAME                                    <-ALL-FMTS
  47 +000044           06 MIDINT                    PIC X(1).                         <-ALL-FMTS
     +000045*                             MIDDLE INITIAL                                <-ALL-FMTS
  48 +000046           06 ADDR1                     PIC X(20).                        <-ALL-FMTS
     +000047*                             ADDRESS LINE 1                                <-ALL-FMTS
  49 +000048           06 ADDR2                     PIC X(20).                        <-ALL-FMTS
     +000049*                             ADDRESS LINE 2                                <-ALL-FMTS
  50 +000050           06 CITY                      PIC X(20).                        <-ALL-FMTS
     +000051*                             CITY                                          <-ALL-FMTS
  51 +000052           06 STATE                     PIC X(2).                         <-ALL-FMTS
     +000053*                             STATE                                         <-ALL-FMTS
  52 +000054           06 ZIP                       PIC X(5).                         <-ALL-FMTS
     +000055*                             ZIP                                           <-ALL-FMTS
  53 +000056           06 FUND                      PIC X(2).                         <-ALL-FMTS
     +000057*                             FUND                                          <-ALL-FMTS
  54 +000058           06 DEPT                      PIC X(3).                         <-ALL-FMTS
     +000059*                             DEPT                                          <-ALL-FMTS
  55 +000060           06 DESCR                     PIC X(50).                        <-ALL-FMTS
     +000061*                             DEPARTMENT                                    <-ALL-FMTS
  56 +000062           06 WKYSAL                    PIC S9(5)V9(2).                   <-ALL-FMTS
     +000063*                             WEEKLY SALARY                                 <-ALL-FMTS
  57  002500 FD  PERS-FILE.
  58  002600 01  PERS-RECORD.
  59  002700     COPY DD-PERSJREC OF PERSJFL.
     +000001*    I-O FORMAT:PERSJREC      FROM FILE PERSJFL    OF LIBRARY DPDMLLIB     PERSJREC
     +000002*                             PERS JOIN LOGICAL FILE                        PERSJREC
     +000003*THE KEY DEFINITIONS FOR RECORD FORMAT  PERSJREC                            PERSJREC
     +000004*  NUMBER                  NAME            RETRIEVAL     TYPE    ALTSEQ     PERSJREC
     +000005*   0001        SOCSEC-NUM                  ASCENDING     AN      NO        PERSJREC
  60 +000006        05      PERSJREC.                                                   PERSJREC
  61 +000007           06 LAST-NAME                 PIC X(15).                        PERSJREC
     +000008*                             LAST NAME                                     PERSJREC
  62 +000009           06 FIRST-NAME                PIC X(10).                        PERSJREC
     +000010*                             FIRST NAME                                    PERSJREC
  63 +000011           06 MIDDLE-INIT               PIC X(1).                         PERSJREC
     +000012*                             MIDDLE INITIAL                                PERSJREC
  64 +000013           06 SOCSEC-NUM                PIC X(9).                         PERSJREC
     +000014*                             SOCIAL SECURITY NUMBER                        PERSJREC
  65 +000015           06 FUND-CODE                 PIC X(2).                         PERSJREC
     +000016*                             FUND                                          PERSJREC
  66 +000017           06 DEPT-CODE                 PIC X(3).                         PERSJREC
     +000018*                             DEPT                                          PERSJREC
  67 +000019           06 TAB-DESC                  PIC X(50).                        PERSJREC
```

Listing 4.14. *(cont.)*

```
5728CB1 R03 M00 900824          AS/400 COBOL Source          DPDMLLIB/PEDISP

 STMT SEQNBR -A 1 B..+....2....+....3....+....4....+....5....+....6....+....7..IDENTFCN  S  COPYNAME

      +000020*                      DEPARTMENT                                         PERSJREC
   68 +000021          06 ADDR-LN1             PIC X(20).                              PERSJREC
      +000022*                      ADDRESS LINE 1                                     PERSJREC
   69 +000023          06 ADDR-LN2             PIC X(20).                              PERSJREC
      +000024*                      ADDRESS LINE 2                                     PERSJREC
   70 +000025          06 ADDR-CITY            PIC X(20).                              PERSJREC
      +000026*                      CITY                                               PERSJREC
   71 +000027          06 ADDR-ST              PIC X(2).                               PERSJREC
      +000028*                      STATE                                              PERSJREC
   72 +000029          06 ADDR-ZIP             PIC X(5).                               PERSJREC
      +000030*                      ZIP                                                PERSJREC
   73 +000031          06 WLKY-SAL             PIC S9(5)V9(2)   COMP-3.                PERSJREC
      +000032*                      WEEKLY SALARY                                      PERSJREC
   74  002800 WORKING-STORAGE SECTION.
   75  002900 01  ONE                 PIC 1 VALUE B'1'.
   76  003000 01  PERS-STATUS         PIC X(02).
   77  003100 01  PERS-STATUS-RED REDEFINES PERS-STATUS.
   78  003200     05  PERS-STATUS-1   PIC X(01).
   79  003300         88  PERS-STATUS-OK      VALUE '0'.
   80  003400         88  PERS-STATUS-END     VALUE '1'.
   81  003500     05  PERS-STATUS-2   PIC X(01).
   82  003600 01  WS-CONTROL.
   83  003700     05  WS-IND          PIC X(02).
   84  003800     05  WS-FORMAT       PIC X(10).
       003900
   85  004000 01  SS-EDIT-AREA.
   86  004100     05  SS-BREAK.
   87  004200         10  SS1-BREAK   PIC X(03).
   88  004300         10  SS2-BREAK   PIC X(02).
   89  004400         10  SS3-BREAK   PIC X(04).
   90  004500     05  SS-DASH.
   91  004600         10  SS1-DASH    PIC X(03).
   92  004700         10  FILLER      PIC X(01)      VALUE '-'.
   93  004800         10  SS2-DASH    PIC X(02).
   94  004900         10  FILLER      PIC X(01)      VALUE '-'.
   95  005000         10  SS3-DASH    PIC X(04).
       005100
       005200
   96  005300 PROCEDURE DIVISION.
       005400
       005500 START-PGM.
   97  005600     OPEN I-O PERS-DSPL  INPUT PERS-FILE.
   98  005700     MOVE ZERO TO IN99 OF PERPRM-O.
   99  005800     MOVE ZERO TO IN98 OF PERPRM-O.
       005900
       006000 DISPLAY-LOOP.
  100  006100     WRITE DSPL-RECORD FORMAT IS 'PERPRM'.
  101  006200     READ PERS-DSPL RECORD.
  102  006300     IF IN03 OF PERPRM-I EQUAL ONE
  103  006400         GO TO CLOSE-FILES.
       006500 LOOP2.
  104  006600     IF IN07 OF PERPRM-I EQUAL ONE
  105  006700         PERFORM 0220-PREV    THRU 0220-EXIT
  106  006800         MOVE ZERO TO IN07 OF PERPRM-I
       006900     ELSE
```

```
5728CB1 R03 M00 900824           AS/400 COBOL Source            DPDMLLIB/PEDISP

 STMT SEQNBR -A 1 B..+....2....+....3....+....4....+....5....+....6....+....7..IDENTFCN  S  COPYNAME

  107  007000          IF IN08 OF PERPRM-I EQUAL ONE
  108  007100              PERFORM 0210-NEXT  THRU 0210-EXIT
  109  007200              MOVE ZERO TO IN08 OF PERPRM-I
       007300          ELSE
  110  007400              MOVE SSNUM    TO SOCSEC-NUM
  111  007500              PERFORM 0200-START  THRU  0200-EXIT
  112  007600              PERFORM 0210-NEXT  THRU  0210-EXIT.
  113  007700      IF PERS-STATUS-END
  114  007800          MOVE ONE TO IN99 OF PERPRM-O
  115  007900          GO TO DISPLAY-LOOP.
  116  008000      IF NOT PERS-STATUS-OK
  117  008100          MOVE ONE TO IN98 OF PERPRM-O
  118  008200          GO TO DISPLAY-LOOP.
  119  008300      PERFORM 0100-SS-EDIT   THRU  0100-EXIT.
  120  008400      MOVE SS-DASH         TO SSEDIT.
  121  008500      MOVE LAST-NAME       TO LSTNAM.
  122  008600      MOVE FIRST-NAME      TO FSTNAM.
  123  008700      MOVE MIDDLE-INIT     TO MIDINT.
  124  008800      MOVE FUND-CODE       TO FUND.
  125  008900      MOVE DEPT-CODE       TO DEPT.
  126  009000      MOVE TAB-DESC        TO DESCR.
  127  009100      MOVE ADDR-LN1        TO ADDR1.
  128  009200      MOVE ADDR-LN2        TO ADDR2.
  129  009300      MOVE ADDR-CITY       TO CITY.
  130  009400      MOVE ADDR-ST         TO STATE.
  131  009500      MOVE ADDR-ZIP        TO ZIP.
  132  009600      MOVE WLKY-SAL        TO WKYSAL.
  133  009700      WRITE DSPL-RECORD FORMAT IS 'PERFLDS'.
  134  009800      READ PERS-DSPL RECORD.
  135  009900      IF IN03 OF PERFLDS-I EQUAL ONE
  136  010000          GO TO CLOSE-FILES.
  137  010100      IF IN07 OF PERPRM-I EQUAL ONE
       010200         OR
       010300         IN08 OF PERPRM-I EQUAL ONE
       010400
  138  010500              GO TO LOOP2.
  139  010600      MOVE ZERO TO IN99 OF PERPRM-O.
  140  010700      MOVE ZERO TO IN98 OF PERPRM-O.
  141  010800      GO TO DISPLAY-LOOP.
       010900
       011000 0100-SS-EDIT.
  142  011100      MOVE SOCSEC-NUM    TO   SS-BREAK.
  143  011200      MOVE SS1-BREAK     TO   SS1-DASH.
  144  011300      MOVE SS2-BREAK     TO   SS2-DASH.
  145  011400      MOVE SS3-BREAK     TO   SS3-DASH.
       011500 0100-EXIT.
       011600      EXIT.
       011700
  146  011800 0200-START.
  147  011900      START PERS-FILE
       012000          KEY NOT LESS THAN SOCSEC-NUM.
       012100 0200-EXIT.
       012200      EXIT.
       012300
  148  012400 0210-NEXT.
```

Listing 4.14. *(cont.)*

```
5728CB1 R03 M00 900824            AS/400 COBOL Source              DPDMLLIB/PEDISP

 STMT SEQNBR -A 1 B..+....2....+....3....+....4....+....5....+....6....+....7..IDENTFCN  S  COPYNAME

  149  012500       READ PERS-FILE NEXT RECORD.
       012600 0210-EXIT.
       012700       EXIT.
       012800
  150  012900 0220-PREV.
  151  013000       READ PERS-FILE PRIOR RECORD.
       013100 0220-EXIT.
       013200       EXIT.
       013300
  152  013400 CLOSE-FILES.
  153  013500       CLOSE  PERS-DSPL
       013600              PERS-FILE.
       013700
       013800 END-PGM.
  154  013900       EXIT PROGRAM.
       014000
       014100
                         * * * * *   E N D   O F   S O U R C E   * * * * *
```

Listing 4.14. *(cont.)*

```
PERSONNEL INQUIRY

SS NUMBER 345

USE F3 TO END PROGRAM. USE ENTER TO ENTER ANOTHER SS NUMBER











03-18     SA        MW        KS        IM        II S1       KB
```

Figure 4.1. PEDISP prompt screen.

```
PERSONNEL INQUIRY

SS NUMBER 345

USE F3 TO END PROGRAM. USE ENTER TO ENTER ANOTHER SS NUMBER

SS NUMBER      345-63-4563
LAST NAME      Robertson
FIRST NAME     Robert          MID INIT
ADDRESS        456 Mill St.

CITY           Wheatcn                     STATE     IL     ZIP     60187

FUND/DEPT      03 - 003
DESCRIPTION         Sheriff

WEEKLY SALARY         545.00

USE F7 TO PAGE BACKWARD, F8 TO PAGE FORWARD




03-15      SA         MW         KS         IM         :I S1         KB
```

Figure 4.2. PEDISP prompt screen and resulting detail screen.

- The SELECT statement uses an additional parameter, SI, which stands for Separate Indicator area. Indicators are not treated as part of the display file, but instead must be explicitly defined by the programmer in WORKING-STORAGE. In this way common indicators are used throughout the program.
- Screen data fields are also redefined in WORKING-STORAGE to eliminate the need for screen data fields to be fully qualified. READ INTO and WRITE FROM are utilized in the Procedure Division.
- Screen I/O is different in that the INDICATORS ARE clause states where the indicators are located in WORKING-STORAGE. Single indicators are set as opposed to the multiple redefined indicators in the inquiry program.
- The logic for the program is to write the prompt display file, then read the same display file to check for responses. The database file is then read to determine if a record exists; if it does, the program loads an update screen; if not, the program loads an add screen. The detail display file is then written and then read so that screen edits can be performed. If edits are unsuccessful, the program loops back to redisplay the screen with errors. This edit loop continues until all errors are corrected. When the screen is correct the database record is written/rewritten, and a clean screen is sent with an 'Update Successful' message, allowing the user to enter another prompt and begin the update cycle again.
- Compile the program in the normal manner (Option 14). When the compile is complete, check the output listing in the output queue for errors. If there are any, correct them and recompile the program.
- To execute the program, enter 'CALL PEDSPL' on the command line. The program will control the workstation until the user ends the execution.

The COBOL source for the program PEDSPL appears in Listing 4.15. Figures 4.3 through 4.6 are four sample screen layouts:

1. The prompt screen.
2. The screen to update an existing record.
3. The screen to add a new record.
4. The resulting completion screen.

```
                                   AS/400 COBOL Source

STMT SEQNBR -A 1 B..+....2....+....3....+....4....+....5....+....6....+....7..IDENTFCN  S  COPYNAME

   1  000100 IDENTIFICATION DIVISION.
   2  000200 PROGRAM-ID.   PEDSPL.
   3  000300 AUTHOR. DML.
   4  000400 DATE-WRITTEN. 07/91.
   5  000500 DATE-COMPILED.

   6  000600 ENVIRONMENT DIVISION.
   7  000700 CONFIGURATION SECTION.
   8  000800 SOURCE-COMPUTER. IBM-AS400.
   9  000900 OBJECT-COMPUTER. IBM-AS400.
  10  001000 INPUT-OUTPUT SECTION.
  11  001100 FILE-CONTROL.
  12  001200     SELECT PERS-DSPL ASSIGN TO WORKSTATION-PEDSPLD-SI
  13  001300         ORGANIZATION IS TRANSACTION
  14  001400         CONTROL-AREA IS WS-CONTROL.
  15  001500     SELECT PERS-FILE ASSIGN TO DATABASE-PERSLFL
  16  001600         ORGANIZATION IS INDEXED
  17  001700         ACCESS IS DYNAMIC
  18  001800         FILE STATUS IS PERS-STATUS
  19  001900         RECORD KEY IS EXTERNALLY-DESCRIBED-KEY.
  20  002000     SELECT TBL-FILE ASSIGN TO DATABASE-PERSTFL
  21  002100         ORGANIZATION IS INDEXED
  22  002200         ACCESS IS RANDOM
  23  002300         FILE STATUS IS TBL-STATUS
  24  002400         RECORD KEY IS EXTERNALLY-DESCRIBED-KEY.
  25  002500 DATA DIVISION.
  26  002600 FILE SECTION.
  27  002700 FD  PERS-DSPL.
  28  002800 01  DSPL-RECORD.
  29  002900     COPY DDS-ALL-FORMATS OF PEDSPLD.
  30 +000001       05  PEDSPLD-RECORD PIC X(138).                                      <-ALL-FMTS
     +000002*  INPUT FORMAT:PERPRM      FROM FILE PEDSPLD     OF LIBRARY DPDMLLIB      <-ALL-FMTS
     +000003*                           NAME PROMPT                                     <-ALL-FMTS
  31 +000004       05  PERPRM-I       REDEFINES PEDSPLD-RECORD.                          <-ALL-FMTS
  32 +000005           06  LSTNAM                 PIC X(15).                             <-ALL-FMTS
     +000006*                           LAST NAME                                       <-ALL-FMTS
  33 +000007           06  FSTNAM                 PIC X(10).                             <-ALL-FMTS
     +000008*                           FIRST NAME                                      <-ALL-FMTS
  34 +000009           06  MIDINT                 PIC X(1).                              <-ALL-FMTS
     +000010*                           MIDDLE INITIAL                                  <-ALL-FMTS
     +000011* OUTPUT FORMAT:PERPRM      FROM FILE PEDSPLD     OF LIBRARY DPDMLLIB      <-ALL-FMTS
     +000012*                           NAME PROMPT                                     <-ALL-FMTS
     +000013*      05  PERPRM-O       REDEFINES PEDSPLD-RECORD.                          <-ALL-FMTS
     +000014*  INPUT FORMAT:PERMSG      FROM FILE PEDSPLD     OF LIBRARY DPDMLLIB      <-ALL-FMTS
     +000015*                           MESSAGES                                        <-ALL-FMTS
     +000016*      05  PERMSG-I       REDEFINES PEDSPLD-RECORD.                          <-ALL-FMTS
     +000017* OUTPUT FORMAT:PERMSG      FROM FILE PEDSPLD     OF LIBRARY DPDMLLIB      <-ALL-FMTS
     +000018*                           MESSAGES                                        <-ALL-FMTS
  35 +000019       05  PERMSG-O       REDEFINES PEDSPLD-RECORD.                          <-ALL-FMTS
  36 +000020           06  CONMSG                 PIC X(50).                             <-ALL-FMTS
     +000021*  INPUT FORMAT:PERFLDS     FROM FILE PEDSPLD     OF LIBRARY DPDMLLIB      <-ALL-FMTS
     +000022*                           PERSONNEL UPDATE                                <-ALL-FMTS
  37 +000023       05  PERFLDS-I      REDEFINES PEDSPLD-RECORD.                          <-ALL-FMTS
  38 +000024           06  SSNUM                  PIC X(9).                              <-ALL-FMTS
     +000025*                           SOCIAL SECURITY NUMBER                          <-ALL-FMTS
```

Listing 4.15. Source for PEDSPL.

```
                                AS/400 COBOL Source

STMT SEQNBR -A 1 B..+....2....+....3....+....4....+....5....+....6....+....7..IDENTFCN  S  COPYNAME

  39 +000026          06 ADDR1                   PIC X(20).                              <-ALL-FMTS
     +000027*                           ADDRESS LINE 1                                   <-ALL-FMTS
  40 +000028          06 ADDR2                   PIC X(20).                              <-ALL-FMTS
     +000029*                           ADDRESS LINE 2                                   <-ALL-FMTS
  41 +000030          06 CITY                    PIC X(20).                              <-ALL-FMTS
     +000031*                           CITY                                             <-ALL-FMTS
  42 +000032          06 STATE                   PIC X(2).                               <-ALL-FMTS
     +000033*                           STATE                                            <-ALL-FMTS
  43 +000034          06 ZIP                     PIC X(5).                               <-ALL-FMTS
     +000035*                           ZIP                                              <-ALL-FMTS
  44 +000036          06 FUND                    PIC X(2).                               <-ALL-FMTS
     +000037*                           FUND                                             <-ALL-FMTS
  45 +000038          06 DEPT                    PIC X(3).                               <-ALL-FMTS
     +000039*                           DEPT                                             <-ALL-FMTS
  46 +000040          06 WKYSAL                  PIC S9(5)V9(2).                         <-ALL-FMTS
     +000041*                           WEEKLY SALARY                                    <-ALL-FMTS
     +000042* OUTPUT FORMAT:PERFLDS     FROM FILE PEDSPLD    OF LIBRARY DPDMLLIB         <-ALL-FMTS
     +000043*                           PERSONNEL UPDATE                                 <-ALL-FMTS
  47 +000044       05 PERFLDS-O       REDEFINES PEDSPLD-RECORD.                          <-ALL-FMTS
  48 +000045          06 SSNUM                   PIC X(9).                               <-ALL-FMTS
     +000046*                           SOCIAL SECURITY NUMBER                           <-ALL-FMTS
  49 +000047          06 ADDR1                   PIC X(20).                              <-ALL-FMTS
     +000048*                           ADDRESS LINE 1                                   <-ALL-FMTS
  50 +000049          06 ADDR2                   PIC X(20).                              <-ALL-FMTS
     +000050*                           ADDRESS LINE 2                                   <-ALL-FMTS
  51 +000051          06 CITY                    PIC X(20).                              <-ALL-FMTS
     +000052*                           CITY                                             <-ALL-FMTS
  52 +000053          06 STATE                   PIC X(2).                               <-ALL-FMTS
     +000054*                           STATE                                            <-ALL-FMTS
  53 +000055          06 ZIP                     PIC X(5).                               <-ALL-FMTS
     +000056*                           ZIP                                              <-ALL-FMTS
  54 +000057          06 FUND                    PIC X(2).                               <-ALL-FMTS
     +000058*                           FUND                                             <-ALL-FMTS
  55 +000059          06 DEPT                    PIC X(3).                               <-ALL-FMTS
     +000060*                           DEPT                                             <-ALL-FMTS
  56 +000061          06 WKYSAL                  PIC S9(5)V9(2).                         <-ALL-FMTS
     +000062*                           WEEKLY SALARY                                    <-ALL-FMTS
  57 +000063          06 MSGLIN                  PIC X(50).                              <-ALL-FMTS
  58  003000 FD  PERS-FILE.
  59  003100 01  PERS-RECORD.
  60  003200     COPY DD-PERSPREC OF PERSLFL.
     +000001*    I-O FORMAT:PERSPREC    FROM FILE PERSLFL    OF LIBRARY DPDMLLIB         PERSPREC
     +000002*                           PERSONNEL FILE                                   PERSPREC
     +000003*THE KEY DEFINITIONS FOR RECORD FORMAT  PERSPREC                             PERSPREC
     +000004*  NUMBER                 NAME              RETRIEVAL    TYPE    ALTSEQ      PERSPREC
     +000005*   0001    LAST-NAME                        ASCENDING    AN      NO         PERSPREC
     +000006*   0002    FIRST-NAME                       ASCENDING    AN      NO         PERSPREC
     +000007*   0003    MIDDLE-INIT                      ASCENDING    AN      NO         PERSPREC
  61 +000008       05   PERSPREC.                                                        PERSPREC
  62 +000009          06 LAST-NAME               PIC X(15).                              PERSPREC
     +000010*                           LAST NAME                                        PERSPREC
  63 +000011          06 FIRST-NAME              PIC X(10).                              PERSPREC
     +000012*                           FIRST NAME                                       PERSPREC
  64 +000013          06 MIDDLE-INIT             PIC X(1).                               PERSPREC
     +000014*                           MIDDLE INITIAL                                   PERSPREC
```

Listing 4.15. *(cont.)*

```
                                    AS/400 COBOL Source

STMT SEQNBR -A 1 B..+....2....+....3....+....4....+....5....+....6....+....7..IDENTFCN  S  COPYNAME

  65 +000015          06 SOCSEC-NUM            PIC X(9).                                  PERSPREC
     +000016*                             SOCIAL SECURITY NUMBER                          PERSPREC
  66 +000017          06 FUND-CODE             PIC X(2).                                  PERSPREC
     +000018*                             FUND                                            PERSPREC
  67 +000019          06 DEPT-CODE             PIC X(3).                                  PERSPREC
     +000020*                             DEPT                                            PERSPREC
  68 +000021          06 ADDR-LN1              PIC X(20).                                 PERSPREC
     +000022*                             ADDRESS LINE 1                                  PERSPREC
  69 +000023          06 ADDR-LN2              PIC X(20).                                 PERSPREC
     +000024*                             ADDRESS LINE 2                                  PERSPREC
  70 +000025          06 ADDR-CITY             PIC X(20).                                 PERSPREC
     +000026*                             CITY                                            PERSPREC
  71 +000027          06 ADDR-ST               PIC X(2).                                  PERSPREC
     +000028*                             STATE                                           PERSPREC
  72 +000029          06 ADDR-ZIP              PIC X(5).                                  PERSPREC
     +000030*                             ZIP                                             PERSPREC
  73 +000031          06 WLKY-SAL              PIC S9(5)V9(2)    COMP-3.                  PERSPREC
     +000032*                             WEEKLY SALARY                                   PERSPREC
  74  003300 FD  TBL-FILE.
  75  003400 01  TBL-RECORD.
  76  003500     COPY DD-PERSTREC OF PERSTFL.
     +000001*    I-O FORMAT:PERSTREC      FROM FILE PERSTFL    OF LIBRARY DPDMLLIB        PERSTREC
     +000002*                             TABLE FILE                                      PERSTREC
     +000003*THE KEY DEFINITIONS FOR RECORD FORMAT  PERSTREC                              PERSTREC
     +000004*  NUMBER              NAME                 RETRIEVAL     TYPE    ALTSEQ      PERSTREC
     +000005*   0001    FUND-CODE                        ASCENDING      AN      NO         PERSTREC
     +000006*   0002    DEPT-CODE                        ASCENDING      AN      NO         PERSTREC
  77 +000007        05  PERSTREC.                                                         PERSTREC
  78 +000008          06 FUND-CODE             PIC X(2).                                  PERSTREC
     +000009*                             FUND                                            PERSTREC
  79 +000010          06 DEPT-CODE             PIC X(3).                                  PERSTREC
     +000011*                             DEPT                                            PERSTREC
  80 +000012          06 TAB-DESC              PIC X(50).                                 PERSTREC
     +000013*                             DEPARTMENT                                      PERSTREC
  81  003600 WORKING-STORAGE SECTION.
  82  003700 01  ONE                    PIC 1 VALUE B'1'.
  83  003800 01  TBL-STATUS             PIC X(02).
  84  003900     88  TBL-STATUS-GOOD    VALUE '00'.
  85  004000 01  PERS-STATUS            PIC X(02).
  86  004100 01  PERS-STATUS-RED REDEFINES PERS-STATUS.
  87  004200     05  PERS-STATUS-1      PIC X(01).
  88  004300         88  PERS-STATUS-OK      VALUE '0'.
  89  004400         88  PERS-STATUS-END     VALUE '1'.
  90  004500         88  PERS-STATUS-DUP     VALUE '2'.
  91  004600     05  PERS-STATUS-2      PIC X(01).
  92  004700 01  WS-CONTROL.
  93  004800     05  WS-IND             PIC X(02).
  94  004900     05  WS-FORMAT          PIC X(10).
      005000
  95  005100 01  BREAK-AREA.
  96  005200     05  STATE-BREAK.
  97  005300         10  STATE-1        PIC X(01).
  98  005400         10  STATE-REST     PIC X(01).
  99  005500     05  CITY-BREAK.
 100  005600         10  CITY-1         PIC X(01).
```

Listing 4.15. *(cont.)*

```
                              AS/400 COBOL Source

STMT SEQNBR -A 1 B..+....2....+....3....+....4....+....5....+....6....+....7..IDENTFCN  S  COPYNAME

 101  005700            10  CITY-REST      PIC X(19).
 102  005800        05  LNAME-BREAK.
 103  005900            10  LNAME-1        PIC X(01).
 104  006000            10  LNAME-REST     PIC X(14).
 105  006100        05  FNAME-BREAK.
 106  006200            10  FNAME-1        PIC X(01).
 107  006300            10  FNAME-REST     PIC X(14).
      006400
 108  006500 01     MESSAGE-AREA.
 109  006600        05  OK-MESSAGE         PIC X(50)
 110  006700            VALUE 'UPDATE COMPLETE. ENTER NEW NAME.'.
 111  006800        05  NEW-REC-MESSAGE  PIC X(50)
 112  006900            VALUE 'NAME NOT ON FILE. ENTER NEW RECORD.'.
 113  007000        05  UPDATE-MESSAGE    PIC X(50)
 114  007100            VALUE 'NAME FOUND. UPDATE FIELDS.'.
 115  007200        05  dup-MESSAGE    PIC X(50)
 116  007300            VALUE 'DUPLICATE SS NUM. RECORD NOT ADDED.'.
      007400
 117  007500 01     IND-AREA.
 118  007600        05  NEW-REC-IND        PIC X(01)  VALUE SPACE.
 119  007700            88  NEW-REC                   VALUE 'Y'.
 120  007800        05  EDIT-IND           PIC X(01)  VALUE SPACE.
 121  007900            88  EDITS-OK                  VALUE SPACE.
 122  008000            88  EDITS-BAD                 VALUE 'Y'.
 123  008100        05  UPDT-IND           PIC X(01)  VALUE SPACE.
 124  008200            88  REC-UPDT                    VALUE 'Y'.
      008300
 125  008400 01     DSPL-INDS.
 126  008500        05  in03               pic 1      indic 03.
 127  008600            88  pgm-end                   value b'1'.
 128  008700        05  in12               pic 1      indic 12.
 129  008800            88  xcl-updt                  value b'1'.
 130  008900        05  in87               pic 1      indic 87.
 131  009000            88  protect-ind               value b'1'.
 132  009100        05  in89               pic 1      indic 89.
 133  009200            88  dept-bad                  value b'1'.
 134  009300        05  in90               pic 1      indic 90.
 135  009400            88  fund-bad                  value b'1'.
 136  009500        05  in91               pic 1      indic 91.
 137  009600            88  zip-bad                   value b'1'.
 138  009700        05  in92               pic 1      indic 92.
 139  009800            88  state-bad                 value b'1'.
 140  009900        05  in93               pic 1      indic 93.
 141  010000            88  city-bad                  value b'1'.
 142  010100        05  in94               pic 1      indic 94.
 143  010200            88  ssnum-bad                 value b'1'.
 144  010300        05  in95               pic 1      indic 95.
 145  010400            88  mi-bad                    value b'1'.
 146  010500        05  in96               pic 1      indic 96.
 147  010600            88  fstnam-bad                value b'1'.
 148  010700        05  in97               pic 1      indic 97.
 149  010800            88  lstnam-bad                value b'1'.
 150  010900        05  in98               pic 1      indic 98.
 151  011000            88  error-ind                 value b'1'.
      011100
```

Listing 4.15. *(cont.)*

```
                                AS/400 COBOL Source

STMT SEQNBR -A 1 B..+....2....+....3....+....4....+....5....+....6....+....7..IDENTFCN  S  COPYNAME

       011200
  152  011300 01  WS-SCREEN-AREA.
       011400
  153  011500     05  WS-SCREEN-1.
  154  011600         10  LSTNAM-WS     PIC X(15).
  155  011700         10  FSTNAM-WS     PIC X(10).
  156  011800         10  MIDINT-WS     PIC X(01).
       011900
  157  012000     05  WS-SCREEN-2.
  158  012100         10  CONMSG-WS     PIC X(50).
       012200
  159  012300     05  WS-SCREEN-3.
  160  012400         10  SSNUM-WS      PIC X(09).
  161  012500         10  ADDR1-WS      PIC X(20).
  162  012600         10  ADDR2-WS      PIC X(20).
  163  012700         10  CITY-WS       PIC X(20).
  164  012800         10  STATE-WS      PIC X(02).
  165  012900         10  ZIP-WS        PIC X(05).
  166  013000         10  FUND-WS       PIC X(02).
  167  013100         10  DEPT-WS       PIC X(03).
  168  013200         10  WKYSAL-WS     PIC S9(5)V99.
  169  013300         10  MSGLIN-WS     PIC X(50).
       013400
  170  013500 PROCEDURE DIVISION.
       013600
       013700 START-PGM.
  171  013800     OPEN I-O PERS-DSPL  PERS-FILE
       013900          INPUT TBL-FILE.
  172  014000     MOVE ALL B'0' TO DSPL-INDS.
       014100
       014200 DISPLAY-LOOP.
  173  014300     MOVE SPACE TO EDIT-IND.
  174  014400     WRITE DSPL-RECORD FROM WS-SCREEN-1
       014500           FORMAT IS 'PERPRM'
       014600           indicators are dspl-inds.
  175  014700     WRITE DSPL-RECORD FROM WS-SCREEN-2
       014800           FORMAT IS 'PERMSG'
       014900           indicators are dspl-inds.
  176  015000     READ PERS-DSPL RECORD INTO WS-SCREEN-1
       015100           FORMAT IS 'PERPRM'
       015200           indicators are dspl-inds.
  177  015300     IF pgm-end
  178  015400         GO TO CLOSE-FILES.
  179  015500     IF xcl-updt
  180  015600         MOVE ALL B'0' TO DSPL-INDS
  181  015700         MOVE SPACE TO CONMSG-WS
       015800                       NEW-REC-IND
       015900                       WS-SCREEN-1
  182  016000         GO TO DISPLAY-LOOP.
  183  016100     PERFORM 0100-EDIT-NAME THRU 0100-EXIT.
  184  016200     IF EDITS-OK
       016300         CONTINUE
  185  016400     ELSE
  186  016500         GO TO DISPLAY-LOOP.
       016600
```

Listing 4.15. *(cont.)*

```
                                   AS/400 COBOL Source

STMT SEQNBR -A 1 B..+....2....+....3....+....4....+....5....+....6....+....7..IDENTFCN  S  COPYNAME

 187  016700        PERFORM 0200-READ-PERS THRU 0200-EXIT.
 188  016800        IF PERS-STATUS-OK
 189  016900            PERFORM 0300-LOAD-SCREEN THRU 0300-EXIT
 190  017000            MOVE UPDATE-MESSAGE TO MSGLIN-WS
      017100        ELSE
 191  017200            MOVE 'Y' TO NEW-REC-IND
 192  017300            PERFORM 0400-INIT-SCREEN THRU 0400-EXIT
 193  017400            MOVE NEW-REC-MESSAGE TO MSGLIN-WS.
      017500
      017600    LOOP2.
 194  017700        MOVE ONE TO IN87.
 195  017800        WRITE DSPL-RECORD FROM WS-SCREEN-2
      017900              FORMAT IS 'PERMSG'
      018000              indicators are dspl-inds.
 196  018100        WRITE DSPL-RECORD FROM WS-SCREEN-3
      018200            FORMAT IS 'PERFLDS'
      018300            INDICATORS ARE DSPL-INDS.
 197  018400        READ PERS-DSPL RECORD INTO WS-SCREEN-3
      018500            FORMAT IS 'PERFLDS'
      018600            INDICATORS ARE DSPL-INDS.
 198  018700        IF pgm-end
 199  018800            GO TO CLOSE-FILES.
 200  018900        IF xcl-updt
 201  019000            MOVE ALL B'0' TO DSPL-INDS
 202  019100            MOVE SPACE TO CONMSG-WS
      019200                          NEW-REC-IND
      019300                          WS-SCREEN-1
 203  019400            GO TO DISPLAY-LOOP.
      019500
 204  019600        PERFORM 0500-EDIT-SCREEN THRU 0500-EXIT.
 205  019700        IF EDITS-OK
 206  019800            IF NEW-REC
 207  019900                PERFORM 0600-MOVE-FLDS THRU 0600-EXIT
 208  020000                PERFORM 0210-WRITE-PERS THRU 0210-EXIT
 209  020100                if ERROR-IND
 210  020200                    move dup-message to msglin-WS
 211  020300                    go to loop2
      020400                else
 212  020500                    MOVE SPACE TO NEW-REC-IND
 213  020600                    MOVE OK-MESSAGE TO CONMSG-WS
      020700            ELSE
 214  020800                PERFORM 0600-MOVE-FLDS THRU 0600-EXIT
 215  020900                PERFORM 0220-REWRITE-PERS THRU 0220-EXIT
 216  021000                if ERROR-IND
 217  021100                    move dup-message to msglin-WS
 218  021200                    go to loop2
      021300                else
 219  021400                    MOVE OK-MESSAGE TO CONMSG-WS
      021500        ELSE
 220  021600            GO TO LOOP2.
      021700
      021800***GET READY FOR NEXT RECORD**********
 221  021900        MOVE ALL B'0' TO DSPL-INDS.
 222  022000        MOVE SPACE TO WS-SCREEN-1
      022100                      WS-SCREEN-3.
```

Listing 4.15. *(cont.)*

```
                                   AS/400 COBOL Source

STMT SEQNBR -A 1 B..+....2....+....3....+....4....+....5....+....6....+....7..IDENTFCN  S  COPYNAME

 223  022200      GO TO DISPLAY-LOOP.
      022300
      022400 0100-EDIT-NAME.
 224  022500      MOVE LSTNAM-WS            TO LNAME-BREAK.
 225  022600      MOVE FSTNAM-WS            TO FNAME-BREAK.
 226  022700      IF LNAME-1 EQUAL SPACE
 227  022800          MOVE ONE TO IN97
 228  022900          MOVE 'Y' TO EDIT-IND.
 229  023000      IF LNAME-1 NUMERIC
 230  023100          MOVE ONE TO IN97
 231  023200          MOVE 'Y' TO EDIT-IND.
 232  023300      IF FNAME-1 EQUAL SPACE
 233  023400          MOVE ONE TO IN96
 234  023500          MOVE 'Y' TO EDIT-IND.
 235  023600      IF FNAME-1 NUMERIC
 236  023700          MOVE ONE TO IN96
 237  023800          MOVE 'Y' TO EDIT-IND.
 238  023900      IF MIDINT-WS NUMERIC
 239  024000          MOVE ONE TO IN95
 240  024100          MOVE 'Y' TO EDIT-IND.
      024200 0100-EXIT.
      024300      EXIT.
      024400
 241  024500 0200-READ-PERS.
 242  024600      MOVE LSTNAM-WS         TO LAST-NAME.
 243  024700      MOVE FSTNAM-WS         TO FIRST-NAME.
 244  024800      MOVE MIDINT-WS         TO MIDDLE-INIT.
 245  024900      READ PERS-FILE.
      025000 0200-EXIT.
      025100      EXIT.
      025200
 246  025300 0210-WRITE-PERS.
 247  025400      WRITE PERS-RECORD.
 248  025500      if pers-status-dup
 249  025600          move one to in98.
      025700 0210-EXIT.
      025800      EXIT.
      025900
 250  026000 0220-REWRITE-PERS.
 251  026100      REWRITE PERS-RECORD.
 252  026200      if pers-status-dup
 253  026300          move one to in98.
      026400 0220-EXIT.
      026500      EXIT.
      026600
 254  026700 0250-READ-TBL.
 255  026800      READ TBL-FILE.
      026900 0250-EXIT.
      027000      EXIT.
      027100
 256  027200 0300-LOAD-SCREEN.
 257  027300      MOVE SPACE             TO CONMSG-WS.
 258  027400      MOVE SOCSEC-NUM        TO SSNUM-WS.
 259  027500      MOVE FUND-CODE OF PERS-RECORD TO FUND-WS.
 260  027600      MOVE DEPT-CODE OF PERS-RECORD TO DEPT-WS.
```

Listing 4.15. *(cont.)*

```
                                AS/400 COBOL Source

STMT SEQNBR -A 1 B..+....2....+....3....+....4....+....5....+....6....+....7..IDENTFCN  S  COPYNAME

 261  027700       MOVE ADDR-LN1        TO ADDR1-WS.
 262  027800       MOVE ADDR-LN2        TO ADDR2-WS.
 263  027900       MOVE ADDR-CITY       TO CITY-WS.
 264  028000       MOVE ADDR-ST         TO STATE-WS.
 265  028100       MOVE ADDR-ZIP        TO ZIP-WS.
 266  028200       MOVE WLKY-SAL        TO WKYSAL-WS.
      028300   0300-EXIT.
      028400       EXIT.
      028500
 267  028600   0400-INIT-SCREEN.
 268  028700       MOVE SPACE           TO CONMSG-WS.
 269  028800       MOVE SPACES          TO SSNUM-WS.
 270  028900       MOVE SPACES          TO FUND-WS.
 271  029000       MOVE SPACES          TO DEPT-WS.
 272  029100       MOVE SPACES          TO ADDR1-WS.
 273  029200       MOVE SPACES          TO ADDR2-WS.
 274  029300       MOVE SPACES          TO CITY-WS.
 275  029400       MOVE SPACES          TO STATE-WS.
 276  029500       MOVE SPACES          TO ZIP-WS.
 277  029600       MOVE ZERO            TO WKYSAL-WS.
      029700   0400-EXIT.
      029800       EXIT.
      029900
 278  030000   0500-EDIT-SCREEN.
 279  030100       MOVE SPACE           TO EDIT-IND.
 280  030200       IF SSNUM-WS NOT NUMERIC
 281  030300           MOVE ONE TO IN94
 282  030400           MOVE 'Y' TO EDIT-IND.
 283  030500       MOVE CITY-WS TO CITY-BREAK.
 284  030600       IF CITY-1 NUMERIC
 285  030700           MOVE ONE TO IN93
 286  030800           MOVE 'Y' TO EDIT-IND.
 287  030900       MOVE STATE-WS TO STATE-BREAK.
 288  031000       IF STATE-1 NUMERIC
 289  031100           MOVE ONE TO IN92
 290  031200           MOVE 'Y' TO EDIT-IND.
 291  031300       IF ZIP-WS NOT NUMERIC
 292  031400           MOVE ONE TO IN91
 293  031500           MOVE 'Y' TO EDIT-IND.
 294  031600       MOVE FUND-WS TO FUND-CODE OF TBL-RECORD.
 295  031700       MOVE DEPT-WS TO DEPT-CODE OF TBL-RECORD.
 296  031800       PERFORM 0250-READ-TBL THRU 0250-EXIT.
 297  031900       IF TBL-STATUS-GOOD
      032000           NEXT SENTENCE
      032100       ELSE
 298  032200           MOVE ONE TO IN90
 299  032300           MOVE ONE TO IN89
 300  032400           MOVE 'Y' TO EDIT-IND.
      032500
      032600   0500-EXIT.
      032700       EXIT.
      032800
 301  032900   0600-MOVE-FLDS.
 302  033000       MOVE SSNUM-WS     TO SOCSEC-NUM.
 303  033100       MOVE FUND-WS      TO FUND-CODE OF PERS-RECORD.
```

Listing 4.15. *(cont.)*

```
                                 AS/400 COBOL Source

STMT SEQNBR -A 1 B..+....2....+....3....+....4....+....5....+....6....+....7..IDENTFCN  S  COPYNAME

 304  033200        MOVE DEPT-WS      TO DEPT-CODE OF PERS-RECORD.
 305  033300        MOVE ADDR1-WS     TO ADDR-LN1.
 306  033400        MOVE ADDR2-WS     TO ADDR-LN2.
 307  033500        MOVE CITY-WS      TO ADDR-CITY.
 308  033600        MOVE STATE-WS     TO ADDR-ST.
 309  033700        MOVE ZIP-WS       TO ADDR-ZIP.
 310  033800        MOVE WKYSAL-WS    TO WLKY-SAL.
      033900    0600-EXIT.
      034000        EXIT.
      034100
 311  034200    CLOSE-FILES.
 312  034300        CLOSE  PERS-DSPL
      034400               PERS-FILE
      034500               TBL-FILE.
      034600
      034700    END-PGM.
 313  034800        EXIT PROGRAM.
      034900
      035000

                        * * * * *   E N D   O F   S O U R C E   * * * * *
```

Listing 4.15. *(cont.)*

```
PERSONNEL UPDATE

ENTER NAME
LAST      Taylor          FIRST C              MIDDLE INITIAL

USE F3 TO END PROGRAM. USE ENTER TO UPDATE, F12 TO CANCEL











04-39     SA        MW        KS        IM        II S1       KB
```

Figure 4.3. PEDSPL prompt screen.

```
PERSONNEL UPDATE

ENTER NAME
LAST       Taylor          FIRST C           MIDDLE INITIAL

USE F3 TO END PROGRAM. USE ENTER TO UPDATE, F12 TO CANCEL


SS NUMBER     908769800
ADDRESS       100 N. State

CITY          Chicago                  STATE     IL   ZIP  60606

FUND/DEPT     01 - 001

WEEKLY SALARY        346.20


NAME FOUND. UPDATE FIELDS.



09-20     SA        MW        KS        IM        II S1       KB
```

Figure 4.4. PEDSPL Update screen.

```
PERSONNEL UPDATE

ENTER NAME
LAST      Roberts          FIRST Michael       MIDDLE INITIAL

USE F3 TO END PROGRAM. USE ENTER TO UPDATE, F12 TO CANCEL


SS NUMBER     234523456
ADDRESS       567 Main St.

CITY          Wheaton                 STATE    IL   ZIP  60187

FUND/DEPT     03 - 003

WEEKLY SALARY     454


NAME NOT ON FILE. ENTER NEW RECORD.




09-20     SA        MW        KS        IM        II S1       KB
```

Figure 4.5. PEDSPL screen to add a new record.

```
PERSONNEL UPDATE

ENTER NAME
LAST                        FIRST                  MIDDLE INITIAL

USE F3 TO END PROGRAM. USE ENTER TO UPDATE, F12 TO CANCEL
UPDATE COMPLETE. ENTER NEW NAME.











04-15     SA        MW        KS        IM        II S1       KB
```

Figure 4.6. Screen resulting from the addition of a new record.

Additional information on COBOL/400 online programming can be found in the following books:

- IBM Manual SC09-1158, *COBOL/400 User's Guide*. This book details ways to write, compile, test, debug, and run COBOL/400 programs.
- IBM Manual SC09-1240, *COBOL/400 Reference*. This book details program structure and Procedure Division statements for successfully running AS/400 COBOL programs.

5

RPG Programming Procedures

The objective of this chapter is to introduce RPG programming principles on the AS/400, geared to an audience of programmers who will be working on the system, and employing a 'learn by doing' approach. Following this introduction is the summary of an RPG/400 exercise, which is the same as the COBOL/400 exercise except for a few slight variations. Be sure to read it carefully.

This chapter will be broken down into sections, which, if applicable, will contain systems examples of the material covered. Included are the following major topics:

- Setup of database files—reference files, physical files, and logical files—with DDS. This is the same as the setup presented in the COBOL/400 exercise.
- RPG/400 batch programming—basic report generation and file updates.
- Setup of screen display files, also with DDS. Again, this matches what was done in COBOL/400.
- RPG/400 online programming—display and update processing.

This chapter is not meant as instruction in the RPG programming language but as a reference tool for using RPG on the AS/400. As with COBOL/400, if the programmer has never worked with RPG or is somewhat rusty on RPG concepts, some sort of review is strongly recommended before this chapter is begun. There are many RPG manuals available to acquaint the programmer with the language, as well as numerous PC-based and in-person classes on the subject.

5.1 AS/400 RPG EXERCISE SUMMARY

The RPG/400 programming exercise closely resembles the COBOL/400 exercise. All source code, DDS, objects, and database files will reside in each programmer's library to minimize problems. If you have already done the COBOL/400 exercise, you may skip steps 1, 2, 3, 6, 7, and 9, as they all relate to the creation of database files. If not, work through all the steps.

The programmer will begin with the creation of a database file, since file creation is so closely linked to program testing:

1. Create an empty physical file as a reference file. For those unfamiliar with COBOL terminology, fields described as 'x' are alphanumeric data, fields described as 's9' are signed numeric data, fields described as '9' are unsigned numeric data, and 'v' indicates an implied decimal point. The source member name will be PERSRFL and should contain the descriptions for the following fields:
   - Last Name—x(15)
   - First Name—x(10)
   - Middle Initial—x(01)
   - SS Number—9(09)
   - Fund—9(02)
   - Department—9(03)
   - Street Address Line 1—x(20)
   - Street Address Line 2—x(20)
   - City—x(20)
   - State—x(02)
   - Zip—x(05)
   - Weekly Salary—s9(5)v99
2. Once the source is entered, the member should be compiled to create its object. Remember that since this is only a reference file, no data will *ever* reside in this object.

3. Before the first RPG/400 program is written, a physical file must be created. This member will be called PERSPFL. Use all the fields from the reference file PERSRFL, in the same order. Make the file keyed, by SS Number (unique). Compile the member to create its object. Data file utility (DFU) may be used through PDM to add data to the database file, but it does very rudimentary edits, so be careful. Be sure to look at the object after the entry operation to ensure that the data was entered properly. Another option for performing this check is to run a Query against the file.
4. Write an RPG/400 batch program, PER003, to print a listing of the PERSPFL database file. Merely read the file in key sequence and print a detail line for each record read. Include SS Number, Last Name, First Name, Middle Initial, Fund, Department, and Weekly Salary on each detail line. Display Edit Weekly Salary (z,zz9.99), and display SS Number with dashes. Put a heading on the report such as 'AS/400 RPG Test Report 1' along with the current date and the page number. Display a final total of the number of database records read.
5. Write another RPG/400 batch program, PER004, using PER003 as a skeleton. This program will update the PERSPFL database and print a report of the updates. Again, read the file sequentially, but update the Weekly Salary field. The value of the update amount will be determined by entry of a PARM into the RPG program via a Control Language program. The PARM should be defined as x(4), both to CL and RPG, but should be moved to a field V9999 in the program. Print the report as in step 4, but do the following:
   - Change the report heading to 'AS/400 RPG Update Report'.
   - Edit the PARM to ensure that it is numeric, displaying an error message on the report and terminating the program if it is not.
   - Add another field to the detail line, displaying Salary both before and after the updates. This will probably necessitate the addition of a second detail line to the report.
   - Display the PARM amount on the report.
   - Audit-trail the number of updates.

6. Create a physical file containing Fund and Department, as previously defined in PERSRFL, and a new field, Department Description (X(50)). This file should be called PERSTFL. After compiling the DDS, use DFU in PDM to load the database.
7. Create a join logical file, PERSJFL, that joins PERSPFL and PERSTFL on Fund and Department. Retain all fields from both files. The primary file will be PERSPFL, and the key to PERSJFL will be SS Number. This join is being done to bring Department Description into the file for the next inquiry program.
8. Write a simple RPG/400 online inquiry program, PEINQY, to run against the join file PERSJFL. Display all fields in PERSJFL, with one database record per screen. Allow for key entry (both partial and full) and paging by SS Number (forward, function key 8; backward, function key 7). Display SS Number with dashes. Set up function key 3 as program exit. Use DDS to create the source for the screen, PEDISPD. If this display file was created for the COBOL/400 exercise, there is no need to re-create it.
9. Create a logical file, PERSLFL, that will contain all fields from PERSRFL. The key to the file will be Last Name, First Name, and Middle Initial. Compile the DDS source to create the logical file. Physical file PERSPFL must exist before the logical path can be created.
10. Write an RPG/400 online update program, PEUPDT, to run against the logical file PERSLFL. Display all fields in PERSLFL, allowing for key entry. Allow changes to existing records as well as the addition of new records. Function key 3 is program exit, and function key 12 cancels the current update, allowing a new key entry. Use DDS to create the source for the screen, PEDSPLD. If this display file was created for the COBOL/400 exercise, there is no need to re-create it. The following edit rules must apply:
    - Changes may not be made to names of existing records.
    - All other fields may be updated.
    - Zip Code, Weekly Salary, Fund, and Department must be numeric.

- Fund and Department must be edited against PERSTFL. PERSTFL must have a corresponding entry.
- SS Number must be numeric, and an error message must be displayed if a duplicate SS number is entered.
- First position(s) of Name fields and City and State fields *may not* be numeric.

5.2 AS/400 DATA DESCRIPTION SPECIFICATIONS—FILES

DDS functions as the mechanism whereby files are described to the AS/400. DDS source code members reside in a source physical file called QDDSSRC inside a user's library. The members in QDDSSRC are compiled to create the objects that can then become the actual files upon which operations can be performed. Additionally, once the members are compiled to become objects, RPG will copy the file layouts into RPG programs when the files are externally defined. The RPG exercise uses four different types of files:

- Reference files—similar to a data dictionary, this file type does not store any physical data but can be used to reference the names and attributes of all the data for a given application. Selected data fields can then be used from the reference file in the creation of physical and logical files in order to maintain consistent naming conventions across files.
- Physical files—data files that can be keyed or not keyed.
- Logical files—files that provide alternate views of a physical file. They can be compared to VSAM alternate keys, but the main difference is that logical file keys need not be contiguous.
- Join logical files—a type of logical file whereby fields from two (or more) physical files can be combined into a single record format for use in an inquiry (only) program.

Refer to Section 4.2 for the specific coding examples required for this exercise.

Additional information on DDS files in RPG can be found in the following books:

- IBM Manual SC21-9659, *Database Guide*. Chapters 2 through 6 explain the setup of physical and logical files very thoroughly.
- IBM Manual SC09-1169, *AS/400 Application Development Tools: Data File Utility User's Guide and Reference*. DFU allows maintenance of database files.
- IBM Manual SC21-9620, *Data Description Specifications Reference*. This manual provides detailed information on DDS, with Chapters 2 and 3 referring specifically to database files.

5.3 AS/400 RPG BATCH PROGRAMMING

RPG/400 in batch mode refers to report and update programs that do *not* use screen layouts for display/maintenance of data. All RPG/400 source code resides in source physical file QRPGSRC inside a user's library. The members in QRPGSRC are compiled to create the objects that can then become the executable programs. The RPG/400 exercise assigns two types of batch programs:

1. A report print program, which merely takes a database file and moves the fields to a print line. Its specifications are detailed in step 4 of the AS/400 RPG exercise summary. This program is set up to run interactively, which means that its execution will tie up the user's AS/400 session until it has finished running. If the program runs quickly, this is not a problem, but if the program is long-running, it is better to submit the job to a batch queue in order to release the terminal.
2. An update and report program, which takes the same database file and does calculations and updates to a numeric field, printing a report with before and after fields. Its specifications are detailed in step 5 of the AS/400 RPG exercise summary. In addition, this program accepts a PARM from an AS/400 data area and is executed in a batch queue by a command connected to a Command Language (CL) program.

Report Print Program

Basically, the report print program sequentially processes a database file and prints the contents of each record on a detail line. The following are pertinent to the coding of this program:

- The source member being edited in QRPGSRC is called PER003, with a TYPE of RPG.
- Make sure you use the prompting (F4) feature while keying in the program. Since RPG has so many types of specifications that are rigidly defined by columns, prompting can substantially ease data entry.
- RPG File Specifications for the externally defined input database file, PERSPFL, must be referenced as such by entry of an 'E' in column 19. File QPRINT, the output report file, is specified normally since it is defined in the program. QPRINT will be the name of the file in the user's output queue when the report is printed.
- RPG Input Specifications for the externally defined file specify the record name, PERSPREC. A record-identifying indicator (in column 19) is used to turn on Indicator 01 for each record read. This is not necessary in this program, but it may be useful in other situations, such as when special processing must be done either before or after all input records have been read.
- The externally defined (via DDS) record description for PERSPREC is automatically placed in the program.
- Calculation specifications are very minimal in this program because report generation is controlled by the normal RPG logic cycle. Since the calculation specifications are executed unconditionally for each input record read, the counter is always incremented by one and each alphanumerically defined Social Security number is moved to a numeric field for ease of output editing.
- The Output Specifications for file QPRINT are defined like any other RPG output file, using the reserved words UDATE for printing the report date and PAGE for printing the page number, as well as normal edit codes for processing numeric fields.
- Once the program is keyed in, it must be compiled (Option 14 from the Work with Members Using PDM screen). After 14 is entered, F4 must be pressed to prompt for RPG/400 compile options. In this way the programmer has the option of controlling the compilation. For example, if he wishes to change the name of the *object* created as a result of the compilation, or the library into which it is compiled, those names can be changed

here. Also, F10 for additional parameters (both source listing options and generation options) allows the programmer to determine what will appear on the output listing. F1 for Help in these instances assists in an explanation of the parameters. The Source Listing option *SECLVL, for example, prints expanded error message text. This is especially helpful when the programmer is new to RPG and/or the AS/400. Generation options assist in the creation of object (executable) code.

- Once the program has compiled, check the output listing in the output queue for errors. If there are any, correct them and recompile the program.
- To execute the program, enter 'CALL PER003' on the command line. Input will be inhibited for a short time since the program is running interactively. The report will be in the user's output queue for review, under the name QPRINT.
- Note that any file(s) being processed by any program must be in the library list of the programmer. If, for example, a production program is being tested, and the programmer wishes to use test files located in a different library, the order of the programmer's library list can be altered by either a CHGLIBL or an ADDLIBLE command. To execute the AS/400 RPG exercise programs, however, programs and data should all reside in the same (the programmer's) library.

The RPG/400 source for the program PER003 is in Listing 5.1. It includes the expansion of the externally defined database file. Listing 5.2 contains a sample of the output report.

Update and Report Program

The update and report program builds on the report print program, using it as a skeleton and adding additional functionality. It sequentially processes a database file, updates a single field on each record based on an external parameter, and prints the contents of each record (both before and after update) on the detail lines. There are certain issues to be aware of with this program:

- The source member being edited in QRPGSRC is called PER004, with a TYPE of RPG.

```
                              IBM AS/400 RPG/400                                                    Page      2
SEQUENCE                                                                    IND    DO    LAST       PAGE   PROGRAM
NUMBER    *...1....+....2....+....3....+....4....+....5....+....6....+....7...*  USE    NUM   UPDATE     LINE   ID
                      S o u r c e   L i s t i n g

     100  F*PROGRAM TO PRINT PERSONNEL REPORT USING EXTERNALLY DEFINED FILES
          H                                                                                             *****
     200  FPERSPFL IP  E                 DISK
           RECORD FORMAT(S):  LIBRARY DPDMLLIB FILE PERSPFL.
                    EXTERNAL FORMAT PERSPREC RPG NAME PERSPREC

     300  FQPRINT  O   F      132      OF      PRINTER

     400  I*
     500  IPERSPREC     01

     500   INPUT  FIELDS FOR RECORD PERSPREC FILE PERSPFL FORMAT PERSPREC.
     500         PERSONNEL FILE
 A000001                                          1  15 LSTNAM                LAST NAME
 A000002                                         16  25 FSTNAM                FIRST NAME
 A000003                                         26  26 MIDINT                MIDDLE INITIAL
 A000004                                         27  35 SSNUM                 SOCIAL SECURITY NUMBER
 A000005                                         36  37 FUND                  FUND
 A000006                                         38  40 DEPT                  DEPT
 A000007                                         41  60 ADDR1                 ADDRESS LINE 1
 A000008                                         61  80 ADDR2                 ADDRESS LINE 2
 A000009                                         81 100 CITY                  CITY
 A000010                                        101 102 STATE                 STATE
 A000011                                        103 107 ZIP                   ZIP
 A000012                                       P 108 1112WKYSAL               WEEKLY SALARY
    1000  C                     ADD  1         CNTR    50       COUNTER
    1100  C                     MOVE SSNUM     SSNUMN  90       NUMERIC SSN

    1200  O*
    1300  OQPRINT  H    08   1P
    1400  O        OR        OF
    1500  O                         UDATE Y    8
    1600  O                                   78 'AS/400 TEST RPG REPORT '
    1700  O                                  126 'PAGE'
    1800  O                         PAGE     132
    1900  O        H    1012 1P
    2000  O        OR        OF
    2100  O                                    9 'LAST NAME'
    2200  O                                   29 'FIRST NAME MI'
    2300  O                                   41 'SOC SEC NUM'
    2400  O                                   49 'FND DPT'
    2500  O                                   64 'ADDRESS LINE 1'
    2600  O                                   85 'ADDRESS LINE 2'
    2700  O                                   96 'CITY'
    2800  O                                  120 'ST ZIP'
    2900  O                                  132 'WKLY SAL'
    3000  O        D 1       01
    3100  O                         LSTNAM    15
```

Listing 5.1. Source for PER003.

```
                                IBM AS/400 RPG/400                                                               Page        3
SEQUENCE                                                                       IND    DO   LAST       PAGE   PROGRAM
NUMBER   *...1....+....2....+....3....+....4....+....5....+....6....+....7...* USE    NUM  UPDATE     LINE   ID

    3200 O                         FSTNAM    26
    3300 O                         MIDINT    28
    3400 O                         SSNUMN    41 'O   -  -    '
    3500 O                         FUND      44
    3600 O                         DEPT      49
    3700 O                         ADDR1     70
    3800 O                         ADDR2     91
    3900 O                         CITY     112
    4000 O                         STATE    116
    4100 O                         ZIP      122
    4200 O                         WKYSAL1  132
    4300 O        T 3      LR
    4400 O                                   50 'END OF REPORT'
    4500 O                                   70 'RECORDS PROCESSED  '
    4600 O                         CNTR  1   80
    4700 O*

         * * * * *   E N D   O F   S O U R C E   * * * * *

         A d d i t i o n a l   D i a g n o s t i c   M e s s a g e s

* 7086      200   RPG PROVIDES BLOCK OR UNBLOCK SUPPORT FOR FILE PERSPFL.
```

Listing 5.1. *(cont.)*

```
 2/03/92                                AS/400 TEST RPG REPORT                                                      PAGE     1

LAST NAME      FIRST NAME MI SOC SEC NUM FND DPT ADDRESS LINE 1       ADDRESS LINE 2      CITY                ST ZIP    WKLY SAL


Taylor         Opie          000-00-0000 07  700 233 Elm St                               Mayberry            NC 44444     300.42
Mertz          Fred       A  040-40-4040 02  003 333 Willow                               Wheaton             IL 60187     294.36
Majkowski      Don           098-76-3456 01  001 123 Cheese Lane                          Green Bay           WI 65655   8,120.46
Ricardo        Lucy       M  111-11-1111 01  001 321 E 68th St.                           New York            NY 10000     203.01
Ricardo        Ricky      A  222-22-2222 01  002 321 E. 68th St.      Apt 1               New York            NY 10000     279.11
Petrie         Rob           222-23-2121 01  001 147 Bonnie Meadow Rd                     New Rochelle        NY 10505   5,075.29
Mertz          Ethel         333-33-3333 02  001 333 Willow                               Wheaton             IL 60187      45.65
Petrie         Laura         456-75-5555 03  003 147 Bonnie Meadow Rd                     New Rochelle        NY 10505     710.53
Taylor         Andy          553-33-3559 01  002 333 Main St                              Mayberry            NC 33333     406.02
Taylor         Bee           555-55-5555 01  001 333 Main St                              Mayberry            NC 33333     203.01
Fife           Barney        666-66-6666 03  003 Boarding House       555 Spruce St       Mayberry            NC 44444     228.36
Brown          Murphy        678-91-2345 01  001 Newsroom                                 Washington          DC 30303     710.53
Campbell       Otis       A  777-77-7777 04  400 County Jail          Suite 1             Mayberry            NC 44444      55.80
Pyle           Gomer         888-88-8888 04  400 Marine Boot Camp                         Ft Pendleton        CA 90909     304.51
Banks          Ernie         909-09-0909 03  003 Wrigley Field                            Chicago             IL 60606   1,435.26
Pyle           Goober        999-99-9999 05  500 Filling Station                          Mayberry            NC 44444      76.10
Anderson       Neal          567-89-6666 01  001 Halas Hall                               Lake Forest         IL 60000  10,150.60

                                  END OF REPORT RECORDS PROCESSED          17
```

Listing 5.2. PER003 output report.

- In the File Specifications the FILE TYPE parameter (column 15) is coded as 'U' for file PERSPFL. This is to indicate that it is an updateable file. Also, the FILE DESIGNATION parameter (column 16) is coded as 'F', which denotes that PERSPFL is a full procedural file. A full procedural file is allowed both sequential and random access in the same program. While this program accesses the file only sequentially, full procedural file processing allows the programmer maximum flexibility.
- Data structures are explicitly defined in the input specifications for work fields used by the program. In this program work fields are defined for each position in the alphanumerically defined parameter, so that each position may be edited for valid numeric values.
- The Calculation Specifications begin with the parameter list statement (*ENTRY PLIST). This statement indicates that a list of parameters is being passed to the program. Those parameters are listed immediately after the *ENTRY PLIST statement. In this case there is a 4-position alphanumeric field being passed to the program, PARAM.
- Exception processing (EXCPT) is used for all print output in the program. This is so that print processing can circumvent the RPG logic cycle. If, as in this program, a nonnumeric parameter is entered, the program stops processing before the first database record is read. With exception output, all output records have TYPE of 'E' in column 15 and a special EXCPT name for each print line in column 32, so that the EXCPT Calculation Specifications can print header, detail, and total lines as required.
- The program is set up as a simple loop. After editing the parameter, the program reads and updates database records and then prints the corresponding detail lines.
- Indicator 99 is used to control the printing of the invalid parameter message. The last record (LR) indicator is also set on when an invalid parameter is encountered , in order to go to end-of-job processing.
- Since the program is called by a CL program, the RETRN statement at its end returns control to the caller. This would be of particular importance if the CL program had additional functions to perform following the call to PER004.

- A data area is created so that the parameter field can be passed to the program. It is created externally to the RPG program, with the command CRTDTAARA. Any updates to the field use the command CHGDTAARA. The value of the data area may be displayed via the command DSPDTAARA. Data areas within library are often used as what could be considered control cards in the mainframe environment.
- A Command Language (CL) program must be created to extract the data area as well as to call the RPG program to execute. The variable associated with the data area must be declared, the data area must be retrieved (with the command RTVDTAARA), and the RPG program must be called. The CL program source must reside in file QCLSRC with a TYPE of CLP (Command Language program) and must be compiled (again, Option 14 from the Work with Members Using PDM screen).
- A command must be created so that the CL program can be executed in the QBATCH subsystem so as not to tie up the workstation while the program is executing. A member in file QCMDSRC must be created with a TYPE of CMD that contains the statement CMD. Then the member must be compiled (Option 14) and F4 must be pressed in order for parameters to be entered. The PROGRAM TO PROCESS COMMAND parameter must contain the name of the CL program created in the previous step. This is the only required parameter.
- The final step for executing the program is command SBMJOB. Press F4 to prompt on the command, entering the command created in the previous step on the COMMAND TO RUN parameter. Other parameters on this screen may be modified, but default values based on the user's job description will be sufficient.

The RPG/400 source for the program PER004, including copybooks, is shown in Listing 5.3. The CL source for program PER004CL and the command source for PER004CMD are shown in Listings 5.4 and 5.5, respectively. Two samples of output reports are also presented:

```
                                   IBM SAA RPG/400                                                                      Page    2
SEQUENCE                                                                             IND   DO   LAST       PAGE   PROGRAM
NUMBER    *...1....+....2....+....3....+....4....+....5....+....6....+....7...*  USE   NUM  UPDATE     LINE   ID
                     S o u r c e   L i s t i n g

     100  F*PROGRAM TO UPDATE PERSONNEL DATA USING PARAMETER SUPPLIED VIA
     200  F*CL PROGRAM
          H
     300  FPERSPFL UF  E           K        DISK                                                    *****
           RECORD FORMAT(S):  LIBRARY DPDMLLIB FILE PERSPFL.
                    EXTERNAL FORMAT PERSPREC RPG NAME PERSPREC
     400  FQPRINT  O   F     132     OF      PRINTER

     500  I*
     600  IPERSPREC     01
     600   INPUT  FIELDS FOR RECORD PERSPREC FILE PERSPFL FORMAT PERSPREC.
     600        PERSONNEL FILE
 A000001                                             1  15 LSTNAM           LAST NAME
 A000002                                            16  25 FSTNAM           FIRST NAME
 A000003                                            26  26 MIDINT           MIDDLE INITIAL
 A000004                                            27  35 SSNUM            SOCIAL SECURITY NUMBER
 A000005                                            36  37 FUND             FUND
 A000006                                            38  40 DEPT             DEPT
 A000007                                            41  60 ADDR1            ADDRESS LINE 1
 A000008                                            61  80 ADDR2            ADDRESS LINE 2
 A000009                                            81 100 CITY             CITY
 A000010                                           101 102 STATE            STATE
 A000011                                           103 107 ZIP              ZIP
 A000012                                         P 108 1112WKYSAL           WEEKLY SALARY
     700  I#WPARM      DS
     800  I                                          1   1 #WP1
     900  I                                          2   2 #WP2
    1000  I                                          3   3 #WP3
    1100  I                                          4   4 #WP4

    1200  C           *ENTRY    PLIST
    1300  C                     PARM           PARAM   4
    1400  C                     MOVE PARAM     #WPARM
    1500  C           #WP1      IFGE *ZEROS                                  B001
    1600  C           #WP2      ANDGE*ZEROS                                   001
    1700  C           #WP3      ANDGE*ZEROS                                   001
    1800  C           #WP4      ANDGE*ZEROS                                   001
    1900  C                     MOVE PARAM     NPARAM  44                     001
    2000  C                     ELSE                                         X001
    2100  C                     SETON                    LR          1        001
    2200  C                     SETON                    99          1        001
    2300  C                     END                                          E001
    2400  C  LR                 GOTO EOF
    2500  C                     EXCPTHEAD1
    2600  C                     EXCPTHEAD2
    2700  C           READ      TAG
    2800  C                     READ PERSPFL                LR     3
    2900  C  LR                 GOTO EOF
```

Listing 5.3. Source for PER004.

```
                                      IBM SAA RPG/400                                                          Page      3
SEQUENCE                                                                       IND    DO    LAST       PAGE    PROGRAM
NUMBER    *...1....+....2....+....3....+....4....+....5....+....6....+....7...*  USE    NUM   UPDATE     LINE    ID

    3000  C                     MOVE WKYSAL    OLDSAL  72
    3100  C                     ADD  1         CNTR    50        COUNTER
    3200  C                     MOVE SSNUM     SSNUMN  90        NUMERIC SSN
    3300  C           1         ADD  NPARAM    PARAM1  54
    3400  C           WKYSAL    MULT PARAM1    WKYSAL
    3500  C                     UPDATPERSPREC
    3600  C                     EXCPTDET1
    3700  C                     EXCPTDET2
    3800  C   OF                EXCPTHEAD1
    3900  C   OF                EXCPTHEAD2
    4000  C                     ADD  1         UCNTR   50        UPDATE COUNTER
    4100  C                     GOTO READ
    4200  C           EOF       TAG
    4300  C                     EXCPTHEAD1
    4400  C                     EXCPTHEAD2
    4500  C                     EXCPTTOT1
    4600  C                     EXCPTTOT2
    4700  C                     RETRN

    4800  O*
    4900  OQPRINT  E    08              HEAD1
    5000  O                             UDATE Y    8
    5100  O                                       78 'AS/400 TEST RPG UPDATE '
    5200  O                                       84 'REPORT'
    5300  O                                      126 'PAGE'
    5400  O                             PAGE     132
    5500  O        E    1012            HEAD2
    5600  O                                        9 'LAST NAME'
    5700  O                                       29 'FIRST NAME MI'
    5800  O                                       41 'SOC SEC NUM'
    5900  O                                       49 'FND DPT'
    6000  O                                       64 'ADDRESS LINE 1'
    6100  O                                       85 'ADDRESS LINE 2'
    6200  O                                       96 'CITY'
    6300  O                                      120 'ST ZIP'
    6400  O        E 1                  DET1
    6500  O                             LSTNAM    15
    6600  O                             FSTNAM    26
    6700  O                             MIDINT    28
    6800  O                             SSNUMN    41 '0   -  -    '
    6900  O                             FUND      44
    7000  O                             DEPT      49
    7100  O                             ADDR1     70
    7200  O                             ADDR2     91
    7300  O                             CITY     112
    7400  O                             STATE    116
    7500  O                             ZIP      122
    7600  O        E 1                  DET2
    7700  O                                       13 'OLD SALARY:'
    7800  O                             OLDSAL1   25
    7900  O                                       39 'NEW SALARY:'
    8000  O                             WKYSAL1   52
    8100  O        E 3                  TOT1
```

Listing 5.3. *(cont.)*

```
                                 IBM SAA RPG/400                                                                Page     4
SEQUENCE                                                                           IND    DO    LAST      PAGE   PROGRAM
NUMBER   *...1....+....2....+....3....+....4....+....5....+....6....+....7...*    USE    NUM   UPDATE    LINE   ID
    8200 O                                  18 'NUMBER OF DATABASE'
    8300 O                                  31 'RECORDS READ'
    8400 O                        CNTR  1   41
    8500 O                                  18 'NUMBER OF DATABASE'
    8600 O                                  78 'RECORDS UPDATED'
    8700 O                        UCNTR 1   87
    8800 O        E 1             TOT2
    8900 O                                  15 'VALUE OF UPDATE'
    9000 O                                  25 'PARAMETER'
    9100 O                        NPARAM1   35
    9200 O                 99     PARAM     35
    9300 O                 99               55  INVALID PARAMETER.
    9400 O                 99               82 'NO UPDATES DONE.'
    9500 O*
 B000000  OUTPUT FIELDS FOR RECORD PERSPREC FILE PERSPFL FORMAT PERSPREC.
 B000000        PERSONNEL FILE
 B000001                          LSTNAM    15  CHAR   15                     LAST NAME
 B000002                          FSTNAM    25  CHAR   10                     FIRST NAME
 B000003                          MIDINT    26  CHAR    1                     MIDDLE INITIAL
 B000004                          SSNUM     35  CHAR    9                     SOCIAL SECURITY NUMBER
 B000005                          FUND      37  CHAR    2                     FUND
 B000006                          DEPT      40  CHAR    3                     DEPT
 B000007                          ADDR1     60  CHAR   20                     ADDRESS LINE 1
 B000008                          ADDR2     80  CHAR   20                     ADDRESS LINE 2
 B000009                          CITY     100  CHAR   20                     CITY
 B000010                          STATE    102  CHAR    2                     STATE
 B000011                          ZIP      107  CHAR    5                     ZIP
 B000012                          WKYSAL   111P PACK  7,2                     WEEKLY SALARY

         * * * * *   E N D   O F   S O U R C E   * * * * *

        A d d i t i o n a l   D i a g n o s t i c   M e s s a g e s
```

Listing 5.3. *(cont.)*

```
                                SEU SOURCE LISTING

SOURCE FILE . . . . . . .  DPDMLLIB/QCLSRC
MEMBER  . . . . . . . . .  PER004CL

SEQNBR*...+... 1 ...+... 2 ...+... 3 ...+... 4 ...+... 5 ...+... 6 ...+... 7 ...+... 8 ...+... 9 ...+... 0
  100            PGM
  301            DCL        VAR(&PER) TYPE(*CHAR) LEN(4) VALUE('    ')
  302            RTVDTAARA  DTAARA(PERVAR) RTNVAR(&PER)
  500            CALL       PGM(PER004) PARM(&PER)
  700            ENDPGM

                         * * * *  E N D  O F  S O U R C E  * * * *
```

Listing 5.4. CL source for PER004CL.

```
                                  SEU SOURCE LISTING

SOURCE FILE . . . . . . .   DPDMLLIB/QCMDSRC
MEMBER  . . . . . . . . .   PER004CMD

SEQNBR*...+... 1 ...+... 2 ...+... 3 ...+... 4 ...+... 5 ...+... 6 ...+... 7 ...+... 8 ...+... 9 ...+... 0
   100 CMD

                      * * * *  E N D  O F  S O U R C E  * * * *
```

Listing 5.5. Command source for PER004CMD.

1. Output for a valid update run (Listing 5.6).
2. Output for a run with an invalid parameter, abnormally terminating processing (Listing 5.7).

Additional RPG/400 Batch Programming Features

Periodically, programs do abend. If they do, a break message usually appears to the individual submitting the job. The program will not continue/stop until a response is entered. In general, the responses are:

- C—cancel processing without a dump.
- R—retry the operation.
- D—cancel processing and dump the RPG identifiers.
- F—cancel processing and dump *all* identifiers.

Any dumps go either to queue QPGMDUMP or queue QEZDEBUG and can be viewed/printed from there.

There is a debugging tool available on the AS/400. It can be started by the command STRDBG and ended by the command ENDDBG. In between, breakpoints can be set, data fields can be interrogated, and so on. The complete list of debug commands can be viewed from the CMDDBG menu. In addition, Chapter 4 of the *RPG/400 User's Guide* leads the programmer through the debug process.

A more structured approach may be used in RPG programming by the use of internal and external subroutines, which help to eliminate some of the GOTOs in programs. Internal subroutines exist inside the RPG program; external subroutines exist outside and are generally for frequently used system-wide functions. Internal subroutines exist within programs by the use of statements BEGSR and ENDSR. The calculation specifications between those two statements consist of the subroutine. Subroutines can be used for print routines, rewrite routines, and various exception-processing routines. In addition, DOW (Do While), DOU (Do Until), and CAS (Case Logic) can be incorporated into the Calculation Specifications to further structure RPG code.

The prompting facility of the AS/400 makes it easier and more understandable to code RPG programs. Prompting is avail-

```
                                              AS/400 TEST RPG UPDATE REPORT                                              PAGE      1
LAST NAME       FIRST NAME MI SOC SEC NUM FND DPT ADDRESS LINE 1        ADDRESS LINE 2         CITY              ST ZIP

Mertz           Fred       A  040-40-4040 02  003 333 Willow                                  Wheaton           IL 60187
  OLD SALARY:    1,136.86   NEW SALARY:     1,142.54
Majkowski       Don           098-76-3456 01  001 123 Cheese Lane                             Green Bay         WI 65655
  OLD SALARY:   31,362.97   NEW SALARY:    31,519.78
Ricardo         Lucy       M  111-11-1111 01  001 321 E 68th St.                              New York          NY 10000
  OLD SALARY:      784.05   NEW SALARY:       787.97
Smith           CCC           123-32-3232 01  001 2323                                        Chicago           IL 60606
  OLD SALARY:    3,441.58   NEW SALARY:     3,458.78
Jones           AA         l  222-22-2223 01  001 123 main st                                 Chicago           il 60606
  OLD SALARY:      344.14   NEW SALARY:       345.86
Ricardo         Ricky      A  222-22-2222 01  002 321 E. 68th St.      Apt 1                  New York          NY 10000
  OLD SALARY:    1,077.96   NEW SALARY:     1,083.34
Petrie          Rob           222-23-2121 01  001 147 Bonnie Meadow Rd                        New Rochelle      NY 10505
  OLD SALARY:   19,601.87   NEW SALARY:    19,699.87
Smith           BBB           232-32-2223 01  001 23323                                       Wheaton           IL 60187
  OLD SALARY:      344.14   NEW SALARY:       345.86
Mertz           Ethel         333-33-3333 02  001 333 Willow                                  Wheaton           IL 60187
  OLD SALARY:      176.26   NEW SALARY:       177.14
Petrie          Laura         456-75-5555 03  003 147 Bonnie Meadow Rd                        New Rochelle      NY 10505
  OLD SALARY:    2,744.19   NEW SALARY:     2,757.91
Taylor          Bee           555-55-5555 01  001 333 Main St                                 Mayberry          NC 33333
  OLD SALARY:      784.05   NEW SALARY:       787.97
Smith           AAA           566-55-5555 01  001 1234                                        Chicago           IL 60606
  OLD SALARY:      344.14   NEW SALARY:       345.86
Anderson        Neal          567-89-6666 01  001 Halas Hall                                  Lake Forest       IL 60000
  OLD SALARY:   39,203.82   NEW SALARY:    39,399.83
Taylor          Andy          666-66-6665 01  002 333 Main St                                 Mayberry          NC 33333
  OLD SALARY:    1,655.78   NEW SALARY:     1,664.05
Fife            Barney        666-66-6666 03  003 Boarding House       555 Spruce St          Mayberry          NC 44444
  OLD SALARY:      881.95   NEW SALARY:       886.35
Brown           Murphy        678-91-2345 01  001 Newsroom                                    Washington        DC 30303
  OLD SALARY:    2,744.19   NEW SALARY:     2,757.91
Campbell        Otis       A  777-77-7777 04  400 County Jail          Suite 1                Mayberry          NC 44444
  OLD SALARY:      215.47   NEW SALARY:       216.54
Pyle            Gomer         888-88-8888 04  400 Marine Boot Camp                            Ft Pendleton      CA 90909
  OLD SALARY:    1,176.05   NEW SALARY:     1,181.93
Stone           Harry         899-88-8888 01  001 123 Bowery                                  New York          NY 10101
  OLD SALARY:    3,441.58   NEW SALARY:     3,458.78
Taylor          Opie          900-00-0000 07  700 233 Elm St                                  Mayberry          NC 44444
  OLD SALARY:    1,160.25   NEW SALARY:     1,166.05
Taylor          C             908-76-9800 01  001 dddd                                        Chicago           IL 60606
  OLD SALARY:      344.14   NEW SALARY:       345.86
Banks           Ernie         909-09-0909 03  003 Wrigley Field                               Chicago           IL 60606
  OLD SALARY:    5,543.27   NEW SALARY:     5,570.98
Pyle            Goober        999-99-9999 05  500 Filling Station                             Mayberry          NC 44444
  OLD SALARY:      293.89   NEW SALARY:       295.35
```

Listing 5.6. Valid update run report.

```
                                        AS/400 TEST RPG UPDATE REPORT                                          PAGE     2
LAST NAME       FIRST NAME MI SOC SEC NUM FND DPT ADDRESS LINE 1       ADDRESS LINE 2       CITY                 ST ZIP

NUMBER OF DATABASE RECORDS READ       23                    RECORDS UPDATED       23
VALUE OF UPDATE PARAMETER      .0050
```

Listing 5.6. *(cont.)*

```
                                          AS/400 TEST RPG UPDATE REPORT                                               PAGE     1
LAST NAME      FIRST NAME MI SOC SEC NUM FND DPT ADDRESS LINE 1       ADDRESS LINE 2       CITY                 ST ZIP


NUMBER OF DATABASE RECORDS READ          0                     RECORDS UPDATED        0
VALUE OF UPDATE PARAMETER     .9NNN INVALID PARAMETER.            NO UPDATES DONE.
```

Listing 5.7. Report of an invalid parameter.

able via the F4 key on any line of code during an RPG/400 edit session. It is available for all specification types. Data is entered into fields corresponding to the columns on the RPG specifications; however, the fields are headed in a meaningful way so that data entry is accomplished simply, without the programmer having to know exact column numbers for fields on RPG specifications. For example, prompting eliminates the need to know whether File Designation on the File Specification belongs in column 15 or column 16. In addition, the AS/400 does rudimentary syntax checking of each line of code to assist in error correction. Specification and corresponding prompt types on the AS/400 include the following:

- H—Control Specifications. Header specifications that contain information about program generation and execution; this is an optional specification when default values are used.
- F—File Description Specifications. Describes all files used in the program.
- E—Extension Specifications. Describes all arrays and tables used in the program.
- L—Line Counter Specifications. Contains information regarding the printing of reports.
- I—Input Specifications. Describes records, fields, data structures, and named constants used in the program.
- C—Calculation Specifications. Describes calculations and the order in which they are processed in the program. Calculation Specifications control many I/O functions.
- O—Output Specifications. Describes records and fields written by the program.
- U—Auto Report Specifications. Used in conjunction with the Auto Report feature, which is not covered in this writeup.

Figures 5.1 and 5.2 are examples of prompt screens for line 3.00 of File Specifications and line 30.00 of Calculation Specifications.

Additional information on RPG/400 batch programming can be found in the following books:

```
Columns . . . :   1 71              Edit                    DPDMLLIB/QRPGSRC
SEU==>                                                               PEUPDT
FMT *  ..... *. 1 ...+... 2 ...+... 3 ...+... 4 ...+... 5 ...+... 6 ...+... 7
       ************** Beginning of data ***********************************
0001.00      F*PROGRAM TO UPDATE PERSONNEL DATA USING EXTERNALLY DEFINED FILES
0002.00      FPERSLFL UF  E            K        DISK                      A
0003.00      FPERSTFL IF  E            K        DISK
0004.00      FPERSPLD CF  E                     WORKSTN
0005.00      E                      ERR       1 3 50
Prompt type . . . FX             Sequence number . . . 0003.00

              File       File          End of                  File
Filename      Type    Designation       File      Sequence    Format
PERSTFL        I           F                                    E
  Mode of          Record
Processing      Address Type       Device      Continuation
                     K             DISK
                      File             File
Exit     Entry       Addition          Condition



F3=Exit   F4=Prompt   F5=Refresh           F11=Previous record
F12=Cancel            F23=Select prompt    F24=More keys
    14-02      SA         MW        KS         IM         II S1        KB
```

Figure 5.1. File Specification prompt screen.

```
  Columns . . . :   1 71          Edit                        DPDMLLIB/QRPGSRC
  SEU==>                                                                PEUPDT
  FMT C  .....CLON01N02N03Factor1+++OpcdeFactor2+++ResultLenDHHiLoEqComments++++
0030.00      C                      MOVE ERR,3     MSGLIN
0031.00      C                      ELSE
0032.00      C                      SETON                       80
0033.00      C                      EXSR INIT
0034.00      C                      MOVE ERR,2      MSGLIN
0035.00      C                      END
0036.00      C           LOOP2      TAG
0037.00      C                      SETON                       87
0038.00      C                      WRITEPERMSG
0039.00      C                      EXFMTPERFLDS
 Prompt type . . .    C     Sequence number . . .  0030.00

Level    N01N02N03 Factor 1     Operation      Factor 2       Result
                                  MOVE         ERR,3          MSGLIN
             Decimal
Length     Positions    H/A   HI   LO   EQ   Comment


F3=Exit    F4=Prompt    F5=Refresh         F11=Previous record
F12=Cancel              F23=Select prompt  F24=More keys

   17-03      SA        MW        KS        IM        II S1      KB
```

Figure 5.2. Calculation Specification prompt screen.

- IBM Manual SC09-1161, *RPG/400 User's Guide*. This book details ways to write, compile, test, debug, and run RPG/400 programs.
- IBM Manual SC09-1089, *RPG/400 Reference*. This book details program structure and is a general reference for RPG/400.
- IBM Manuals SC21-9775 through SC21-9779, *CL Reference*, Volumes 1-5. These books provide detailed information about each CL command on the AS/400.
- IBM Manual SC21-8076, *Command Reference Summary*. This book summarizes the commands in the *CL Reference*.

5.4 AS/400 DATA DESCRIPTION SPECIFICATIONS—SCREENS

This section reviews AS/400 DDS for display file (screen) creation.

DDS is the mechanism that describes screens to the AS/400. DDS source code members reside in a source physical file called QDDSSRC inside a user's library. The members in QDDSSRC are compiled to create the objects that are the actual display files upon which operations can be performed. Additionally, once members are compiled to become objects, RPG will copy the screen layouts into the RPG programs when the files are externally defined. The RPG exercise creates two screens:

1. An inquiry-only screen, which displays data from a database file.
2. An update screen, which allows adds and updates to a database file.

The simplest way to code DDS for screens is to first review the specifications for the RPG exercise. Step 8 describes the inquiry program, and step 10 describes the update program. Screen formats will be the same as those used in the COBOL/400 exercise. Then review the reference material described at the end of this section, particularly Chapter 8 in the *RPG/400 User's Guide*. It is important to see exactly how the screen layouts interact with the RPG statements in order to get the total picture.

Refer back to Section 4.4 for the specific coding examples required for this exercise.

Additional information on DDS screens in RPG can be found in the following books:

- IBM Manual SC21-9620, *Data Description Specifications Reference*. This manual provides detailed information on DDS, with Chapter 4 devoted specifically to display files.
- IBM Manual SC09-1161, *RPG/400 User's Guide*. Chapter 8, in particular, explains the use of WORKSTN files.
- IBM Manual SC09-1171, *Application Development Tools: Screen Design Aid User's Guide and Reference*. This guide steps the user through this AS/400 utility, which helps in the creation of screens by creating DDS source as the user 'paints' the screen. This can be used *after* the user has gained some familiarity with and understanding of basic DDS.

5.5 AS/400 RPG ONLINE PROGRAMMING

RPG/400 in online mode refers to inquiry and update programs that use display stations for display/maintenance of data. All RPG/400 source code resides in source physical file QRPGSRC inside a user's library. The members in QRPGSRC are compiled to create the objects, which can then become the executable programs. The RPG/400 exercise assigns two types of online programs:

1. Inquiry program—merely takes a database file and moves the fields to the screen according to key fields entered by the user. The specifications for the program are detailed in step 8 of the AS/400 RPG exercise summary. It is set up to run interactively, which means that it will tie up an AS/400 session until the user ends it.
2. Update program—based on key fields entered by the user; database records can either be added or updated. The specifications for the program are detailed in step 10 of the AS/400 RPG exercise summary. Like the inquiry program, it is set up to run interactively.

Inquiry Program

The inquiry program displays database records based on key fields entered on a prompt screen. Many of the characteristics of RPG/400 in the batch environment are similar to RPG/400 in the online environment, but because of the use of display files (discussed in Section 5.4), there are some unique programming considerations, including the following:

- The source member being edited in QRPGSRC is called PEINQY, with a TYPE of RPG.
- The File Specification for PEDISPD, the display file, indicates a FILE TYPE of 'C', which stands for combined input-output file. In addition, the DEVICE parameter is set to WORKSTN, signifying that the file is processed via a workstation device. Display files must also be defined as full procedural files. Note also that the display file is the same one used in the COBOL/400 exercise.
- The Input Specifications indicate a data structure for a redefined field, SSNUM. SSNUM exists in file PERSJFL and, in the data structure, is redefined to be three fields. The three fields are used to display-edit the Social Security number on the output screen. Had the SSNUM field been defined as numeric in the database, the display-editing for the field could have been done in the DDS for the display file (via an edit word) instead of in the RPG program.
- A second data structure, #WORK, is specified in the Input Specifications. #WORK is used to display-edit field SSNUM.
- The Calculation Specifications are set up as a basic loop in which the prompt screen is displayed, with detail records displayed based on the entry on the prompt screen.
- The EXFMT operation with a record name writes, then reads the specified format of the display file.
- Function keys 03 (End Program), 07 (Read Previous Record), and 08 (Read Next Record) are defined in the display file and control the program's processing. They are used as Indicators 03, 07, and 08.
- Indicators 98 and 99, which are used as resulting indicators for invalid I/O functions, are defined and controlled by the display file (PEDISPD).

- Operation SETLL (Set Lower Limit) positions the database file at the next record with a key greater than or equal to that specified in the statement. The operation can point to a record either by a specific or a generic key. Note that a database read must still be done in order to actually access the record pointed to by the SETLL.
- READ (Read the Next Record Sequentially) and READP (Read the Previous Record Sequentially) are used to actually access the database records based on the function key pressed.
- Repetitive processes are executed by subroutines, such as I/O and display-edit processes.
- No Output Specifications are coded in the program—all outputs are handled by the WORKSTN file.
- After the program is keyed in, it must be compiled (Option 14 from the Work with Members Using PDM screen). After entering 14, press F4 to prompt for RPG/400 compile options. They are the same as those discussed in Section 5.3.
- Once the program has been compiled, check the output listing in the output queue for errors. If there are any, correct them and recompile the program.
- To execute the program, enter 'CALL PEINQY' on the command line. The program will control the workstation until the user ends its execution.
- Note that if the program goes into a loop (or otherwise ties up the workstation), the user can press the ALT/SYSRQ keys to start an alternate session. When the System Request Menu is displayed, Option 2 (End Previous Request) should be selected. Perhaps at this point the programmer should utilize the debugging features available, which were detailed in Section 5.3.
- The file(s) being processed by any program must be in the library list of the programmer. If, for example, a production program is being tested, and the programmer wishes to use test files located in a different library, the order of the programmer's library list can be altered either by a CHGLIBL command or by an ADDLIBLE command. For the AS/400 RPG exercise programs to execute, however, programs and data should all reside in the same (the programmer's) library.

The RPG/400 source for the program PEINQY is shown in Listing 5.8. Figures 5.3 and 5.4 show the following two sample screen layouts:

1. The prompt screen.
2. The prompt screen plus the resulting detail screen.

Update Program

The update program builds on the inquiry program, using it as a skeleton and adding additional functionality. It adds or updates database records based on key fields entered on a prompt screen, incorporating edit logic and use of a second database file for edit purposes. The programming techniques used in this program are as follows:

- The source member being edited in QRPGSRC is called PEUPDT, with a TYPE of RPG.
- There are three files described in the File Specifications: the logical view of the database (PERSLFL), the display file (PEDSPLD), and the table database file against which entered data is validated (PERSTFL). Note that PERSLFL has an 'A' in the File Addition field (column 66) on its File Specification to denote that records may be added to the database. Also, PEDSPLD is the same as that utilized in the COBOL/400 exercise.
- Following the File Specifications are the Extension Specifications. Extension Specifications describe the compile time array used for error messages in this program. The Extension Specifications detail the name of the array (ERR), the number of entries in each input record (1), the number of entries in the array (3), and the length of each entry (50 positions). The error array is coded following the source code for the program and is noted by '**' in columns 1–3 of the statement *prior* to the error messages. The error messages are moved to screen fields by the specification of the explicit entry number in the ERR array in the Calculation Specifications.
- The Input Specifications include redefinitions of several database fields so that edits may be done to prevent invalid data from being written to databases.

```
                         IBM SAA RPG/400                                                                              Page        2
SEQUENCE                                                                                  IND    DO    LAST        PAGE   PROGRAM
NUMBER    *...1....+....2....+....3....+....4....+....5....+....6....+....7...*  USE    NUM   UPDATE      LINE   ID
                        S o u r c e   L i s t i n g

     100  F*PROGRAM TO DISPLAY PERSONNEL DATA USING EXTERNALLY DEFINED FILES
          H                                                                                                    *****
     200  FPERSJFL IF  E           K        DISK
           RECORD FORMAT(S):  LIBRARY DPDMLLIB FILE PERSJFL.
                    EXTERNAL FORMAT PERSJREC RPG NAME PERSJREC

     300  FPEDISPD CF  E                    WORKSTN
           RECORD FORMAT(S):  LIBRARY DPDMLLIB FILE PEDISPD.
                    EXTERNAL FORMAT PERPRM RPG NAME PERPRM
                    EXTERNAL FORMAT PERFLDS RPG NAME PERFLDS


 A000000   INPUT  FIELDS FOR RECORD PERSJREC FILE PERSJFL FORMAT PERSJREC.
 A000000         PERS JOIN LOGICAL FILE
 A000001                                           1  15 LSTNAM               LAST NAME
 A000002                                          16  25 FSTNAM               FIRST NAME
 A000003                                          26  26 MIDINT               MIDDLE INITIAL
 A000004                                          27  35 SSNUM                SOCIAL SECURITY NUMBER
 A000005                                          36  37 FUND                 FUND
 A000006                                          38  40 DEPT                 DEPT
 A000007                                          41  90 DESCR                DEPARTMENT
 A000008                                          91 110 ADDR1                ADDRESS LINE 1
 A000009                                         111 130 ADDR2                ADDRESS LINE 2
 A000010                                         131 150 CITY                 CITY
 A000011                                         151 152 STATE                STATE
 A000012                                         153 157 ZIP                  ZIP
 A000013                                       P 158 1612WKYSAL               WEEKLY SALARY
 B000000   INPUT  FIELDS FOR RECORD PERPRM FILE PEDISPD FORMAT PERPRM.
 B000000         SSN PROMPT
 B000001                                           1   1 *IN03                END OF PROGRAM
 B000002                                           2   2 *IN07                PREVIOUS RECORD
 B000003                                           3   3 *IN08                NEXT RECORD
 B000004                                           5   5 *IN98                FILE ERROR. PRESS RESET, THEN ENTER OR F3
 B000005                                           4   4 *IN99                FILE AT TOP OR BOTTOM.     PRESS RESET, THEN ENTER
 B000006                                           6  14 SSNUM                SOCIAL SECURITY NUMBER
 C000000   INPUT  FIELDS FOR RECORD PERFLDS FILE PEDISPD FORMAT PERFLDS.
 C000000         PERSONNEL DISPLAY
 C000001                                           1   1 *IN03                END OF PROGRAM
 C000002                                           2   2 *IN07                PREVIOUS RECORD
 C000003                                           3   3 *IN08                NEXT RECORD
     400  ISSNUM      DS
     500  I                                        1   3 SS1
     600  I                                        4   5 SS2
     700  I                                        6   9 SS3
     800  I#WORK      DS
     900  I                                        1   3 #SSE1
    1000  I                                        4   4 #SSD1
    1100  I                                        5   6 #SSE2
    1200  I                                        7   7 #SSD2
    1300  I                                        8  11 #SSE3

    1400  C           PROMPT    TAG
```

Listing 5.8. Source for PEINQY.

```
                                  IBM SAA RPG/400                                                         Page        3
SEQUENCE                                                                          IND    DO    LAST        PAGE    PROGRAM
NUMBER    *...1....+....2....+....3....+....4....+....5....+....6....+....7...*  USE    NUM   UPDATE      LINE    ID
    1500  C                    EXFMTPERPRM                                                   02/04/92
    1600  C   03               GOTO EOJ                                                      02/04/92
    1700  C          CONT      TAG                                                           02/04/92
    1800  C   07               EXSR PREV                                                     02/04/92
    1900  C   08               EXSR NEXT                                                     02/04/92
    2000  C  N07N08            EXSR START                                                    02/04/92
    2100  C  N07N08            EXSR NEXT                                                     02/04/92
    2200  C                    SETOF                     0708            1 2                 02/04/92
    2300  C   98               GOTO PROMPT                                                   02/07/92
    2400  C   99               GOTO PROMPT                                                   02/07/92
    2500  C                    EXSR SSN                                                      02/04/92
    2600  C                    EXFMTPERFLDS                                                  02/04/92
    2700  C   03               GOTO EOJ                                                      02/04/92
    2800  C   07               GOTO CONT                                                     02/07/92
    2900  C   08               GOTO CONT                                                     02/07/92
    3000  C                    GOTO PROMPT                                                   02/04/92
    3100  C          EOJ       TAG                                                           02/04/92
    3200  C                    SETON                     LR              1                   02/05/92
    3300  C          PREV      BEGSR                                                         02/04/92
    3400  C                    READPPERSJREC               9899            2 3               02/04/92
    3500  C                    ENDSR                                                         02/04/92
    3600  C          NEXT      BEGSR                                                         02/04/92
    3700  C                    READ PERSJREC               9899            2 3               02/04/92
    3800  C                    ENDSR                                                         02/04/92
    3900  C          START     BEGSR                                                         02/04/92
    4000  C          SSNUM     SETLLPERSJREC             9898            1 2                 02/04/92
    4100  C                    ENDSR                                                         02/04/92
    4200  C          SSN       BEGSR                                                         02/04/92
    4300  C                    MOVE SS1       #SSE1                                          02/04/92
    4400  C                    MOVE '-'       #SSD1                                          02/04/92
    4500  C                    MOVE SS2       #SSE2                                          02/04/92
    4600  C                    MOVE '-'       #SSD2                                          02/04/92
    4700  C                    MOVE SS3       #SSE3                                          02/04/92
    4800  C                    MOVE #WORK     SSEDIT                                         02/04/92
    4900  C                    ENDSR                                                         02/04/92
 D000000   OUTPUT FIELDS FOR RECORD PERPRM FILE PEDISPD FORMAT PERPRM.
 D000000         SSN PROMPT
 D000001                           *IN98       2  CHAR    1              FILE ERROR. PRESS RESET, THEN ENTER OR F3
 D000002                           *IN99       1  CHAR    1              FILE AT TOP OR BOTTOM.     PRESS RESET, THEN ENTER
 E000000   OUTPUT FIELDS FOR RECORD PERFLDS FILE PEDISPD FORMAT PERFLDS.
 E000000         PERSONNEL DISPLAY
 E000001                           SSEDIT     11  CHAR   11
 E000002                           LSTNAM     26  CHAR   15              LAST NAME
 E000003                           FSTNAM     36  CHAR   10              FIRST NAME
 E000004                           MIDINT     37  CHAR    1              MIDDLE INITIAL
 E000005                           ADDR1      57  CHAR   20              ADDRESS LINE 1
 E000006                           ADDR2      77  CHAR   20              ADDRESS LINE 2
 E000007                           CITY       97  CHAR   20              CITY
 E000008                           STATE      99  CHAR    2              STATE
 E000009                           ZIP       104  CHAR    5              ZIP
 E000010                           FUND      106  CHAR    2              FUND
 E000011                           DEPT      109  CHAR    3              DEPT
```

Listing 5.8. *(cont.)*

```
                                IBM SAA RPG/400                                                                   Page       4

SEQUENCE                                                                      IND    DO    LAST       PAGE   PROGRAM
NUMBER    *...1....+....2....+....3....+....4....+....5....+....6....+....7...* USE    NUM   UPDATE     LINE   ID

 E000012                        DESCR     159  CHAR   50                     DEPARTMENT
 E000013                        WKYSAL    166  ZONE  7,2                     WEEKLY SALARY

          * * * * *   E N D   O F   S O U R C E   * * * * *

         A d d i t i o r a l   D i a g n o s t i c   M e s s a g e s
```

Listing 5.8. *(cont.)*

```
PERSONNEL INQUIRY

SS NUMBER 876

USE F3 TO END PROGRAM. USE ENTER TO ENTER ANOTHER SS NUMBER




   03-18     SA        MW        KS        IM        II S1       KB
```

Figure 5.3. Prompt screen.

```
PERSONNEL INQUIRY

SS NUMBER 876

USE F3 TO END PROGRAM. USE ENTER TO ENTER ANOTHER SS NUMBER

SS NUMBER       876-54-3210
LAST NAME       Allen
FIRST NAME      Brad            MID INIT
ADDRESS         123 E. Oak St.

CITY            Chicago                   STATE      IL   ZIP   60601

FUND/DEPT       01-001
DESCRIPTION        Candy

WEEKLY SALARY         900.00

USE F7 TO PAGE BACKWARD, F8 TO PAGE FORWARD



    03-15     SA        MW        KS        IM        II S1      KB
```

Figure 5.4. Prompt screen and resulting detail screen.

- Ninety-nine indicators are available to the RPG/400 program. If there are numerous indicators being used in the program and they are not well documented by comments within the program, the programmer will encounter many difficulties in determining their meanings. In this program the indicators are documented in the program source prior to the beginning of the Calculation Specifications.
- Function keys 03 (End Program) and 12 (Cancel Update) are defined as command attention (CA) keys in the DDS for the display file. Because they are defined as CA keys, on an I/O to the display file, use of valid F keys does *not* transmit data back to the program. If, on the other hand, the F keys were defined as CF (command function) keys, data *would* be transmitted back to the program.
- The logic for the heart of the program is in the Calculation Specifications. To begin with, the prompt display format is written, then the display file is read to check for responses. The database file is then read to determine if a record exists; if it does, the program loads an update screen; if not, the program loads an add screen. The detail display format is then written and then read so that screen edits can be performed. If the edits are unsuccessful, the program loops back to redisplay the screen with errors. This edit loop continues until all errors are corrected. When the screen is correct, the database record is written/rewritten, and a clean screen is sent with an 'Update Successful' message, allowing the user to enter another prompt and begin the update cycle again.

  The Calculation Specifications in the program contain several concepts worth reviewing. They are as follows:

  - In RPG/400 indicators can be referenced as data fields as well as, in the normal manner, indicators conditioning the execution of calculation statements. The equivalent statement for SETON of an indicator is to MOVE the value 1 to it, and the equivalent statement for SETOF is to MOVE the value 0 to it. The *IN array is a series of 1-byte indicators numbered 1 through 99, corresponding to the 99 indicators available to the RPG program. Items in the indicator array can be referenced as a normal item in an array—for example, Indicator 46 is referenced as *IN,46 in a Calculation Specifications statement. Use of indicators as data fields is especially helpful in conditional operations such as DOW (Do While), DOU (Do Until), IFxx (If statements), and CAS (Case Logic), where routines are executed based on the VALUE of a data field rather than the on–off STATUS of an indicator.

- The EXFMT statement functions as a WRITE and then a READ to a workstation file. In this program EXFMTs are not used. Explicit WRITEs and READs are done because the display file contains three formats: a prompt format into which the search criteria are keyed, a message format that functions as an output-only screen, and an update format into which all data fields are keyed. At any given time formats are written and then only the format required for data entry/editing is read.
- Data fields onscreen and in the database are never explicitly MOVE'd from one place to another in the program. This is because the display file PEDSPLD uses as its reference file the database file PERSLFL via the REF statement in DDS. Descriptions of all data fields in the display file are retrieved from PERSLFL.
- The KLIST parameter concatenates several fields from a database file for use as a composite key for I/O to the file. While in DDS the keys to files are explicitly specified; in RPG this is the only way to gather these fields to obtain the key to a database as a single field.
- Repetitive processes are executed by subroutines, such as I/O functions and edit routines.
- Nested IFs are used for much of the processing. All IFs have corresponding ENDs, and they are organized from the inside out.
- UPDAT and WRITE statements must reference RECORD names when using externally defined database files.

• No Output Specifications are coded in the program.
• Compile the program in the normal manner (Option 14). Once the program has been compiled, check the output listing in the output queue for errors. If there are any, correct them and recompile the program.

- To execute the program, enter 'CALL PEUPDT' on the command line. The program will control the workstation until the user ends the execution.

The RPG/400 source for the program PEUPDT is in Listing 5.9. Following the source code are the compile-time array (Listing 5.10) plus four sample screen layouts:

1. The prompt screen (Figure 5.5).
2. The screen to update an existing record (Figure 5.6).
3. The screen to add a new record (Figure 5.7).
4. The resulting completion screen (Figure 5.8).

Additional information on RPG/400 online programming can be found in the following books:

- IBM Manual SC09-1161, *RPG/400 User's Guide*. This book details ways to write, compile, test, debug, and run RPG/400 programs. Chapter 8 goes into some detail on WORKSTN files, and Chapter 12 has a number of worthwhile RPG/400 program examples.
- IBM Manual SC09-1089, *RPG/400 Reference*. This book details program structure and is a general reference for RPG/400.

```
                                   IBM SAA RPG/400                                                                    Page      2
SEQUENCE                                                                          IND    DO    LAST       PAGE   PROGRAM
NUMBER   *...1....+....2....+....3....+....4....+....5....+....6....+....7...*   USE    NUM   UPDATE     LINE   ID
                    S o u r c e   L i s t i n g

     100  F*PROGRAM TO UPDATE PERSONNEL DATA USING EXTERNALLY DEFINED FILES
          H                                                                                               *****
     200  FPERSLFL UF  E           K        DISK                         A
           RECORD FORMAT(S):  LIBRARY DPDMLLIB FILE PERSLFL.
                    EXTERNAL FORMAT PERSPREC RPG NAME PERSPREC

     300  FPERSTFL IF  E           K        DISK
           RECORD FORMAT(S):  LIBRARY DPDMLLIB FILE PERSTFL.
                    EXTERNAL FORMAT PERSTREC RPG NAME PERSTREC

     400  FPEDSPLD CF  E                    WORKSTN
           RECORD FORMAT(S):  LIBRARY DPDMLLIB FILE PEDSPLD.
                    EXTERNAL FORMAT PERPRM RPG NAME PERPRM
                    EXTERNAL FORMAT PERMSG RPG NAME PERMSG
                    EXTERNAL FORMAT PERFLDS RPG NAME PERFLDS

     500  E                    ERR     1   3 50

 A000000   INPUT  FIELDS FOR RECORD PERSPREC FILE PERSLFL FORMAT PERSPREC.
 A000000         PERSONNEL FILE
 A000001                                       1  15 LSTNAM              LAST NAME
 A000002                                      16  25 FSTNAM              FIRST NAME
 A000003                                      26  26 MIDINT              MIDDLE INITIAL
 A000004                                      27  35 SSNUM               SOCIAL SECURITY NUMBER
 A000005                                      36  37 FUND                FUND
 A000006                                      38  40 DEPT                DEPT
 A000007                                      41  60 ADDR1               ADDRESS LINE 1
 A000008                                      61  80 ADDR2               ADDRESS LINE 2
 A000009                                      81 100 CITY                CITY
 A000010                                     101 102 STATE               STATE
 A000011                                     103 107 ZIP                 ZIP
 A000012                                   P 108 1112WKYSAL              WEEKLY SALARY
 B000000   INPUT  FIELDS FOR RECORD PERSTREC FILE PERSTFL FORMAT PERSTREC.
 B000000         TABLE FILE
 B000001                                       1   2 FUND                FUND
 B000002                                       3   5 DEPT                DEPT
 B000003                                       6  55 DESCR               DEPARTMENT
 C000000   INPUT  FIELDS FOR RECORD PERPRM FILE PEDSPLD FORMAT PERPRM.
 C000000         NAME PROMPT
 C000001                                       1  15 LSTNAM              LAST NAME
 C000002                                      16  25 FSTNAM              FIRST NAME
 C000003                                      26  26 MIDINT              MIDDLE INITIAL
 D000000   INPUT  FIELDS FOR RECORD PERMSG FILE PEDSPLD FORMAT PERMSG.
 D000000         MESSAGES
 E000000   INPUT  FIELDS FOR RECORD PERFLDS FILE PEDSPLD FORMAT PERFLDS.
 E000000         PERSONNEL UPDATE
 E000001                                       1   9 SSNUM               SOCIAL SECURITY NUMBER
 E000002                                      10  29 ADDR1               ADDRESS LINE 1
 E000003                                      30  49 ADDR2               ADDRESS LINE 2
```

Listing 5.9. Source for PEUPDT.

```
                                   IBM SAA RPG/400                                                                      Page      3
SEQUENCE                                                                          IND    DO    LAST       PAGE   PROGRAM
NUMBER    *...1....+....2....+....3....+....4....+....5....+....6....+....7...*   USE    NUM   UPDATE     LINE   ID
 E000004                                          50  69 CITY                     CITY
 E000005                                          70  71 STATE                    STATE
 E000006                                          72  76 ZIP                      ZIP
 E000007                                          77  78 FUND                     FUND
 E000008                                          79  81 DEPT                     DEPT
 E000009                                          82  882WKYSAL                   WEEKLY SALARY
     600  ILSTNAM     DS
     700  I                                        1   1 LNAM1
     800  I                                        2  15 LNAM2
     900  IFSTNAM     DS
    1000  I                                        1   1 FNAM1
    1100  I                                        2  10 FNAM2
    1200  ICITY       DS
    1300  I                                        1   1 CITY1
    1400  I                                        2  20 CITY2
    1500  ISTATE      DS
    1600  I                                        1   1 STAT1
    1700  I                                        2   2 STAT2
    1800  IZIP        DS
    1900  I                                        1   1 ZIP1
    2000  I                                        2   2 ZIP2
    2100  I                                        3   3 ZIP3
    2200  I                                        4   4 ZIP4
    2300  I                                        5   5 ZIP5
    2400  ISSNUM      DS
    2500  I                                        1   1 SSNUM1
    2600  I                                        2   2 SSNUM2
    2700  I                                        3   3 SSNUM3
    2800  I                                        4   4 SSNUM4
    2900  I                                        5   5 SSNUM5
    3000  I                                        6   6 SSNUM6
    3100  I                                        7   7 SSNUM7
    3200  I                                        8   8 SSNUM8
    3300  I                                        9   9 SSNUM9

    3400  **  PROGRAM INDICATORS ARE SET UP AS FOLLOWS:                                              *****
    3500   *  03  -  PF KEY 03 - END OF JOB                                                               S
    3600   *  12  -  PF KEY 12 - CANCEL UPDATE
    3700   *  70  -  SCREEN EDIT INDICATOR
    3800   *  75  -  NO PERSONNEL RECORD FOUND
    3900   *  80  -  ADD NEW RECORD
    4000   *  87  -  PROTECT SOCIAL SECURITY NUMBER ON SCREEN DISPLAY
    4100   *  89  -  EDIT ERROR ON SCREEN - DEPT
    4200   *  90  -  EDIT ERROR ON SCREEN - FUND
    4300   *  91  -  EDIT ERROR ON SCREEN - ZIP
    4400   *  92  -  EDIT ERROR ON SCREEN - STATE
    4500   *  93  -  EDIT ERROR ON SCREEN - CITY
    4600   *  94  -  EDIT ERROR ON SCREEN - SS NUMBER
    4700   *  95  -  EDIT ERROR ON SCREEN - MIDDLE INITIAL
    4800   *  96  -  EDIT ERROR ON SCREEN - FIRST NAME
    4900   *  97  -  EDIT ERROR ON SCREEN - LAST NAME
    5000   *  98  -  FILE ERROR ON I/O TO DATABASE

    5100  C           PROMPT    TAG
```

Listing 5.9. *(cont.)*

```
                                    IBM SAA RPG/400                                                                 Page      4

SEQUENCE                                                                                  IND   DO    LAST       PAGE   PROGRAM
NUMBER   *...1....+....2....+....3....+....4....+....5....+....6....+....7...*            USE   NUM   UPDATE     LINE   ID

    5200 C                     SETOF                     12                               1
    5300 C                     WRITEPERPRM
    5400 C                     WRITEPERMSG
    5500 C                     READ PERPRM                     LR                              3
    5600 C   03                GOTO EOJ
    5700 C   12                GOTO PROMPT
    5800 C                     EXSR EDTNAM
    5900 C   97                GOTO PROMPT
    6000 C   96                GOTO PROMPT
    6100 C   95                GOTO PROMPT
    6200 C                     EXSR READPR
    6300 C           *IN,75    IFEQ '0'                                                         B001
    6400 C                     MOVE ERR,3     MSGLIN                                             001
    6500 C                     MOVE *BLANKS   CONMSG                                             001
    6600 C                     ELSE                                                             X001
    6700 C                     SETON                     80                               1      001
    6800 C                     EXSR INIT                                                         001
    6900 C                     MOVE ERR,2     MSGLIN                                             001
    7000 C                     END                                                              E001
    7100 C           LOOP2     TAG
    7200 C                     SETON                     87                               1
    7300 C                     WRITEPERMSG
    7400 C                     WRITEPERFLDS
    7500 C                     READ PERFLDS                    LR                              3
    7600 C   03                GOTO EOJ
    7700 C           *IN,12    IFEQ '1'                                                         B001
    7800 C                     EXSR SETOFF                                                       001
    7900 C                     MOVE *BLANKS   CONMSG                                             001
    8000 C                     SETOF                     80                               1      001
    8100 C                     GOTO PROMPT                                                       001
    8200 C                     END                                                              E001
    8300 C                     EXSR EDTSCR
    8400 C           *IN,70    IFEQ '0'                                                         B001
    8500 C           *IN,80    IFEQ '1'                                                         B002
    8600 C                     EXSR WRITE                                                        002
    8700 C           *IN,98    IFEQ '0'                                                         B003
    8800 C                     MOVE ERR,1     CONMSG                                             003
    8900 C                     EXSR SETOFF                                                       003
    9000 C                     GOTO PROMPT                                                       003
    9100 C                     ELSE                                                             X003
    9200 C                     GOTO LOOP2                                                        003
    9300 C                     END                                                              E003
    9400 C                     ELSE                                                             X002
    9500 C                     EXSR REWT                                                         002
    9600 C           *IN,98    IFEQ '0'                                                         B003
    9700 C                     MOVE ERR,1     CONMSG                                             003
    9800 C                     EXSR SETOFF                                                       003
    9900 C                     GOTO PROMPT                                                       003
   10000 C                     ELSE                                                             X003
   10100 C                     GOTO LOOP2                                                        003
   10200 C                     END                                                              E003
   10300 C                     END                                                              E002
```

Listing 5.9. *(cont.)*

```
                                        IBM SAA RPG/400                                                          Page      5
SEQUENCE                                                                                IND    DO    LAST      PAGE   PROGRAM
NUMBER    *...1....+....2....+....3....+....4....+....5....+....6....+....7...*         USE    NUM   UPDATE    LINE   ID
   10400  C                  ELSE                                                               X001
   10500  C                  GOTO LOOP2                                                          001
   10600  C                  END                                                                E001
   10700  C          EOJ     TAG
   10800  C                  SETON                     LR                          1
   10900  C          EDTNAM  BEGSR
   11000  C          LNAM1   IFEQ *BLANKS                                                       B001
   11100  C          LNAM1   ORGT *ZEROS                                                         001
   11200  C                  SETON                     7097                        1 2           001
   11300  C                  END                                                                E001
   11400  C          FNAM1   IFEQ *BLANKS                                                       B001
   11500  C          FNAM1   ORGT *ZEROS                                                         001
   11600  C                  SETON                     7096                        1 2           001
   11700  C                  END                                                                E001
   11800  C          MIDINT  IFGT *ZEROS                                                        B001
   11900  C                  SETON                     7095                        1 2           001
   12000  C                  END                                                                E001
   12100  C                  ENDSR
   12200  C          READPR  BEGSR
   12300  C          PKEY    CHAINPERSPREC             7598                        1 2
   12400  C                  ENDSR
   12500  C          INIT    BEGSR
   12600  C                  MOVE *BLANKS   SSNUM
   12700  C                  MOVE *BLANKS   ADDR1
   12800  C                  MOVE *BLANKS   ADDR2
   12900  C                  MOVE *BLANKS   CITY
   13000  C                  MOVE *BLANKS   STATE
   13100  C                  MOVE *BLANKS   ZIP
   13200  C                  MOVE *BLANKS   FUND
   13300  C                  MOVE *BLANKS   DEPT
   13400  C                  MOVE *ZEROS    WKYSAL
   13500  C                  MOVE *BLANKS   CONMSG
   13600  C                  ENDSR
   13700  C          EDTSCR  BEGSR
   13800  C                  SETOF                     70                          1
   13900  C          SSNUM1  IFLT *ZEROS                                                        B001
   14000  C          SSNUM2  ORLT *ZEROS                                                         001
   14100  C          SSNUM3  ORLT *ZEROS                                                         001
   14200  C          SSNUM4  ORLT *ZEROS                                                         001
   14300  C          SSNUM5  ORLT *ZEROS                                                         001
   14400  C          SSNUM6  ORLT *ZEROS                                                         001
   14500  C          SSNUM7  ORLT *ZEROS                                                         001
   14600  C          SSNUM8  ORLT *ZEROS                                                         001
   14700  C          SSNUM9  ORLT *ZEROS                                                         001
   14800  C                  SETON                     7094                        1 2           001
   14900  C                  END                                                                E001
   15000  C          CITY1   IFLT *ZEROS                                                        B001
   15100  C                  ELSE                                                               X001
   15200  C                  SETON                     7093                        1 2           001
   15300  C                  END                                                                E001
   15400  C          STAT1   IFLT *ZEROS                                                        B001
   15500  C                  ELSE                                                               X001
   15600  C                  SETON                     7092                        1 2           001
   15700  C                  END                                                                E001
```

Listing 5.9. *(cont.)*

```
                                     IBM SAA RPG/400                                                        Page        6

SEQUENCE                                                                   IND    DO    LAST        PAGE    PROGRAM
NUMBER     *...1....+....2....+....3....+....4....+....5....+....6....+....7...* USE    NUM   UPDATE      LINE    ID

   15800  C          ZIP1      IFLT *ZEROS                                        B001
   15900  C          ZIP2      ORLT *ZEROS                                         001
   16000  C          ZIP3      ORLT *ZEROS                                         001
   16100  C          ZIP4      ORLT *ZEROS                                         001
   16200  C          ZIP5      ORLT *ZEROS                                         001
   16300  C                    SETON                     7091            1 2      001
   16400  C                    END                                                E001
   16500  C                    EXSR TABLE
   16600  C                    ENDSR
   16700  C          REWT      BEGSR
   16800  C                    UPDATPERSPREC               98              2
   16900  C                    ENDSR
   17000  C          WRITE     BEGSR
   17100  C                    WRITEPERSPREC               98              2
   17200  C                    ENDSR
   17300  C          TABLE     BEGSR
   17400  C          TKEY      CHAINPERSTREC             9098            1 2
   17500  C   90               SETON                     7089            1 2
   17600  C                    ENDSR
   17700  C          SETOFF    BEGSR
   17800  C                    SETOF                     127075          1 2 3
   17900  C                    SETOF                     8087            1 2
   18000  C                    ENDSR
   18100  C          PKEY      KLIST
   18200  C                    KFLD           LSTNAM
   18300  C                    KFLD           FSTNAM
   18400  C                    KFLD           MIDINT
   18500  C          TKEY      KLIST
   18600  C                    KFLD           FUND
   18700  C                    KFLD           DEPT
 F000000   OUTPUT FIELDS FOR RECORD PERSPREC FILE PERSLFL FORMAT PERSPREC.
 F000000         PERSONNEL FILE
 F000001                            LSTNAM    15  CHAR    15                 LAST NAME
 F000002                            FSTNAM    25  CHAR    10                 FIRST NAME
 F000003                            MIDINT    26  CHAR     1                 MIDDLE INITIAL
 F000004                            SSNUM     35  CHAR     9                 SOCIAL SECURITY NUMBER
 F000005                            FUND      37  CHAR     2                 FUND
 F000006                            DEPT      40  CHAR     3                 DEPT
 F000007                            ADDR1     60  CHAR    20                 ADDRESS LINE 1
 F000008                            ADDR2     80  CHAR    20                 ADDRESS LINE 2
 F000009                            CITY     100  CHAR    20                 CITY
 F000010                            STATE    102  CHAR     2                 STATE
 F000011                            ZIP      107  CHAR     5                 ZIP
 F000012                            WKYSAL   111P PACK   7,2                 WEEKLY SALARY
 G000000   OUTPUT FIELDS FOR RECORD PERPRM FILE PEDSPLD FORMAT PERPRM.
 G000000         NAME PROMPT
 H000000   OUTPUT FIELDS FOR RECORD PERMSG FILE PEDSPLD FORMAT PERMSG.
 H000000         MESSAGES
 H000001                            CONMSG    50  CHAR    50
 I000000   OUTPUT FIELDS FOR RECORD PERFLDS FILE PEDSPLD FORMAT PERFLDS.
 I000000         PERSONNEL UPDATE
 I000001                            SSNUM      9  CHAR     9                 SOCIAL SECURITY NUMBER
 I000002                            ADDR1     29  CHAR    20                 ADDRESS LINE 1
 I000003                            ADDR2     49  CHAR    20                 ADDRESS LINE 2
```

Listing 5.9. *(cont.)*

```
                                  IBM SAA RPG/400                                                                      Page        7
SEQUENCE                                                                                   IND     DO     LAST       PAGE    PROGRAM
NUMBER      *...1....+....2....+....3....+....4....+....5....+....6....+....7...*         USE     NUM    UPDATE     LINE    ID
 I000004                          CITY        69   CHAR    20                            CITY
 I000005                          STATE       71   CHAR     2                            STATE
 I000006                          ZIP         76   CHAR     5                            ZIP
 I000007                          FUND        78   CHAR     2                            FUND
 I000008                          DEPT        81   CHAR     3                            DEPT
 I000009                          WKYSAL      88   ZONE   7,2                            WEEKLY SALARY
 I000010                          MSGLIN     138   CHAR    50

            * * * * *   E N D   O F   S O U R C E   * * * * *

           A d d i t i o n a l   D i a g n o s t i c   M e s s a g e s

* 7089       400    RPG PROVIDES SEPARATE INDICATOR AREA FOR FILE PEDSPLD.
```

Listing 5.9. *(cont.)*

```
                                      IBM SAA RPG/400

SEQUENCE
 NUMBER     *...+....1....+....2....+....3....+....4....+....5....+....6....+....7....+....8

                   C o m p i l e - T i m e   T a b l e s

 Table/Array  . . . . . . :   ERR

    18900   UPDATE COMPLETE. ENTER NEW NAME.
    19000   NAME NOT ON FILE. ENTER NEW RECORD.
    19100   NAME FOUND. UPDATE FIELDS
```

Listing 5.10. Compile-time array.

```
PERSONNEL UPDATE

ENTER NAME
LAST       Smith              FIRST James        MIDDLE INITIAL

USE F3 TO END PROGRAM. USE ENTER TO UPDATE, F12 TO CANCEL










    04-43     SA       MW        KS        IM        II S1      KB
```

Figure 5.5. Prompt screen.

```
PERSONNEL UPDATE

ENTER NAME
LAST      Smith              FIRST James          MIDDLE INITIAL

USE F3 TO END PROGRAM. USE ENTER TO UPDATE, F12 TO CANCEL


SS NUMBER     123456789
ADDRESS       123 Main Street

CITY          Glen Ellyn               STATE     IL   ZIP   60137

FUND/DEPT     01 - 001

WEEKLY SALARY        300.00


NAME FOUND. UPDATE FIELDS



      09-20    SA       MW       KS       IM       II S1      KB
```

Figure 5.6. Update screen.

```
PERSONNEL UPDATE

ENTER NAME
LAST      Smith              FIRST Robert       MIDDLE INITIAL

USE F3 TO END PROGRAM. USE ENTER TO UPDATE, F12 TO CANCEL


SS NUMBER      987098709
ADDRESS        1223 Oak St

CITY           Chicago                STATE     IL   ZIP   60606

FUND/DEPT      01 - 001

WEEKLY SALARY      900


NAME NOT ON FILE. ENTER NEW RECORD.




    16-25     SA       MW       KS       IM       II S1      KB
```

Figure 5.7. Add screen.

```
PERSONNEL UPDATE

ENTER NAME
LAST                        FIRST              MIDDLE INITIAL

USE F3 TO END PROGRAM. USE ENTER TO UPDATE, F12 TO CANCEL
UPDATE COMPLETE. ENTER NEW NAME.









     04-15      SA         MW         KS         IM         II S1        KB
```

Figure 5.8. Completion screen.

6

Miscellaneous Information

The objective of this chapter is to present some miscellaneous information on the AS/400, including some of the differences between mainframe and AS/400 processing. This is certainly not an exhaustive list, and anyone working on the AS/400 will come up with a list of his or her own.

Job Queues. On the AS/400, job queues and finding jobs within queues can be somewhat difficult. While the command WRKOUTQ is used to work with all output queues, many times it is difficult to determine which queue to look at when there are numerous output queues in the system. Some users have output queues in their own libraries, prefixed by their userids. Most other jobs go to generic output queues that can be set up in a variety of ways. In one environment output queues are referenced by the day of the week. For example, HKOQTHUJOB contains jobs for the previous Thursday. The daily job queues generally remain active for one week, or for a specified period of time, through the execution of a CL program to change daily queues. Queue PRT01 contains jobs routed to the system printer. Job queues can also be set up for specific applications so that logs for all users of those applications reside in common queues.

DSPLOG. DSPLOG allows the user to view the history log on the system, which can be very useful in debugging. For example, the progress of an AS/400 application started remotely by a mainframe program can be monitored via the history log. The command DSPLOG is used to begin, and the user should hit PF4 to prompt on the screen. The log is called QHST, and default parameters can be used or searches can be limited by beginning date and time, end date and time, or various jobs and/or users.

CICS versus AS/400 Interactive Programming. CICS coding on the mainframe requires a great deal of specialized coding skills. For example:

- Displaying a screen in CICS first requires the programmer to generate screen macro code and assemble it. It then requires the programmer to insert non-COBOL code into COBOL programs in order to process the screen(s).
- Special CICS code is required for file I/O.
- The COBOL programs then have to be precompiled to translate the CICS code into code that can be deciphered by the COBOL compiler.
- Numerous system tables must be updated in order for the CICS programs and transactions to be executed. In addition, all files must be identified to the CICS region.
- CICS applications themselves must run in a specific CICS region.

The AS/400, on the other hand, allows the programmer to utilize existing COBOL skills along with the standardized coding techniques of DDS. For example:

- DDS is used for file creation and screen generation, which makes for an easy transition.
- Normal COBOL coding techniques and normal verbs (read, write, etc.) are used to receive and send screen formats or to perform file I/O.
- Minor variations in I/O statements indicate data formats for either multiple part screens or multiple record layout files.
- No special regions or tables need to be allocated for AS/400 interactive programs; interactive programs run in the AS/400 subsystem QINTER. Nevertheless, special subsystems by application may be set up as needed.
- AS/400 interactive code is very much geared toward the use

of indicators. This probably stems from the fact that the AS/400 started as an outgrowth of System 3X processes that utilize RPG code, and RPG uses indicators extensively.

The IBM AS/400 COBOL manuals have good explanations and examples of interactive processing. In addition, future operating-system enhancements will include a version of CICS that will run on the AS/400, which may help mainframe programmers making the transition to the AS/400 from other systems.

QUSRTOOL. The QUSRTOOL library is available on all AS/400s. It is part of the base system package and is an invaluable source of AS/400 information. QUSRTOOL contains source programs that have been developed by AS/400 users over the last several years to improve productivity and enhance performance. It is sent with the system by IBM at installation time, but its contents are not guaranteed; it is merely supplied in good faith. No executable modules are sent, and any programs in the library are subject to compilation errors. A variety of maintenance and subroutine modules are available, as are a number of sample programs. For example, user tool source programs are available for job schedule reporting, converting message files to database files, backing up files since the last save, and copying job logs. Source file QATTINFO in QUSRTOOL contains descriptive information on many QUSRTOOL functions.

Subfiles. The concept of subfiles is something unique in the AS/400 environment. Subfiles are groups of like records that are either written to or read from a workstation device, utilized in an interactive mode. For example, a subfile may be populated by a read of a number of database records that are then written to it. Then the subfile is written to the display device in a single write operation. This is particularly useful in inquiry situations where one screen contains summary information from many database records. In addition, subfiles are useful in high-volume data entry environments where multiple data records are processed on a screen as a single subfile. The subfile is read from the display device in one operation, and each record within the subfile can be processed/edited individually. Subfiles have special requirements both in DDS and in applications coding, and can be used both in COBOL/400 and RPG/400.

Index